Indiana
Bird Watching

A Year-Round Guide

Published by Cool Springs Press, a Division of Thomas Nelson, Inc., P. O. Box 141000, Nashville, Tennessee, 37214.

Thompson, Bill, 1962-
    Indiana bird watching : a year-round guide / Bill Thompson III and the staff of Bird watcher's digest.
       p. cm.
    Includes bibliographical references (p.   ) and index.
    ISBN 1-59186-169-1
    1. Bird watching--Indiana. 2. Birds--Indiana. I. Bird watcher's digest. II. Title.
QL684.I5T49 2005
598'.07'234772—dc22

                                           2004029831

First Printing 2005
Printed in the United States of America
10 9 8 7 6 5 4 3 2 1

Managing Editor: Billie Brownell
Interior Designer: Bill Kersey, Kersey Graphics
Production Artist: S.E. Anderson
Map and Icon Illustrator: Heather Lynch
Sighting Notes Illustrator: Julie Zickefoose

Cool Springs Press books may be purchased in bulk for educational, business, fundraising, or sales promotional use. For information, please email SpecialMarkets@ThomasNelson.com.

Visit the Thomas Nelson website at **www.thomasnelson.com**

Photography Credits

Arthur Morris/Birds as Art: Front cover top photo (sandhill crane); front cover middle photo (northern cardinal); intro photo page 6 (northern cardinal); Pages 7; 9; 10; 12; 15; 16; 17 (both photos); 18; 19; 20; 23 (cerulean warbler); 24 (great egret); 25 (peregrine falcon); 26 (sandhill crane)

Cliff Beitel: Front cover featured photo (Carolina chickadee); Pages 8; 22 (black-bellied plover); 23 (Caspian tern)

Tom Vezo: Pages 14; 21; 25 (pileated woodpecker)

Maslowski Photography: Pages 24 (Henslow's sparrow); 26 (short-eared owl)

Robert McCaw: Front cover bottom photo (bobolink); Page 22 (bobolink)

Brian Henry: Back cover bottom photo (Eastern bluebird)

Barth Schorre: Back cover top photo (scarlet tanager)

Indiana
Bird Watching

A Year-Round Guide

Bill Thompson, III
and the staff of

COOL SPRINGS PRESS
A Division of Thomas Nelson Publishers
Since 1798

www.thomasnelson.com

Dedication and Acknowledgements

Dedication

To my parents, Bill and Elsa Thompson, who were bird watching *way* before it was cool and who had the courage and optimism to launch *Bird Watcher's Digest* in the living room of our home back in 1978. Thank you, Mom and Dad, for opening the door to my lifelong passion for birds and bird watching.

To Julie, Phoebe, and Liam (my own little family) who make each day sweeter than the last.

And to my siblings, Andy and Laura, for always being there for me.

Acknowledgements

There's no such thing as "too many cooks spoiling the broth" when creating a book. From the outset I leaned on and drew upon the talents of publishing professionals and birding experts in creating this book. At *Bird Watcher's Digest*: Deborah Griffith (special editorial blue ribbon), Heather Lynch (map design kudos), Andy Thompson, Ann Kerenyi, Linda Brejwo, Bob Carlsen, Elsa "Catbird" Thompson, Helen Neuberger, Susan Hill, Joyce Abicht, Laura Kammermeier, and Katherine Koch deserve my never-ending thanks for covering for me at *BWD* so I could stay home and write.

Andy Thompson, Charles Kirkwood, and Russell Galen made early and important contributions to the launching of this book.

My deep gratitude to the folks at Cool Springs Press—especially Billie Brownell, Hank McBride, David Dunham, and Roger Waynick—for their enthusiasm, guidance, and support. Thanks also to the many people who helped in the development of this book "behind the scenes"—to Jamie Chavez for her copyediting expertise, to Bill Kersey for his art direction, and to S.E. Anderson for pulling it all together.

Helping me with the content creation were Norma Siebenheller, Howard Youth, and Julie Zickefoose, three peerless bird authors. Without them I'd still be laboring over a smoking-hot laptop.

Neil Case lent his expertise in creating the "Welcome to Bird Watching in Indiana" chapter and I'm mighty grateful for his help. Neil says, "I can't remember a time when I wasn't interested in birds. My parents weren't bird watchers but they knew the common birds, taught me those, and bought bird books for me. My grandfather let me use his field glasses, 4x, I think."

Neil Case worked for the Indiana Department of Natural Resources from November, 1965 to March 1, 1991, at the Jasper-Pulaski Fish and Wildlife Area, the Upper Wabash Reservoirs, and as the manager of one of those reservoirs, the Salamonie. He has written "Outdoor Notes," a weekly newspaper column, since May 1977. Now retired, Neil and his wife Mona travel widely in the United States and Canada, "bird watching everywhere we go."

Creating a book requires a lot of "cooks" and I am grateful for everyone's contributions. Any errors or omissions contained herein are the responsibility of the author (me).

Finally, thank *YOU* for reading this book. I hope our paths cross someday in a beautiful natural place where there are lots and lots of birds. What could be better?

—*Bill Thompson, III*

Table of Contents

Welcome to Bird Watching
in Indiana . . . Neil Case

Indiana, according to the state motto, is "The Crossroads of America." Travelers from the East, Northeast, or even Southeast who go to Chicago or head farther west cross Indiana. And, of course, travelers from Chicago or farther west who are going east also cross the state. People from Michigan, Wisconsin, and Ontario cross Indiana going to Florida—many of them to spend the winter and cross it again returning home in spring. Many birds, too, cross the Hoosier State when they migrate south in fall and again when they fly north in spring.

Indiana could also be called a meeting place for birds and plants. There are birds that are common to the East, to the North, to the South, and some that are usually seen farther west.

To the earliest explorers going west and to the trappers and settlers who followed, most of the territory that became the state of Indiana was forested. It was a land of Indians and white-tailed deer, turkeys, and ruffed grouse. The trees that shaded those early travelers were the same as the trees they had seen in Ohio: maples, beech, chestnut, sycamore, tulip, cottonwood, willows, and many more.

In the northern part of the territory were also trees that were common in Michigan, pines and spruces. Where the land was poorly drained in the north there were tamaracks. In swampland along the Ohio River in the south there were those well-known trees of the Deep South, bald cypress.

As those early travelers continued west, if they noticed the species of trees they would have found that the maples and beech in the central and northern part of the territory became scarcer, and that oaks and hickories increased. In the west-central part of the state, near the line that now separates Indiana and Illinois, they would have emerged in places from the forest and entered the tallgrass prairie. To the north they would have encountered swamp, then extensive wetlands with tracts of prairie. As they struggled through the swamps and marshes in summer they would have been plagued by hordes of mosquitoes. Those who managed to get through this inhospitable area would have come to a series of ridges, then, at the far north, sand dunes and finally the shores of Lake Michigan.

Being a land of forest, Indiana was a land of forest birds. There were thrushes and warblers, vireos and woodpeckers. There were turkeys and ruffed grouse. Early settlers were said to be able to shoot turkeys from the windows of their cabins.

Prothonotary warbler (male)

Great flocks of passenger pigeons flew over the state, landing at times to feed on beechnuts and to roost at night. On the wetlands of the northwest in spring and fall there were flocks of ducks, geese, and shorebirds. Some of these birds stayed and raised young in the state. Sandhill cranes and a few whooping cranes nested in the wetlands of northern Indiana. Greater prairie-chickens bred in the prairies.

According to Russell Mumford and Charles Keller in *The Birds of Indiana*, there were Carolina parakeets in southern Indiana. There is no record of ivory-billed woodpeckers being seen in Indiana but there is one specimen in the Miami County Museum in Peru, Indiana, that may have been collected in the state along the Ohio River.

John James Audubon visited southern Indiana on at least four occasions: in 1807, 1810, 1819, and 1822. Alexander Wilson, sometimes called the father of American ornithology, was in Louisville, Kentucky, in March 1810 and must have at least visited Indiana.

Settlement brought clearing and, in the north and central sections of the state, draining of the land. Farms and villages were established, then

Carolina chickadee

towns and cities. Forest in the north and central regions and in part of the south was reduced to farm woodlots and strips of woods along streams and rivers. The Grand Kankakee Marsh in the northwest and Gene Stratton-Porter's Limberlost in the east-central region were drained. Corn and wheat, then corn and soybeans replaced the trees where the land was level enough for cultivation. Where the land was too hilly for agriculture, it was often used as small dairy farms with pastures and hayfields.

As settlements expanded, more trees were felled and woodland birds decreased in Indiana. The passenger pigeon and Carolina parakeet disappeared, not just in Indiana, of course, but everywhere. Wild turkeys, ruffed grouse, and white-tailed deer were gone, too, though not extinct. Bald eagles no longer nested in the state though a few were occasionally seen, usually along the shore of Lake Michigan. Prairie-chickens were still seen at one small bit of remaining prairie into the 1960s, then they, too, were gone. Ducks and geese decreased, as well.

Sandhill cranes stopped nesting in the state. Some still gathered at a remnant of marsh in the northwest in spring and fall but their numbers were counted in hundreds where there once had been thousands. Whooping cranes were completely gone from Indiana. In fact, whooping cranes almost followed the passenger pigeon and Carolina parakeet into extinction, but were saved due to extensive presentation efforts.

Remnants of the original forest cover remain in Indiana, however, and so do most of the bird species. Some of those remnants are protected today in state parks and forests, in state fish and wildlife areas and nature preserves. There are the Hoosier National Forest, Lake Michigan National Lakeshore, and the three National Wildlife Refuges, (Big Oaks, Muscatatuck, and Patoka River).

The Nature Conservancy, ACRES (a Fort Wayne-based organization that protects 50 nature preserves in fourteen Northeast Indiana counties), and other private organizations have acquired and are preserving or restoring some of

Wild turkey

Indiana's natural areas. A group named Friends of the Limberlost is acquiring bits of land that were once part of that broad swampland and are reflooding sections, attempting to re-establish that habitat.

Its location and the remaining and re-established natural areas still make Indiana a meeting place for the ranges of birds of East, West, North, and South. The nesting area of the black-capped chickadee, a more northern-nesting species, meets and overlaps the range of the closely related Carolina chickadee from farther south. Scarlet tanagers breed in Indiana and, in the southern part of the state, so does the summer tanager. Prothonotary warblers and golden-winged warblers nest in the Hoosier State. Pileated woodpeckers have increased and now nest across the state. Wild turkeys, ruffed grouse, and white-tailed deer have been successfully reintroduced and are now numerous enough that there are hunting seasons for them.

Eastern meadowlarks are more common in the state but western meadowlarks are occasionally found in the northwestern corner of Indiana. Horned larks breed here, and dickcissel nests have been found in appropriate grassland habitat. Yellow-headed blackbirds have been seen in the northwest part of the state.

Forty years ago only a few hundred sandhill cranes gathered in spring and fall at the Jasper-Pulaski State Fish and Wildlife Area in northwest Indiana. But conservation efforts have increased their numbers since then. Now several thousand gather in spring and as many as 30,000 have been seen in fall at J-P, as the area is called by Hoosier birders. A few sandhill cranes now nest in the northern part of the state. It's good to have such an impressive creature living and breeding in Indiana once again.

Bald eagles and peregrine falcons have been reintroduced and nest once more in Indiana. Whooping cranes are being hatched and raised in captivity and some of them have been taught to follow ultralite aircraft at the Necedah National Wildlife Refuge in Wisconsin. In fall, they are led by plane across Indiana, headed south to the Chassohowitzka National Wildlife Refuge in Florida. One stopping point on their journey south has been the Muscatatuck National Wildlife Refuge in Indiana.

From Florida the whooping cranes of Necedah and Chassohowitzka return in spring, on their own, to Wisconsin. A few have been seen with sandhill cranes in spring in Indiana, and many Hoosier birders eagerly watch for their passing.

In *Indiana Birds and Their Haunts*, published in 1979, Charles E., Shirley A., and Timothy C. Keller wrote that 363 species of birds might be seen in Indiana and that 166 species have nested here. Those numbers have increased in the ensuing decades. The "splitting" of species by the naming committee of the American Ornithologists Union has caused part of this but vagrant birds have also turned up and been added to the state bird list.

Rare and improbable birds, at least in Indiana, that have been seen here are Pacific loon, Ross's goose, Eurasian wigeon, king eider, Mississippi kite, pomarine, parasitic and long-tailed jaegers, laughing, Thayer's and Franklin's gulls, scissor-tailed flycatcher, northern shrike, Kirtland's warbler, and Le Conte's and clay-colored sparrows. Even magnificent frigatebirds have been found in Indiana. One was seen along the shore of Lake Michigan and one was shot in Shelby County in south-central Indiana in 1896, according to early ornithological records.

Indiana, it seems, lives up to its title as "The Crossroads of America" both for people and birds. It's a meeting place of birds and bird watchers from north and south, east and west.

Tips for Successful Birding in Indiana

- *Start with bird feeding.* There's nothing quite as enjoyable for a bird watcher as being able to enjoy the birds from the comfort of your patio or living room. Indiana offers some of the best bird feeding in North America year-round, especially in winter when our resident chickadees, titmice, cardinals, American goldfinches, house finches, song sparrows, and white-breasted nuthatches are augmented by our winter-only feeder birds, including dark-eyed juncos, white-crowned, white-throated, and tree sparrows, purple finches, and perhaps pine siskins or evening grosbeaks. Summer feeder highlights include ruby-throated hummingbirds and Baltimore orioles, as well as our backyard nesting birds.

- *Tune in to migration.* Spring and fall migrations bring huge influxes of birds into Indiana—birds that just pass through the Hoosier State on their way northward to breed (in spring) or southward to spend the winter (in fall). On a mid-May morning, any woodlot in the state might hold more than two dozen warbler species. Any bit of grassland habitat in late fall might have eight or ten sparrow species. Winter brings waterfowl, eagles, and other raptors. Late summer means shorebirds already heading south from their short Arctic breeding season. Indiana birders know the seasonal ebb and flow of our birds and they time their field trips to catch these natural phenomena.

- *Connect with a bird club.* Indiana has a rich, enthusiastic, and diverse community of bird and nature enthusiasts. There are active bird clubs in every part of the state. Start by contacting the Indiana Audubon Society (see Resources on page 31). Join a local bird club or group of bird watchers on an outing—beginners are always welcomed. This is one of the best ways to learn about the fantastic birding opportunities our state has to offer.

- *Keep a list.* Record your bird sightings in a journal, in your field guide, on your computer, or in a notebook. Your records will help you to chart your progress as a bird watcher, and they will provide lots of enjoyment for years to come when you read through them and remember favorite birds and favorite birding adventures.

- *Dress for success.* Indiana has many challenges for the aspiring bird watcher, including weather extremes, insects, and troublesome plants (poison ivy). In extremely cold winter weather, dressing in layers is vital, and it's always wise to wear *more* clothing than you think you'll need. In summer the heat, sun, and insects can make life miserable if you are not prepared by bringing plenty of water, a hat and sunscreen, and protective clothing or insect repellent. Veteran birders often keep these items handy in their vehicle for themselves, and to share with other, less-prepared birders.

Enjoy Indiana's birds! Our state is rich with birds, wonderful birding hotspots, and some of the world's most friendly bird watchers. Get out there and experience all of them!

Black vulture

Ecoregions of Indiana

There are three primary ecoregions in Indiana, if we view the state from a bird or habitat distribution perspective. Going from north to south in Indiana, these are the Lake Plain, the Till Plain, and the Hill Country.

To residents of southern Indiana, anyone who lives north of Shelbyville, Franklin, or Martinsville is a flatlander. Those cities are south of Indianapolis. That puts approximately the northern two-thirds of the state in the category of flat land.

The northern two-thirds of Indiana *is* fairly flat. But it is not uniformly so and is usually divided into two geographic regions, a northern region called the Lake Plain and a southern region, approximately the central third of the state, called the Till Plain.

The Lake Plain

The Lake Plain is a region of small hills and many lakes in the east and center of Indiana. Typical birds of the Lake Plain ecoregion include great blue heron, Canada goose, red-tailed hawk, American kestrel, mourning dove, killdeer, chimney swift, northern flicker, downy woodpecker, tree and barn swallows, blue jay, American crow, black-capped chickadee, white-breasted nuthatch, American robin, European starling, yellow warbler, eastern meadowlark, red-winged blackbird, American goldfinch, and house finch.

There are at least one thousand natural lakes in this area and before agricultural draining there were many more. The largest of these lakes is Lake Wawasee, at 3,600 acres. Other lakes that are big enough for recreational boating are James, Maxinkuckee, Shafer, and Tippecanoe. Much of the shoreline of each of these lakes, and many of the smaller lakes, is lined with houses and summer cottages. Ducks swim, feed, and loaf on the water in spring and fall. Mallards nest along the shores. Canada geese are common throughout the Lake Plain, much to the annoyance of many lakeshore property owners.

Rivers in the northern part of the state are the Maumee, which flows northeast, the St. Joseph, Pigeon, Eel, and Tippecanoe, which flow southwest or west and then southwest, and the Elkhart and Kankakee, which flow west. All the rivers are rather shallow except after heavy or prolonged rain. All are crooked except where they have been dredged and straightened.

Where the banks have not been cleared, the rivers in northern Indiana are corridors of trees through farmland—excellent bird habitat. But the banks have been cleared in many areas and cultivated fields often extend to the banks. There the water is the color of the earth that lines its banks, which is eroded into the river by every rain. There are stretches of muddy shores and there are shorebird-friendly mudflats most of the year.

The northwest and west section of the Lake Plain might almost be considered a separate region. More level and not as well drained as the rest of the Lake Plain, it was wetlands and prairie, in many places wet prairie. The Grand Kankakee River Marsh is estimated to have at one time covered one thousand square miles extending across northwest Indiana and into Illinois.

In spring, summer, and fall pioneers struggling to cross the wetlands described flocks of ducks and geese rising in clouds ahead of them. Sandhill cranes and a few whooping cranes and trumpeter swans and dozens of species of shorebirds nested in this marshland. Prairie-chickens were abundant on the drier land, the patches of dry prairie.

Scattered remnants of the Grand Kankakee River Marsh and of other marshland and prairie in northwest Indiana remain. The State Department of Natural Resources manages four Fish and Game Areas in northwest Indiana and there is bit of prairie called Hoosier Prairie. The flocks of ducks, geese, sandhill cranes, and shorebirds still visit the remaining plots of marsh and wet prairie in spring and fall. Some of these birds stay and nest. But sadly for Indiana's bird watchers, the whooping cranes, trumpeter swans, and prairie-chickens are long gone.

The extreme northwest part of this region, and of the state, is a series of ridges and sand dunes that give way to the shore of Lake Michigan. Here is Dunes National Lakeshore and Indiana Dunes State Park. It is here, along the lakeshore, that many birds rare to Indiana are seen.

The Till Plain
The central region of the state, the Till Plain, is more level than either north or south. Typical birds for the Till Plain are similar to those of the Lake Plain ecoregion, except that Carolina chickadee replaces the black-capped, and two other more southerly-distributed species, red-bellied woodpecker and northern cardinal, become more common. It's more nearly flat-land. Ironically, the highest elevation in the state, 1,285 feet above sea level, is in Randolph County in the eastern part of this region.

The Wabash River originates in Ohio and flows northwest across a bit of this region into the northern, then southwest back into and across the central region of Indiana. In the west-central part of the state the Wabash becomes the boundary between Indiana and Illinois and flows generally south.

The Eel River flows from the northeast into the Wabash, the Salamonie, and Mississinewa from the southeast and the Tippecanoe from the north. The White River flows southwest through the central part of this region, through Indianapolis, and joins the Wabash in south-west Indiana. All these waterways serve as migration corridors during spring and fall and as feeding and loafing habitat for ducks and Canada geese.

Both the Lake Plain and Till Plain are agricul-tural areas. But there are many towns and cities. Several of the cities—Indianapolis, Fort Wayne, South Bend, and Gary—are the largest in the state. The area around Gary is a sprawling industrial complex.

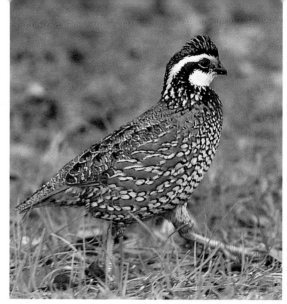

Northern bobwhite (male)

The forests of pioneer days are gone from the Till Plain. Trees in the regions now are in farm woodlots, in parks, along the rivers and streams, and in places by the shores of the region's many lakes.

Glaciers flowed across the Lake Plain and the Till Plain during the Pleistocene Epoch. They left scattered rocks and deposits of sand and gravel. The soil is fertile and in many places it is deep. The central and east areas of the Lake Plain tend to have smaller farms and dairy farms. The west area of the Lake Plain and the Till Plain have larger farms, though nowhere do they compare with the broad fields of Illinois and Iowa.

The Hill Country
A bit more than the southern third of Indiana is known as the Hill Country. The great glaciers rode over the east and west of this region but this was the southern limit of their extent. Here the ice sheets were not as thick or as heavy as in the northern part of the state. They didn't level the land as much and left it more rugged, less suitable for agriculture. Still, much of the land was cleared and farms established, although ero-sion was a major problem.

The glaciers did not cover the center of the southern region of Indiana. Here are the steepest hills in the state, with ravines, bluffs, and rock outcroppings. Here you'll find Brown County with its famous fall display of leafy color, and Brown County State Park and Lake Monroe, the largest lake in the state, an artificial reservoir created by a dam. Farther south is Hoosier National Forest, along with several state forests.

To the east, in the southern region, is Muscatatuck National Wildlife Refuge and still farther east is Big Oaks National Wildlife Refuge. To the southwest in this region is the Patoka River National Wildlife Refuge.

Brown County State Park is not the only State Park in southern Indiana. There are Clifty Falls, Harmonie, McCormick's Creek, Shades, Shakamak, Spring Mill, Turkey Run, Versailles, and Whitewater. Each was designated a park because of its rugged terrain, scenic beauty, and abundant wildlife.

The southern boundary of the state, the line between Indiana and Kentucky, is the Ohio River. Historically this region featured low falls, rapids, and great bluffs. Along this river, and along the lower part of the Wabash, were extensive cypress swamps, where wood ducks once nested in large numbers. There were huge rookeries of herons and egrets. In winter there were flocks of mallards and other ducks.

Typical birds of today's Indiana Hill Country include green heron, Canada goose, wood duck, turkey vulture, red-tailed hawk, northern bobwhite, mourning dove, red-bellied woodpecker, downy woodpecker, barn swallow, American crow, Carolina chickadee, tufted titmouse, American redstart, and northern cardinal.

As with the wetlands and the prairie of the northwest, only remnants of the cypress swamps are left. Even in those remnants, many of the trees were cut. Stumps of the great trees, some of bald cypress sixteen feet across, are reminders of what the forests used to be.

But not all of Indiana's abundant natural beauty is gone. Pieces of the original ecoregions remain in state parks and forests and in fish and wildlife areas and nature preserves. As mentioned previously, the Nature Conservancy, ACRES, and other groups have acquired some natural areas. Friends of the Limberlost are re-establishing

flooding of some of that swampland. And there are a variety of national and state parks and wildlife refuges.

Eighty-seven percent of Indiana was originally covered by deciduous forest. One pioneer who left an account of crossing the state described a feeling of confinement that dampened the spirits as they traveled through the forest. Today less than 5 percent of the state is covered by forest; instead of a vast stand of trees, wooded areas are small plots now, except in larger tracts in Hoosier National Forest and several state forests.

More than 80 percent of the original wetlands of Indiana, including many small lakes, were drained. But more lakes have been created. The largest lakes in the state now are artificial reservoirs created by dams, such as Monroe, Brookville, Patoka, Mississinewa, Salamonie, and J. Edward Roush.

Though only bits of the original cover of Indiana remain, the topography is largely the same except for drainage projects, reservoirs, and development. The ecoregions are now areas created by development: agricultural areas where once there was forest, wetland, and prairie; urban areas and cities; and even houses and cottages around many of the lakes.

Yet there are still birds and other animals in all seasons. While some species of birds have declined, others have increased. Robins, cardinals, and eastern meadowlarks are undoubtedly more numerous now than in pioneer days. There are more starlings, house sparrows, and house finches. Sandhill cranes now nest in the state again. Bald eagles, wild turkeys, peregrine falcons, and white-tailed deer have been successfully re-established and breed here once more. A program to establish Canada geese in the state has succeeded, perhaps too well for some.

The variety of terrain and cover, however, still provides habitats for many bird species. Indiana's location as a crossroads in the east-central part of the United States makes it a place where bird watchers can see the common eastern and midwestern species, as well as northern, southern, and a few western species.

Indiana Bird Watching by Season

Spring

Spring in Indiana, as everywhere in the Midwest, is unpredictable. There are often warm, sunny days in February or even January that make us think of spring. But such days are nearly always followed by more days of freezing temperatures, ice, and often snow. However, by the end of February, in spite of vicissitudes of weather, buds on trees are swelling and the first bird migrants have arrived.

The outline of spring included in this chapter generally applies to the central part of Indiana. In the southern part, along the Ohio River, events may be a month earlier while in the north; along the shore of Lake Michigan, they may be weeks or nearly a month later.

Robins are spotted toward the end of February or early in March. Their presence is often reported in newspaper stories announcing the beginning of spring. Flocks of male red-winged blackbirds (perhaps better harbingers of spring's arrival) drift over the countryside during the day and roost at night in cattails of marshes or around the shores of lakes. Meadowlarks and bluebirds return and begin singing and courting.

The first robin in the yard, or bluebird along a country road, or flock of red-winged blackbirds is a signal to start visiting lakes and marshes looking for waterfowl and other waterbirds. Wood ducks, mallards, blue-winged teal, a few other species and, of course, Canada geese nest in Indiana, but many more pass through to more northern nesting grounds. March is the time when leaves begin to open and the bird watcher in Indiana who wants a big annual list goes out looking for the ducks, geese, and early shorebirds.

March is also a time to visit woods to see early wildflowers as well as birds. Bloodroot, spring beauty, hepatica, and many more flowers bloom while sunlight still shines through leafless branches and warms the ground. Resident woodland birds such as blue jays, downy, hairy, and red-bellied woodpeckers, chickadees, tufted titmice, and white-breasted nuthatches are selecting territories, singing or calling, and even beginning to build nests.

This is when sandhill cranes visit the Jasper-Pulaski Fish and Wildlife Area in northwest Indiana. The cranes are never as numerous there in spring as on peak days in fall, but the fortunate bird watcher may still see several thousand of these spectacular birds at dusk as they gather to roost at "J-P."

March, the windy month, is the time to check the direction of the wind. Go to the fields on clear days when the wind is from the south and watch the sky: On a warm day when thermals are rising there may be hawks—red-tailed and broad-winged hawks, northern harriers, merlins, Cooper's and sharp-shinned hawks—flying over. There may also be flocks of ducks, geese, and

Broad-winged hawk

sandhill cranes. With the sandhills, there is an ever-greater chance of seeing a whooping crane on its return flight to the Necedah Refuge in Wisconsin.

Indiana does not have a birding hotspot to compare with Whitefish Point in Michigan, or Hawk Mountain, Pennsylvania, or Duluth, Minnesota. But the shore of Lake Michigan at the northwest corner of the state and the area near it can provide a long list of waterfowl and other waterbirds, shorebirds, gulls, raptors, and songbirds in March, April, or even early in May.

Most of the birds that visit Indiana only in winter leave in March. Dark-eyed juncos and tree sparrows disappear from the bird feeders, headed north to breed. Pine siskins, redpolls, and evening grosbeaks leave those fortunate birders who have enjoyed these erratic, unpredictable visitors. The flocks of Lapland longspurs and snow buntings that have occasionally been found along country roads are gone but Indiana's horned larks have begun nesting.

Dandelions begin to bloom in March and mourning doves, robins, and bluebirds begin to nest. Brown thrashers return and sing to announce their territories. Tree swallows appear toward the end of the month, followed by purple martins.

April is a month of constant change and activity among plants and birds. Trees are blossoming, their leaves opening. Many red-winged blackbirds have deserted the flocks and divided marshes and fields into territories, each bird singing and flashing its epaulets in its chosen kingdom. The females return. Most other resident summer birds are back. Baltimore orioles, catbirds, song sparrows, chipping sparrows, indigo buntings, killdeer, and many more are announcing territories, choosing mates, and nesting.

Barn swallows return and circle over fields and lakes and marshes during the day, swooping in

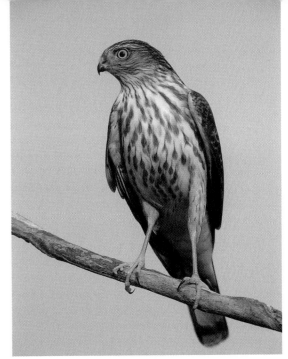

Sharp-shinned hawk

and out of barns and other buildings that have open windows or doors, already prospecting for satisfactory places to plaster up their nests of mud. Bank swallows and rough-winged swallows join the barn swallows in what seems like nearly nonstop daily aerial patrolling for insects.

The end of April or the first of May is the time when Hoosier bird watchers go for their Big Days. Then they hope to see lingering waterfowl and shorebirds on and around lakes and marshes, warblers and other songbirds in the woods, and grassland birds in the fields. On a day early in May it is possible to find thirty species of warbler, half a dozen species of vireo, and a dozen birds named sparrow.

As May progresses, the migrants that pass through or over Indiana disappear. Only summer resident birds remain and most of them are busy with families. There are goslings and ducklings on lakes and ponds, young killdeer in fields. Fledgling, spot-breasted robins follow their parents on lawns in yards and parks, begging noisily. By the end of May the leaves on the trees are all open and mosquitoes are almost unbearable around wetlands at dusk and dawn. Summer has arrived.

Summer

The pace of life appears to slow in summer. The green leaves of trees and bushes seem to be unchanging. Growing crops of corn and soybeans look the same day after day though there is noticeable change from one week to the next. The migrating birds that pass through the state are gone.

Nesting birds no longer show the frenetic activity of pairing. By June the dawn bird chorus is greatly reduced in volume, variety, and duration. Song sparrows still sing before the sun appears. Robins, brown thrashers, and cardinals greet the sun. Meadowlarks whistle from pasture fenceposts but the songs are brief. Many of the birds have nestlings to feed. Mourning doves and robins are incubating or even beginning to feed second broods.

There are more and more young birds about in June. Juvenile spot-breasted robins prospect lawns for worms, having to find their own food as their parents incubate the eggs of second broods. There are bob-tailed redwings in hayfields and the cattails of marshes. Young mallards

Mourning dove

and wood ducks follow their mothers across the water of lakes and marshes. Immature Canada geese look nearly as big as their parents. Young killdeer are nearly grown.

Bird watchers in Indiana who keep their feeders stocked in summer have bird families coming for handouts. Cardinals, song sparrows, and chipping sparrows that visit feeders are followed by one or two fledglings, which the adult birds stuff at these bird cafeterias. Occasionally a song or chipping sparrow will be feeding a young cowbird that is much bigger than it is. Barn swallows in their nests are nearly crowding each other out.

By the end of June many birds only sing or call sporadically, though our red-eyed and warbling vireos continue to sing throughout the day. A walk through the woods can be a quiet, nearly silent, time unless the wind is blowing, shaking leaves and rattling branches. Birds will be hard to spot as they move quietly through the screen of leaves.

In July the weather is likely to be the same day after day, except when it rains: pleasant in the early morning and evening, hot the rest of the day. Puffy, white cumulus clouds appear in the morning and often build into giant thunderheads by afternoon. Sometimes there are thunderstorms, with lightning and thunder, and occasionally brief torrential showers.

Red-tailed hawks and turkey vultures circle in the rising air currents beneath the clouds. Swallows swirl about, high and low, at times barely skimming the grass in pastures and hayfields. They actually scoop water from the surface of lakes and ponds on still days, leaving wakes of ripples as they drink on the fly.

In July adult starlings begin to lose their iridescent breeding plumage. By the end of the month, they are brown and speckled, and their bills have changed from yellow to blackish-brown. Their colors match the colors of their fledglings. Flocks of starlings fly about the countryside, landing like swarms of locusts in pastures and other grassy fields, feeding on the insects there.

Red-eyed vireo

Shorebirds that nested farther north, such as yellowlegs, dowitchers, and a host of little sandpipers, reappear on the shore of Lake Michigan, then the shores of lakes in Indiana. These birds have molted into post-breeding plumage and are migrating, already on the way south, although it might seem early, to us, for the onset of fall migration.

In August there are multitudes of red-winged blackbirds as well as starlings. The blackbird crowds grow as flock joins flock until, as they fly, they appear from the distance like wisps of smoke drifting across the sky. There may be tens of thousands, hundreds of thousands in a single flock. At night the flocks fly to communal roosts, usually dense stands of cattails. As they collect in trees around the roost at dusk their calling creates a din that drowns out all other sound.

At night flocks come together to roost, often in the cattails of a marsh or in a large shade tree.

Late in July and in August, when most other birds have finished nesting for the year, goldfinches are just beginning. From the heads of thistles going to seed they get down to line the nests they build in saplings in fence rows and scrubby fields. As the goldfinches begin to incubate eggs, swallows are flocking, often perching on power lines like rows of clothespins.

Interestingly, as redwings flock they separate by sex. There are groups of males and there are groups of females, but there are no flocks of males and females. At night they also roost separately. In the roosts, though male and female redwings don't intermingle, either group may also contain starlings, common grackles, brown-headed cowbirds, robins, and tree, barn, bank, and rough-winged swallows.

Mallard (male)

Autumn

Blooming Joe Pye weed, New England aster, the first goldenrod, poison ivy, Virginia creeper, and sumac leaves turning red all signal the beginning of autumn in Indiana. Walnut leaves turn yellow and begin to fall. Bird watchers notice the changing colors of the leaves as they struggle to identify the passing peep sandpipers and look for the first migrating warblers.

Autumn in Indiana is a time of birds disappearing as well as appearing. Catbirds and brown thrashers, Baltimore orioles, rose-breasted grosbeaks, and scarlet tanagers disappear. Unlike spring when the date of first appearance of a species is noted, the date of disappearance is rarely known. One day the bird watcher just notices the catbirds are gone from the bushes around the yard, the brown thrashers from the trees along the stream, the tanagers from the woods—and that they haven't been seen in days. Yellow warblers and common yellowthroats are also gone.

In September, people with hummingbird feeders begin to wonder how soon they should bring those feeders in. Some people become concerned that having their feeders out may be the

Gray catbird

reason a few hummingbirds are still there and that those birds may be caught by an early frost. This, however, is a myth: keeping your hummingbird feeders out will in fact help fuel these tiny migrants on their long journey south.

By the end of September, goldenrod blossoms are fading as the plants go to seed. The leaves of walnut trees have fallen, though there are still nuts on the trees. Cottonwoods have lost their leaves except a few which crown the very top. Maples and tulip trees, oaks and hickories, and dogwoods and other trees have lost their green and turned to yellow and orange, red and brown. While the trees are changing to their brightest colors, warblers are passing through, many in their dullest colors.

Fall migration of songbirds is far different than spring migration. In spring those birds were in breeding plumage, the warblers so brightly colored they have been called butterflies of the bird world. They were singing. They seemed full of energy, ever active, easy to spot but difficult to get a good look at as they flitted about. In fall many are in faded plumage. They look dull and shop-worn. They don't sing though they do call occasionally, the warblers with faint lisps and *seeps*. They appear to move more slowly, more deliberately; the warblers and vireos almost seem to be sneaking through the tree branches.

October is the peak of fall color in Indiana. It's then or early in November that Hoosiers go to Brown County in southern Indiana to enjoy the color and the weather. October's bright blue weather is not just a saying but usually a fact. The temperature dips, there is often frost at night toward the end of the month, but the temperatures during the day are mild. Mosquitoes, flies, and other insect pests no longer bother us when we're outdoors.

In October and into November flocks of ducks and geese are migrating through. This is a good time for bird watchers in the state to visit the Indiana Dunes and look for birds that are rare visitors, perhaps a brant or a Eurasian wigeon, a glaucous or Iceland gull. For birders who don't

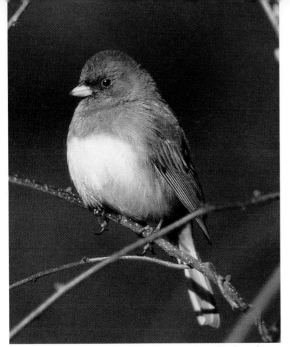

Dark-eyed junco

want to travel that far or risk being there when the wind is uncomfortably strong and cold, any lake in the state may be visited to view flocks of waterfowl.

Fall, of course, is the season when hunters as well as bird watchers look for ducks and geese. Deer hunters are also out and birders should be aware of this when walking in the woods. Hunting seasons are set annually but are usually fairly liberal in Indiana. The wise birder will take note of them, not just for personal safety, but also because if there are duck hunters at a marsh or lake there won't be ducks or geese.

As in spring, when the weather is fair and the wind favorable (blowing from the north in fall), bird watchers can go out in the country and watch for birds flying over. They may see flocks of ducks or geese or even sandhill cranes. They can watch for a white whooping crane among the gray sandhills. They may see red-tailed, broad-winged, Cooper's, and sharp-shinned hawks, northern harriers, and a bald eagle or even two or three. Golden eagles have been seen in Indiana during late fall and winter.

Late October and early November is the time when bird watchers from Indiana, Illinois, Michigan, and Wisconsin and even farther afield make a trip to the Jasper-Pulaski Fish and Wildlife Area to see the sandhill cranes. Unlike spring, when the rush is on to find prime nesting spots, in fall the birds gather and stay, often for a couple of weeks or longer as others keep arriving. They feed in harvested grain fields around the area during the day, gather in the evening in a field called the goose pasture, and soon after dusk fly to shallow marshes on the property where they roost, standing in the water. Anywhere from 10,000 to 30,000 sandhill cranes may be at Jasper-Pulaski at the peak, usually early in November. Late afternoon is the best time to visit; find an observation platform, then stand, watch, and listen as the birds gather. Stay until nearly dark to see and hear as the birds take off, *en masse*, to fly out to the marshes.

To see more of the cranes, get there earlier and drive around the surrounding country looking for small flocks standing and feeding in harvested grain fields or flying across the sky, often quite low. Staying at a motel in a nearby town enables birders to get out before dawn to see the birds leave the roost. Watch as they stream out in all directions and separate into small flocks of only a few hundred each. Watch closely for a white one—a whooping crane.

As long as the experiment establishing a migratory flock of whooping cranes—that summer at Wisconsin's Necedah National Wildlife Refuge and winter at the Chassohowitzka Refuge in Florida—continues, bird watchers in Indiana can check the news to learn of the progress of these birds as they cross the state. Often the news includes a viewing site and time where birders can go to see the ultralite aircraft leading the cranes.

By the end of November the more common birds that nest farther north and that winter in Indiana have arrived. Dark-eyed juncos and American tree sparrows have become regular visitors at bird feeders. Red-breasted nuthatches are scattered and uncommon but there are some every year and the bird watcher who has one coming to a feeder is considered lucky.

Thanksgiving passes and with it, it seems, autumn.

Winter

December is usually a drab month in Indiana, a cold month. Leaves are nearly all gone from the trees. They blanket the ground where they have not been raked up. Weeds and wildflowers along the sides of roads create a miniature forest of yellow and brown stems. The fields of corn and soybeans are gone, replaced by fields of stubble or dark earth where the ground has been plowed. Frost puts a glitter on the leaves and stems and stubble at dawn but the glitter disappears soon after the sun comes up.

The most common birds, in December and throughout the winter, are year-round residents such as cardinals, blue jays, house sparrows, house finches, American goldfinches, chickadees, titmice, white-breasted nuthatches, and downy, hairy, and red-bellied woodpeckers. They are seen at nearly every bird feeder, joined there by winter visitors, the juncos and tree sparrows, and occasionally, a few white-crowned sparrows.

There are flocks of starlings about and sometimes a gaggle of these insatiable birds will descend on a feeder. There are stragglers, too; perhaps a small flock of red-winged blackbirds, or robins in woods where there are berries still on the branches, a few bluebirds in a brush-lined fencerow, or a mourning dove or two. The starlings will be around all winter, while the other birds may be gone after the first snow.

Canada geese are on the lakes and rivers. There are a few mallards and sometimes other ducks, until ice puts a lid on lakes and ponds and marshes. A few great blue herons and occasionally a belted kingfisher linger until ice covers the water. Bird watchers look for all these stragglers and try to keep track of them so they can list them on Christmas Bird Counts, held between late December and early January.

There are crows and red-tailed hawks and a few kestrels. There are great horned owls, barred owls, and eastern screech-owls though these are rarely seen. Late in December, however, the great horned owls call often at dusk. Their hoots are meant for each other, but they also let birders know that the owls are about and beginning their late-winter nesting cycle.

Winter weather in Indiana is as unpredictable as the most erratic winter birds. There may be snow as early as November or not until January; in some years there is a lot of snow, and some years almost none. Often snow blankets the entire state, but sometimes it is limited to the "snow belt," an area in the north around the shores of Lake Michigan.

Whether there is snow or not, there are Cooper's and sharp-shinned hawks in Indiana in winter. Though not numerous, individual birds are sometimes conspicuous as they hang about the vicinity of a particular bird feeder, perching nearby, swooping in now and then and snatching a chickadee or goldfinch or other bird feeding there. Though a natural, even exciting event, such raids are usually decried by the feeder owner.

Winter is a quiet time outdoors, particularly when there is snow on the ground and ice on the rivers as well as the lakes and ponds. It can be,

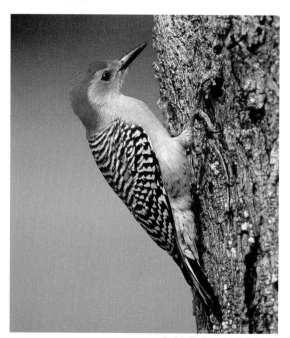

Red-bellied woodpecker (male)

and frequently is, an unexciting time for bird watchers. But for the birder willing to roam about the countryside there is always the chance of seeing a "good" bird or even a flock of them. The usual red-tailed hawk perched on the branch of a tree or on a power pole may, after a closer look, turn out to be a rough-legged hawk. A flock of horned larks seen flying over a field, if followed and checked, may have Lapland longspurs in its midst. Flocks in windswept fields should always be checked for flashes of white when they fly, for there is always the chance of seeing snow buntings, particularly in the northern part of the state.

Northern saw-whet owl

There are other winter wanderers, too, erratic, unpredictable birds that add a bit of suspense to birding when the weather is cold, the days are short, and, often, snow covering the ground. Some of these birds are solitary and some travel in flocks like the snow buntings.

A few snowy owls are seen in Indiana every winter. Rare anywhere in the state, they are especially rare south of Indianapolis. Short-eared owls are also seen nearly every winter, almost always (like snowies) in the northern half of the state. Usually these owls are seen singly but occasionally there is a small group of them. They hunt during the day in overcast weather and may remain in the same area most of the winter, often roosting in a stand of pines or other evergreen trees.

Two more species of owl are seen in Indiana, usually in winter (though both have been known to nest in the state). But it's in winter that bird watchers walk through pine plantations looking for pellets and the tell-tale whitewash of owl droppings, searching the branches overhead when they find them. There they may find a northern saw-whet owl, often at eye level, usually wide-eyed, staring back and showing no fear. Or a birder searching evergreens may spot a long-eared owl perched higher up.

Flocks of little seed-eating birds in Indiana during winter may be pine siskins or redpolls. Every bird in a flock of redpolls should be checked through binoculars, because a hoary redpoll is always possible among the commons. Other birds seen sometimes in flocks here during winter are evening grosbeaks and both red and white-winged crossbills.

Siskins, redpolls, evening grosbeaks, and crossbills are irruptive, seen outside their usual range in large number some years. Certainly this describes the appearance of these birds in Indiana. Hoosier bird watchers speak of "the winter of the siskins" (or redpolls or evening grosbeaks), a winter when the birds indicated seemed to have been everywhere.

Nearly every year there is a period of warm weather, a winter thaw, in January or February. At this time, bird watchers who have been content to do their birding through the windows of their homes, watching birds at their feeders, get out in the woods and around the fields and think of spring. They may find that the old nest of a pair of red-tailed hawks is now occupied by a great horned owl. They won't be able to see into the elevated nest, but they'll know that the owl has eggs. This, even more than the weather, will make them think of spring—but it's too early. Even though the owl is incubating, winter is not over. Nor is the possibility of seeing a rare winter visitor, perhaps a northern shrike, a northern goshawk, or a small flock of pine grosbeaks. And spring, along with the return of our favorite migrants, is not far off.

Indiana's Ten Must-See Birds

Black-bellied Plover
Pluvialis squatarola

This is a chunky bird, larger than a robin, smaller than a crow. In spring it has a black face, throat, and belly, a short, thick black bill, black legs and feet, and a black back flecked with white. In flight the black-bellied plover shows black "armpits" under its wings, a good field mark for identifying distant birds. Only a golden plover resembles it and the color of the golden's back is completely different, a more golden hue.

In fall the black on a black-bellied plover's breast is gone except for the bill, legs, and feet and is replaced by mottled gray, giving the bird a much less impressive appearance than it has in spring and summer.

As a bird of passage in Indiana, black-bellied plovers may be seen on the muddy shores of any lake or in a muddy farm field anywhere in the state in spring when they are migrating north, or in late summer or early fall when they are on the way south. Scanning appropriate habitat during spring migration is a fruitful way to find these shorebirds. They seem to have an uncanny ability to blend into a muddy field or shoreline in spite of their large size (11¹/₂ inches). The black-bellied plover is a fairly rare sighting in Indiana, usually just a single bird, though small flocks are occasionally seen along the shore of Lake Michigan during spring and fall migrations.

Bobolink
Dolichonyx oryzivorus

In breeding plumage, the male bobolink is a reverse of the usual dark above, light below most birds display: his face and throat are black, while the back of his head is cream colored. The breast and belly are black and the shoulders and rump are white with buffy steaks down its back—a kind of backward tuxedo look. The female is another little brown bird, more buffy or yellow than most sparrows.

A bird of grassy fields, the bobolink has profited by the clearing of forests in Indiana. As fields replace forests, it's become a common bird in the northern part of the state, somewhat less common in the central part. There's been a decline in recent years, perhaps due to the increased use of cold-hardy hay plantings that permit earlier hay cuttings—while the bobolinks are on the nest. Now birders take note of fields where bobolinks still nest in Indiana. These include sites where remnant prairie is preserved or where large grasslands have been left uncut, such as at Big Oaks National Wildlife Refuge near Madison in southern Indiana.

One of spring's most beautiful sights is the fluttering flight song display of the male bobolink as he courts a female hidden in the grass and announces his "turf" to rival males. His bubbling, babbling song is spring music to the ears of bird watchers everywhere.

Caspian Tern

Sterna caspia

A tern looks like a streamlined version of a gull, with more slender, pointed wings. The Caspian tern is a large one (21 inches long), longer than some gulls, with a proportionately larger head. It is white overall with a black cap and black wingtips, and a dark-red bill with a black tip. Eastern North America's only other large white tern, the royal tern, is smaller than the Caspian, and is rarely found inland away from salt water.

Caspian terns are migrants that go north through Indiana in spring and pass through again headed south in fall. They are seen regularly in both spring and fall along the shores of Lake Michigan. They are also seen frequently on lakes and reservoirs in the state, or along rivers, sometimes resting on a snag in the water, sometimes flying twenty or more feet above the water, then suddenly plunging in to catch a fish.

From a distance, the Caspian tern appears to be a very large white gull. Though the Caspian is a very gull-like bird, its flight style is lighter and more buoyant than a gull's and its wings appear more angled and tapered toward the wingtips than a gull's wings. Gulls and terns may be seen together, loafing on a sandbar, along a dam wall, or lakeshore, so it pays to check carefully through flocks of resting gulls.

Caspian terns spend the winter months along the southern coasts of the United States.

Cerulean Warbler

Dendroica cerulea

This is a treetop forager, easily heard but hard to spot among the leaves as it sings its high, buzzy song that sounds like teazel, teazel, teazel, ti ti ti zeeee. If a bright sky above doesn't turn it into a silhouette, the male is easy to identify, blue above with a white throat and two white wing bars, white below with a blue-black necklace and streaks along the sides. The female is yellowish-green above, yellowish-gray below and lacks the necklace and streaking.

An early writer of birds in Indiana, Amos W. Butler, considered this one of the most common birds in the extensive forests of the state. Now, even where forest remains, this is an uncommon-to-rare spring and summer bird except in a few places, one being the Big Oaks National Wildlife Refuge north of Madison in southeast Indiana. Several population studies are ongoing all across the eastern United States seeking answers for this bird's rapid decline.

The cerulean warbler prefers dry oak or deciduous woods for its nesting habitat. Forest fragmentation and other habitat loss, both here in North America and in the Central and South American tropical forests where it winters, have reduced the population of this warbler to a fraction of its original numbers. This makes this warbler species a prize find for Indiana birders and one that many actively seek out each spring and summer when the cerulean is in our midst. Winter finds the cerulean amid the tropical forests of Central America with no plans to return to Indiana until the following spring.

Great Egret
Ardea alba

In Indiana only the great blue heron and sandhill crane stand taller than this long-necked, long-legged white bird. The little blue heron is approximately the same length (an immature little blue is also white). But the yellow bill and dark legs and feet set the great egret apart from the little blue and the smaller cattle and snowy egrets.

Stories of plume hunters decimating great and snowy egrets in their rookeries in the South (particularly in Florida), and the drastic decline of the species make people think of these as southern birds. But they once nested in significant numbers in rookeries along the Ohio River in southern Indiana and in the Grand Kankakee Marsh in northwest Indiana. As in the South, they declined drastically and almost disappeared from the state, but this decline was due as much and possibly more to loss of habitat as it was to hunting. The shallow water areas where they fed were drained; trees where they nested were cut.

However, great egrets have made a comeback in Indiana as well as in other states. Though not as numerous as in pioneer days, today they once more nest in a few places in the state. Almost certainly they are more widespread now than in pioneer days, because they are wanderers when not nesting and can be seen at any marsh or pond, either wading, perched in a tree, or on the shore.

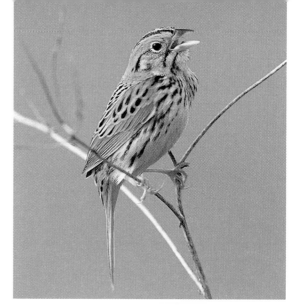

Henslow's Sparrow
Ammodramus henslowii

The Henslow's sparrow is one of those frustrating, intriguing LBJs (little brown jobs). A bird of open grassland, it's difficult to get a good look at it—often it is only glimpsed as it spurts up out of the grass, flies a short distance, and then drops back out of sight. It's described as a large-headed sparrow with gray marks on the face and a gray stripe through the crown.

The best time to see and identify a Henslow's sparrow is in spring and summer when it's singing. Then it perches at the top of a stem of grass and, though its appearance is nondescript, its song is distinctive (though it isn't much of a song)—an unmusical, lisping, two-note *tssi-slip!*, almost like a dry hiccup or the call of some insect. Bird watchers unfamiliar with this song might ignore it as insect background noise, which is certainly present in these grassland habitats. The song of the grasshopper sparrow, another of Indiana's rare grassland nesters, is equally insectlike.

This bird is rare and local over most of Indiana. However, it is common in spring and summer in the Big Oaks National Wildlife Refuge in southeast Indiana and a significant nesting population can be found at Chinook Fish and Wildlife Area near Brazil. Many of the reclaimed strip mines in Indiana have become suitable habitat for Henslow's sparrow and the birds seem to be thriving in these areas.

Peregrine Falcon
Falco peregrinus

In Indiana—where there are no prairie falcons—this large falcon with the dark helmet and back and spotted, almost banded lower breast and belly is unmistakable. The peregrine is the largest falcon regularly seen in Indiana. Though a merlin resembles it, the merlin is markedly smaller, more slender, and lacks the look of power of the peregrine. With just a few strokes of its long, tapered wings a peregrine falcon can reach a high rate of flight speed. When diving or stooping upon prey from above, peregrines can—with the help of gravity—reach speeds of up to 200 miles per hour.

Historical nesting records of peregrines in Indiana are hard to find, but the bird was reported regularly during migration, particularly along the shore of Lake Michigan in fall. With the extensive use of DDT following World War II, though, the peregrine disappeared from Indiana as a migrant and from the eastern half of the United States as a breeding bird.

Peregrines, however, have been successfully reintroduced to the state in an urban setting that, ironically, closely resembles the cliffside habitat in which peregrines normally nest. As in other states, they were released in cities after it was found they would nest on the ledges of tall buildings and prey upon starlings and pigeons. Peregrines now nest in Indianapolis, Ft. Wayne, and Gary, and are sometimes seen, though rarely, outside the cities. Migrant peregrines are still encountered in spring and fall along Lake Michigan and at other sites where hawk migration is regularly monitored.

Pileated Woodpecker
Dryocopus pileatus

The pileated is a woodpecker that is nearly as big as a crow. It is a large, mostly black-and-white bird. Both male and female pileateds have a flaming red crest and a white stripe through the face and down the neck. Males have a red moustache on the cheek, while females show a black moustache.

When it decides to make noise the pileated woodpecker is loud. Its repetitive *ack-ack-ack-ack-ack* call can be heard for long distances even in thick woods. When excavating a nest hole, drilling for insect prey on a tree, or doing some territorial drumming, the pileated's large chisel-like bill can sound exactly like an axe hitting a tree trunk. Yet, when this largest of Indiana's woodpeckers chooses to, it can be almost silent as it swoops through the trees.

In pioneer days this bird was reported to be common in Indiana, as might be expected with so much of the land covered in deep forest. As the forests were cut, the species declined until early in the last century there were suggestions that the pileated, like its relative the ivory-billed woodpecker, might become extinct. But the pileated has adapted. Though not numerous, it is far from rare and is now found in woodlots, in residential areas and parks where there are shade trees, and in trees along streams and rivers, as well as in the remaining large forests of the state. Some backyard feeders have been visited by pileateds, often for hunks of suet or specially made bird dough.

25

Sandhill Crane

Grus canadensis

The sandhill crane and great blue heron are both tall, long-necked, long-legged, gray birds, but an adult sandhill has a red forehead, a heron's is white, and an immature sandhill has a rusty head and neck. In flight, a crane flies with neck extended giving it a cross shape, while the heron folds its neck back and flies with its head nearly on its shoulders.

Aldo Leopold, forester, conservationist, educator, and author, called the sandhill crane "wilderness incarnate." Whether it's heard, then seen, as it flies high overhead, or seen feeding in a harvested grain field or standing in the shallow water of a marsh, it is an impressive symbol of wildness.

Sandhill cranes nested in the marshes of the north and northwest of Indiana in pioneer days. When those wetlands were nearly all drained, the cranes stopped breeding here. But they still migrated across the state, flying from nesting areas in Wisconsin, Minnesota, and Canada to wintering grounds in Georgia and Florida in fall, returning north in spring. They began using the Jasper-Pulaski State Fish and Wildlife Area in northwest Indiana as a staging area. In 1944, approximately 700 gathered there. Since then, the number has increased year by year until now 20,000 or more may be seen there in early November.

Sandhill cranes are also nesting once more in the north of the Hoosier State. The nests are widely scattered and not numerous but nearly every year nests are found and reported.

Short-eared Owl

Asio flammeus

The feather tufts that give this owl its name are tiny and seldom seen, creating a round-headed look, much like a barred owl. In fact, these ear tufts are usually only visible on perched birds that are alert and excited. But the short-eared has streaking around the face and on the throat (instead of barring), and yellow eyes (not brown), which easily distinguish it from the barred. Additionally, the short-eared owl is a bird of grassy, open fields, not woodlands, the preferred habitat of the barred owl.

Short-eared owls have nested in Indiana infrequently in the past, but now they are largely erratic winter visitors. A bird watcher driving about the Indiana countryside on a cloudy day in winter may spot one, or a small, loose-knit group of them, flying as buoyantly as a butterfly, fairly bouncing along in the air. Short-eared owls fly low over the ground as they hunt for mice and voles. They use both sight and sound to locate their prey, wheeling and hovering, then pouncing once an unfortunate rodent reveals its location. Walking through a grassy field, you may flush this owl, because they roost on the ground, often in a loose colony. If you flush a short-eared from its daytime roost, scan the ground for pellets. These are regurgitated balls of fur and bones, the indigestible parts of its diet.

In winter, short-eared owls may skirmish with one another over prime hunting habitat. During these episodes you may hear the owl's hoarse, doglike call. The Indiana Dunes is one spot where short-eared owls may be found.

Indiana's Ten Best Bird-Watching Spots

Indiana Ecoregions

☐ TILL PLAIN

☐ HILL COUNTRY

☐ LAKE PLAIN

Key Code

1. Jasper-Pulaski State Fish and Wildlife Area
2. Indiana Dunes National Lakeshore
3. Willow Slough State Fish and Wildlife Area
4. Kankakee State Fish and Wildlife Area
5. Pigeon River State Fish and Wildlife Area
6. Salamonie Reservoir
7. Big Oaks National Wildlife Refuge
8. Muscatatuck National Wildlife Refuge
9. Patoka River National Wildlife Refuge
10. Hovey Lake State Fish and Wildlife Area

---

❼

Big Oaks National Wildlife Refuge

1661 West JPG Niblo Road
Madison, IN 47250
www.midwest.fws.gov/bigoaks

From 1940 to 1995 this was a U.S. Army Base, the Jefferson Proving Grounds. Shells, rockets, and bombs were tested here, which has left many areas of the property where there are unexploded shells and bombs. Since the cost of cleaning up those areas is prohibitive, the refuge has large areas that are unsafe and are "Off Limits." Visitors are permitted on the refuge only in the safe areas, and only on Monday and Friday, April through November, and on the second and fourth Saturdays of those months. Each visitor is given a safety briefing and must sign a form acknowledging that he or she understands the restrictions and the reasons for them.

In spite of the limitations and safety hazards, Big Oaks is worth a birder's time. It combines grasslands and woodlands that produce the highest nesting populations of Henslow's sparrows and cerulean warblers in the state. Turkeys and deer are common in the woodlands and many other species frequent these habitats. There is also a 165-acre lake that attracts good numbers of waterfowl in spring and summer.

Hovey Lake State Fish and Wildlife Area
15010 SR 69 South
Mt. Vernon, IN 47620
(812) 838-2927

This is an oxbow lake of more than 4,000 acres along the Ohio River. Oxbows are created when a big, curving bend of a river is cut off, usually when the river changes course during a powerful flood, leaving behind an oxbow. The lake has many bald cypress trees growing where it is most shallow and around the shore in places.

The cypress and the expanse of water attract ducks, geese, double-crested cormorants, little blue and great blue herons, black-crowned and yellow-crowned night herons, and snowy egrets in summer and fall, though the egrets don't nest here. Bald eagles do, however, and recently a pair of ospreys nested here. In spring, fall, and winter there can be many waterfowl, and in spring (on those certain days that bird watchers dream about), the trees can be full of migrant warblers.

Indiana Dunes National Lakeshore (and surrounding area)
1100 North Mineral Springs Road
Porter, IN 46304
(219) 926-7561

Indiana Dunes State Park
1600 North 25 East
Chesterton, IN 46304
(219) 926-1952

This is a combination of the National Lakeshore, Indiana Dunes State Park, and tracts of private land along the shore of Lake Michigan from Gary to Michigan City. Inland from the shoreline are the sand dunes, including Big Baldy, a huge, active dune that is slowly moving south, burying an oak woodlot. There are bird-filled wetland woods, bogs, and areas of wetland prairie. The lakeshore and diversity of habitat attracts a variety of birds. Many rarities for Indiana have been seen here including scoters, jaegers, glaucous, Iceland, little, and Sabine's gulls, and black-legged kittiwake. Snowy owls, boreal chickadees, and hoary redpolls have also been sighted. On a broad sandy beach in Michigan City and from a stone jetty and breakwater there, harlequin ducks, king eiders, and purple sandpipers have been spotted in winter. Most rare birds have been spotted in this area in fall, but rarities can occur in spring and winter, too.

Jasper-Pulaski State Fish and Wildlife Area
5822 North Fish and Wildlife Lane
Medaryville, IN 47975
(219) 843-4841

The greatest birding spectacle in Indiana is the gatherings of sandhill cranes at Jasper-Pulaski, or J-P. This area of woodlands, fields, and shallow lakes is a staging area in spring and especially in fall for thousands of sandhill cranes. Bird watchers from Indiana and surrounding states make annual fall trips to J-P in late October or early November when they may see and hear 30,000 of these great gray birds gathering at dusk in a field before flying out to roost standing in the shallow water of the lakes. Now, with whooping cranes migrating from Wisconsin, there is an increasing chance of seeing one or more of these endangered birds with the sandhills at J-P. Observation platforms make long-distance viewing of the birds easier. J-P is also a place of migrating waterfowl in spring and fall, and some of the ducks of several species stay in spring to nest. There are marsh birds, too. At times in spring the woodland trees are alive with warblers. Then, too, there are vireos, flycatchers, and thrushes to delight sharp-eyed bird watchers.

Kankakee State Fish and Wildlife Area

4320 West Toto Road
P.O. Box 77
North Judson, IN 46366
(574) 896-3522
www.in.gov/dnr/fishwild/publications/kank.htm#wild

Once this was part of the extensive Kankakee River Marsh, a natural wonder covering hundreds of thousands of acres in this region of Indiana. The concentrations of ducks, geese, and shorebirds are said to have "blackened the skies" before the area was settled. Much of the Kankakee was drained for agriculture in the late 1800s. What remains today—just a fraction of the original—is still excellent for bird watching. The Yellow River flows into the Kankakee River here. There is riverbank woodland (good for warblers, vireos, tanagers, and orioles in spring and summer), wet marshy areas (good for rails and shorebirds), and low fields (sparrows and meadowlarks) that are flooded frequently. It's a place to see waterfowl and shorebirds in spring. In fall, due to intensive waterfowl hunting around the property, it is closed to prevent ducks from being flushed out to waiting hunters. Call ahead to determine access to the best birding areas.

Muscatatuck National Wildlife Refuge

12985 East U.S. Highway 50
Seymour, IN 47274
www.midwest.fws.gov/muscatatuck

This is river bottomland that was once hardwood forest. The forest was largely cleared for timber and the land converted to agriculture. But farming was difficult because of annual spring flooding and poor drainage that left the land wet long after the flood subsided. Now the land is managed through planting, controlled burning, and water-level manipulation to provide forest, wetland, and grassland habitat for birds and wildlife.

The Muscatatuck River flows through the refuge, fed by streams and natural springs, and there are both natural and artificial shallow impoundments. This habitat attracts many ducks, especially wood ducks, and Canada geese in addition to other waterbirds and wildlife. Summer tanager and blue grosbeak, generally more southern species uncommon in Indiana, have nested here. For several years there has been a resident pair of bald eagles.

Patoka River National Wildlife Refuge

510 West Morton Box 217
Oakland City, IN 47660
(812) 749-3199
www.midwest.fws.gov/patokariver/

This is a growing property in southern Indiana, presently between 5,000 and 6,000 acres with a goal of becoming 22,000 acres as land becomes available and there is money for purchase. Like Muscatatuck, this is a river bottomland habitat and is managed extensively for waterfowl, particularly wood ducks. The overall management objective, more limited than at Muscatatuck, is primarily the restoration of the bottomland hardwood forests. However, the Cane Ridge Unit of the refuge has the largest nesting population of interior least terns east of the Mississippi River. Many bird watchers visit Patoka River National Wildlife Refuge in early summer especially to see this federally endangered species.

Other birds to look for here include American woodcock, wild turkey, scarlet tanager, yellow warbler, common yellowthroat, Louisiana water-thrush, Carolina chickadee, and red-headed and pileated woodpeckers. Spring and fall migrations are the most active periods for birds, but summer and winter can be productive as well.

⑤

Pigeon River State Fish and Wildlife Area

8310 East 300 North
Box 71
Mongo, IN 46771
(260) 367-2164

This is a long, narrow state wildlife area comprising 11,605 acres along seventeen miles of the Pigeon River. It has farmland, scrubby pastureland, prairie plantings, wetlands, forest, and impoundments for waterfowl resting areas. Always a place for large numbers of waterfowl in spring and fall, it is becoming a fall staging area for sandhill cranes with several hundred there in recent years. It is also a good place to see migrating shorebirds. Look for them along any exposed mudflats and along the edges of wetlands. Spring mornings can offer rewarding warbler watching in Pigeon River's woodlands, especially along the river itself. As with other Indiana State Fish and Wildlife Areas, Pigeon River is managed for hunting and fishing. During fall waterfowl hunting season, large areas are closed to nonhunters, so it is advisable to call ahead for information about seasonal access.

⑥

Salamonie Reservoir

9214 West-Lost Bridge West
Andrews, IN 46702
(260) 468-2125

This is a flood-control reservoir, the center one of three created by dams that hold water to prevent flooding on the upper reaches of the Wabash River. The reservoir varies from 976 acres in winter to 2,855 in summer, with a maxi-mum flood-holding capacity of 9,000 acres. The land around the reservoir is river bluffs, agricultural fields, former agricultural fields now growing up to brush and trees, planted prairie plots, and woodlots. Drawdown of the water creates vast mudflats in late fall and winter, so check these areas for shorebirds. In summer the lake is used extensively by boaters, so the birding opportunities are diminished. When the water level goes above the summer level for flood control, there is flooding of fields and woods. There are smaller impoundments, ponds and marshes, around the reservoir.

The diversity of habitat and the annually fluctuating water level make this a place of waterbirds, shorebirds, woodland birds, and birds of open fields.

③

Willow Slough State Fish and Wildlife Area

2042 South 500 West
Morocco, IN 47963
(219) 285-2704
www.in.gov/dnr/fishwild/publications/willow.htm

This is an area of woodland, prairie, marsh, and lake, an area where once the forest gave way to prairie and marsh. Such variety of habitat attracts a variety of birds, of course: waterfowl, gulls, terns, herons, rails, grassland birds, vireos, warblers, thrushes, flycatchers, and swallows—Willow Slough gets them all. A number of rare species for Indiana have been seen at Willow Slough, including Ross's goose, black rail, yellow-headed blackbird, and Smith's longspur, a tundra-nester from the Far North that passes through during spring and fall migrations.

Osprey and bald eagle can be seen here, and this is also an excellent place to listen for owls at night. As a state fish and wildlife area, Willow Slough is managed for hunting, fishing, camping, and other outdoor activities. Call ahead to check on access—some areas are closed during the various hunting seasons.

Resources for Indiana Bird Watchers

Indiana Audubon Society

2505 East Maynard Drive
Indianapolis, IN 46227
www.indianaaudubon.org
The Indiana Audubon Society is the oldest conservation organization continuously operating in Indiana. It is not a chapter of the National Audubon Society, but an independent statewide organization.

Official State Bird Checklist

www.indianaaudubon.org/ibrc/offcklst.htm

Globally Important Bird Areas in Indiana

www.abcbirds.org/iba/indiana.htm

National Parks and Wildlife Refuges

Indiana Dunes National Lakeshore
(219) 926-7561 x225
www.nps.gov/indu

Muscatatuck National Wildlife Refuge
(812) 522-4352
http://midwest.fws.gov/Muscatatuck

State Parks and Wildlife Areas

Indiana's Division of State Parks and Reservoirs
www.IN.gov/dnr/parklake/parks/

Indiana Fish and Wildlife Areas
www.in.gov/dnr/fishwild/about/18areas.htm

Indiana Birding Websites

Indiana Audubon Society Online Birding Guide
www.indianaaudubon.org/guide

Conservation and Rescue Organizations

Chipper Woods Bird Observatory
10329 North New Jersey Street
Indianapolis, IN 46280
www.wbu.com/chipperwoods/index.htm
CWBO is a federal and state non-profit organization. Their mission is to bring good science to the conservation of birds and their habitats through scientific research, scientific training, and educational programs.

Indiana Bluebird Society
P.O. Box 356
Leesburg, IN 46538
www.nabluebirdsociety.org

Brown County Bluebird Society
P. O. Box 660
Nashville, IN 47448

Soarin' Hawk Avian Rescue
P. O. Box 13698
Fort Wayne, IN 46865
(260) 241-0134
www.soarinhawk.org/rehab/index_msie.html
A not-for-profit service to serve northeast Indiana's injured or orphaned birds of prey.

The Mary Gray Bird Sanctuary
3497 South Bird Sanctuary Road
Connersville, IN 47331
(765) 827-0908
www.indianaaudubon.org/AboutUs/Mary Gray.htm
Located in Fayette County, the sanctuary has more than seven hundred acres of forest, meadow, prairie, and ponds.

The Nature Conservancy's Indiana Field Office
1505 North Delaware Street, Suite 200
Indianapolis, IN 46202
(317) 951-8818
http://nature.org/wherewework/north
america/states/indiana/

Indiana National Audubon Chapters on the Web

Amos W. Butler Audubon Society
www.amosbutleraudubon.org

Dunes-Calumet Audubon Society
www.dunes-calumetaudubon.org/

Robert Cooper Audubon Society
http://bsu.edu/web/audubon

Evansville Audubon Society
www.evvaudubon.org

Knob and Valley Audubon Society
www.kavaudubon.org/

Potawatomi Audubon Society
www.alco.org/audubon/

Sassafras Audubon Society
www.bloomington.in.us/~audubon/

South Bend-Elkhart Audubon Society
www.sbeaudubon.org/

Tippecanoe Audubon Society
www.tippeaudubon.org/

Indiana Bird Clubs and Audubon Societies

American Midland Naturalist
University of Notre Dame
Notre Dame, IN 46556

East Central Audubon Society
210 South Hutchinson Avenue
Muncie, IN 47303

Mississinewa Audubon Club
6586 South 150 East
Jonesboro, IN 46938

Star Country Acres Bird Club
82 East 700 N-27
LaFontaine, IN 46940

Sycamore Audubon Society
P.O. Box 2716
West Lafayette, IN 47996

Wabash Valley Audubon Society
P. O. Box 2338
Terre Haute, IN 47802

West Central Indiana Bird Club
RR 1, Box 235 A
Carbon, IN 47837

Getting Started in Bird Watching

Bird watching, or birding, is one of North America's fastest-growing and most popular hobbies. According to a recent survey by the U.S. Fish & Wildlife Service, there are as many as 44 million bird watchers in the United States. Back in 1978, when my family began publishing Bird Watcher's Digest in our living room, bird watching was still considered a bit odd. The image many people associated with bird watching was Miss Jane Hathaway of The Beverly Hillbillies. Fortunately, that stereotype is long gone now, and our culture has come to embrace bird watching as an enriching, exciting pursuit—one that can be done with little expense and enjoyed almost anywhere at any time.

Why Do We Watch Birds?

Birds have inspired humans for thousands of years. Birds can fly—something we humans have mastered only in the past 100 years. Birds have brilliant plumage, and some even change their colors seasonally. Birds are master musicians, singing beautiful and complex songs. They possess impressive physical abilities—hovering, flying at high speeds, and withstanding extreme weather conditions, as well as the rigors of long migration flights. Birds also have behav-iors to which we can relate, such as intense courtship displays, devotion to their mates, and the enormous investment of effort spent in raising their young. Sound familiar? In short, birds are a vivid expression of life, and we admire them because they inspire us. This makes us want to know them better and to bring them closer to us. We accomplish this by attracting them to our backyards and gardens, and by using optics to see them more clearly in an "up close and personal" way.

Early Bird Study

Before the advent of modern optics that help us view birds more closely, humans used a shotgun approach to bird watching. Literally. Famed ornithologist and bird artist John James Audubon was the first European to document many of the North American bird species in the early 1800s. He did so by shooting every unfamiliar bird he encountered. Having a bird in the hand allowed him to study it closely and draw it accurately. This was an excellent method of learning a lot about birds quickly, but it was rather hard on the birds. This method of bird study continued largely unchecked until the

Millions of Americans enjoy bird watching.

early 1900s, when the effects of market hunting on birds became unhappily apparent. In 1934, a young bird enthusiast and artist named Roger Tory Peterson published *A Field Guide to the Birds*, with a system of arrows showing key field marks on the plumage of each species. This enabled a person to identify a bird from a distance, with or without the aid of magnifying optics. Modern bird watching was born, and it was no longer necessary to shoot birds in order to positively identify them. The era of shotgun ornithology was over.

Modern Bird Watching

Bird watching today is about seeing or hearing birds and then using these clues to identify them. To reach this identification, we use two important tools of the bird-watching trade: binoculars and a field guide. The binoculars (or perhaps a *spotting scope*, which is a telescope especially designed for nature watching) help you to get a closer, clearer look at the bird. The field guide helps you interpret what you see so that you can identify the bird species.

I like to say that we live in the golden era of bird watching. When I started birding more than 35 years ago, feeders, seed, birdhouses, and other supplies were hard to come by—we had to make our own. Now they are available in almost any store. We can buy a field guide or a book like the one you're holding in any bookstore. We can try out optics at camera stores, outdoor suppliers, and at birding festivals. We can learn about birds in special bird courses, on the Internet, in magazines, or from CD-ROMs, DVDs, and videos. We can join a local or state bird club and meet new bird-watching friends. We can take birding tours to far-off places.

Select binoculars that feel good in your hands and are easy to use.

There's never been a better time to become a bird watcher. So let's get started!

Basic Gear

If you're just starting out as a birder, you may need to acquire the basic tools—binoculars and a field guide.

Binoculars

You may be able to borrow optics from a friend or family member, but if your interest takes off, you'll certainly want to have your own binoculars to use anytime you wish. Fortunately, a decent pair of binoculars can be purchased for less than $100, and some really nice binoculars can be found used on the Internet or through a local bird club for just a bit more. The magnification powers that are commonly used for bird watching are 7x, 8x, and 10x. This is always the first number listed in the binoculars' description, as in 8x40. The second number refers to the size of the objective lens (the big end) of the binocular. The bigger the second number, the brighter the view presented to your eye. In general, for bird-watching binoculars the first number should be between 7x and 10x, and the second number should be between 30 and 45.

Try to find binoculars that are easy and comfortable to use. Make sure they focus easily, giving you a clear image, and that they are comfortable to hold (not too large or heavy) and fit your eye spacing. Every set of eyes is different, so don't settle for binoculars that just don't feel right. The perfect pair of binoculars for you should feel like a natural extension of your hands and eyes. Over time you will become adept at using your optics and, with a little practice, you'll be operating them like a pro.

Field Guide

When choosing a field guide, you'll need to decide what type of birding you'll be doing and where you plan to do it. If nearly all of your bird watching will be done at home, you might want to get a basic field guide to the backyard birds of your region, or at least a field guide that limits its scope to your half of the continent. Many field guides are offered in eastern (east of the Rocky Mountains) and western (from the

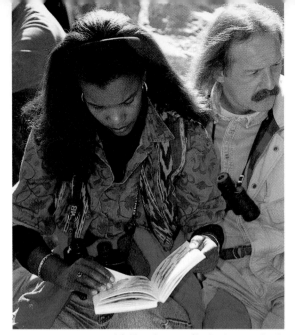
A field guide is one of birding's essential tools.

Rockies west) versions. These geographically limited formats include only those birds that are commonly found in that part of the continent, rather than continent-wide guides that include more than 800 North American bird species. Choose a field guide that is appropriate for you, and you'll save a lot of searching time—time that can be better spent looking at birds!

It Starts at Home

Most bird watchers like to start out at home, and this usually means getting to know the birds in your backyard. A great way to enhance the diversity of birds in your yard is to set up a simple feeding station. Even a single feeder with the proper food can bring half a dozen or more unfamiliar bird species into your yard. And it's these encounters with new and interesting birds that make bird watching so enjoyable.

Start your feeding station with a feeder geared to the birds that are already in your backyard or garden. For most of us this will mean a tube or hopper feeder filled with sunflower seeds. Place the feeder in a location that offers you a clear view of bird activity, but also offers the birds some nearby cover in the form of a hedge, shrubs, or brush pile into which the birds can fly when a predator approaches. I always set our feeding stations up opposite our kitchen or living room windows because these are the rooms in which we spend most of our daylight hours,

and because these rooms have the best windows for bird watching. We'll discuss bird feeding and attracting in greater detail in the next section.

Once you've got a basic feeder set up outside, you'll need to get yourself set up inside your house. You've probably already selected the best location for viewing your feeder. Next you should select a safe place to store your binoculars and field guide—somewhere that is easily accessible to you when you suddenly spot a new bird in your backyard. At our house we keep binoculars hanging on pegs right next to our kitchen windows. This keeps them handy for use in checking the feeders or for heading out for a walk around our farm.

Keeping Your Bird List

Most bird watchers enjoy keeping a list of their sightings. This can take the form of a written list, notations inside your field guide next to each species' account, or in a special journal meant for just such a purpose. There are even software programs available to help you keep your list on your computer. In birding, the most common list is the *life list*. A life list is a list of all the birds you've seen at least once in your life. Let's say you noticed a bright, black-and-orange bird in your backyard willow tree one morning, then keyed it out in your field guide to be a male Baltimore oriole. This is a species you'd never seen before, and now you can put it on your life list. List keeping can be done at any level of involvement, so keep the list or lists that you enjoy. I like to keep a property list of all the species we've seen at least once on our 80-acre farm. Currently, that list is at 181 species, but I'm always watching for something new to show up. I also update my North American life list a couple of times a year, after I've seen a new bird species.

Bird Watching Afield

Sooner or later you may want to expand your bird-watching horizons beyond your backyard bird feeders. Birding afield—away from your own home—can be a wonderfully exhilarating experience. Many beginning bird watchers are shy about venturing forth, afraid that their inexperience will prove embarrassing, but there's really no reason to feel this way. The best way to begin

Ten Tips for Beginning Bird Watchers

1. Get a decent pair of binoculars, ones that are easy for you to use and hold steady.

2. Find a field guide to the birds of your region (many guides are divided into eastern and western editions). Guides that cover all the birds of North America contain many birds species uncommon or entirely absent from your area. You can always upgrade to a continent-wide guide later.

3. Set up a basic feeding station in your yard or garden.

4. Start with your backyard birds. They are the easiest to see, and you can become familiar with them fairly quickly.

5. Practice your identification skills. Starting with a common bird species, note the most obvious visual features of the bird (color, size, shape, and patterns in the plumage). These features are known as field marks and will be helpful clues to the bird's identity.

6. Notice the bird's behavior. Many birds can be identified by their behavior—woodpeckers peck on wood, kingfishers dive for small fish, and swallows are known for their graceful flight.

7. Listen to the bird's sounds. Bird song is a vital component to birding. Learning bird songs and sounds takes a bit of practice, but many birds make it pretty easy for us. For example, chickadees and whip-poor-wills (among others) call out their names. The Resources section of this book contains a listing of tools to help you to learn bird songs.

8. Look at the bird, not at the book. When you see an unfamiliar bird, avoid the temptation to put down your binoculars and begin searching for the bird in your field guide. Instead, watch the bird carefully for as long as it is present—or until you feel certain that you have noted its most important field marks. Then look at your field guide. Birds have wings, and they tend to use them. Your field guide will still be with you long after the bird has gone, so take advantage of every moment to watch an unfamiliar bird while it is present.

9. Take notes. No one can be expected to remember every field mark and description of a bird. But you can help your memory and accelerate your learning by taking notes on the birds you see. These notes can be written in a small pocket notebook, in the margins of your field guide, or even in the back of this book.

10. Venture beyond the backyard and find other bird watchers in your area. The bird watching you'll experience beyond your backyard will be enriching, especially if it leads not only to new birds, but also to new birding friends. Ask a local nature center or wildlife refuge about bird clubs in your region. Your state ornithological organization or natural resources division may also be helpful. Bird watching with other birders can be the most enjoyable of all.

birding away from the backyard is to connect with other local bird watchers via your local bird club. Most parts of North America have local or regional bird clubs, and most of these clubs offer regular field trips. Bird watchers are among the friendliest people on the planet, and every bird club is happy to welcome new prospective members. If you don't know how to find a local bird club, ask your friends and neighbors if they know any bird watchers, check the telephone directory, search the Internet, or ask at your area parks, nature centers, and wild bird stores.

Getting out in the field with more experienced bird watchers is the fastest way to improve your skills. Don't be afraid to ask questions ("How did you know that was an indigo bunting?"). Don't worry if you begin to feel overwhelmed by the volume of new information—all new bird watchers experience this. When it happens, relax and take some time to simply watch. In time you'll be identifying birds and looking forward to new challenges and new birds.

Feeding and Housing

Birds need four basic things to live: food, water for drinking and bathing, a safe place to roost, and a safe place to nest. These vital elements are actually quite easy for you to offer to birds, even if your backyard is small.

Food

Bird feeding is a good place to start your bird-attracting efforts. It's wise to begin with a single feeder, such as a hopper feeder or tube feeder filled with black-oil sunflower seeds. The black-oil sunflower seed is the most common type of sunflower seed available, because it's the seed type that most of our feeder birds can readily eat. Think of it as the hamburger of the bird world. The black-oil sunflower seed has a thin shell (easy for seed-eating birds to crack) and a large, meaty seed kernel inside. As you can see from the seed preference chart on page 147, many backyard bird species eat sunflower seeds.

Other excellent foods for birds include: mixed seed (a blend that normally includes millet,

Pictured from the top down: Black-oil sunflower seed, peanuts, mixed seed, and cracked corn.

milo, cracked corn, and other seeds), sunflower bits (shells removed), peanuts (best offered unsalted and without the shell), suet or suet cakes, cracked corn, thistle seed (also known as Niger or nyjer seed), safflower seed, nectar (for hummingbirds), mealworms, fruits, and berries. Bird feeding varies from region to region—don't be afraid to experiment with new feeders or food. Birds will vote with their bills and stomachs and will let you know their preferences

Eating the food at feeders is not the only way birds find sustenance. A backyard or garden that includes natural food sources for birds—such as seed-producing flowering plants and fruit-bearing trees and shrubs—will further enhance its attractiveness to birds. In fact, it's often the natural features of a backyard habitat that attract the birds' attention rather than the bird feeders. Read the Bird-Friendly Plants section on page 162 for more specific suggestions.

Feeder Types

It's important to match the foods and feeders to each other, as well as to the birds you wish to attract. Sunflower seed works in a wide variety of feeders, including tube, hopper, platform, and satellite or excluder feeders (that permit small birds to feed, but exclude larger birds), as well as for ground feeding. Mixed seed does not work as well in tube or hopper feeders for a couple of reasons. First of all, the birds that prefer mixed seed tend to be ground feeders, so it's less natural for them to go to an elevated feeder for food. Secondly, elevated feeder designs (such as tubes or hoppers) are built to dole out seed as it is eaten and the smaller size of most mixed seed kernels causes excess spillage. Mixed seed works best when offered on a platform feeder or when scattered on the ground.

A fruit feeder will attract orioles, tanagers, and other fruit feeders.

take a few days or even a few weeks before they recognize your offering as a source of food. Sooner or later, a curious chickadee, finch, or sparrow will key into the food source, and the word will spread along the local bird "grapevine."

Housing for Birds

Almost every bird species builds or uses some type of nest to produce and rear its young. However, only a small fraction of our birds use nest boxes provided by humans. Birds that use next boxes or birdhouses are called *cavity nesters*, because they prefer to nest inside an enclosed space, such as hole excavated in a tree, as many woodpeckers do. Nest boxes simulate a natural cavity, but they have the added advantage (for humans) of our being able to place them in a convenient spot. To the birds' advantage, we can protect the nest box from predators, bad weather, and other problems.

When purchasing your feeders and foods, make sure they will work effectively with each other. Specialty foods such as suet, peanuts, thistle (Niger), mealworms, fruit, and nectar require specific feeders for the best results for you and the birds. The Food and Feeder Chart on page 147 is a great place to start.

Being a landlord to the birds is a thrilling experience. You are treated to an intimate peek inside the lives of your "tenants" and rewarded with the presence of their offspring, if nesting is successful. To help ensure the nesting success of your birds you need to provide the proper housing in an appropriate setting, and you should monitor the housing during the nesting season.

Your Feeding Station

Place your feeding station in a spot that is useful and attractive to you and the birds. When we moved into our farmhouse, we looked out all the windows before choosing a spot for our feeding station. You may want to do the same thing. After all, the whole point of bird feeding is to be able to see and enjoy the birds. From the birds' perspective, your feeders should be placed adjacent to cover—a place they can leave from and retreat to safely and quickly if a predator appears. This cover can be a woodland edge, brushy area or brush pile, hedges or shrubs, or even a weedy fencerow. If your yard is mostly lawn, consider creating a small island of cover near your feeding station. This will greatly enhance the feeders' appeal to birds.

The Right Housing

Two factors are key to providing the right nest box for your birds: the size of the housing and

Male northern cardinals eat sunflower seed from a hopper-style feeder.

Be patient. You've spent the money and effort to put up feeders, but don't expect immediate dividends. Birds are creatures of habit, and it may

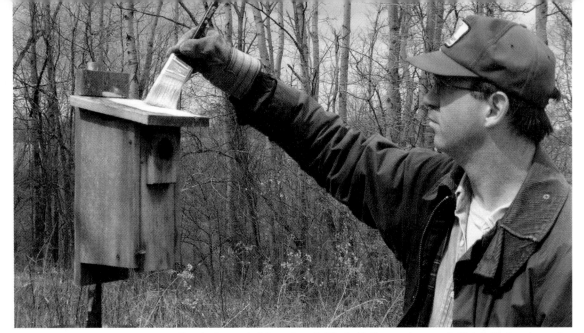

Exterior latex stain helps prolong the life of a birdhouse and protects the birds inside from the weather.

the size of the entry hole. Not all cavity nesters are picky about the interior dimensions of the cavity, except when it is excessively big or small. But the size of the entry hole is important because it can effectively limit the entrance of large, aggressive nest competitors, predators, and inclement weather. For example, an entry hole with a diameter of 1½ inches on a bluebird nest box will permit entry by bluebirds and many smaller birds, including chickadees, titmice, nuthatches, wrens, and tree swallows. But this same size keeps European starlings out and prevents them from usurping the box.

Use the Nest Box Chart (page 148) to help you determine the appropriate nest box details for your backyard birds. Whether you build your own birdhouses or buy them at your local wild bird products supplier, see page 40 for a few tips for "landlords" that you will want to consider.

An Appropriate Setting

Place your nest boxes where they will be most likely to be found and used by birds. Bluebirds and swallows prefer nest sites in the middle of large, open, grassy areas. Wrens, chickadees, nuthatches, flycatchers, woodpeckers, and other woodland birds prefer sites that are in or adjacent to woodlands. Robins, phoebes, Carolina wrens, barn swallows, and purple martins prefer to nest near human dwellings, perhaps for the protection from predators that we provide.

Monitoring Your Nest Boxes

By taking a weekly peek inside your nest boxes, you will stay abreast of your tenants' activities, and you'll be able to help them raise their families successfully. During most of the year, your birdhouses will appear to be empty. This does not mean that the boxes are going unused. In fact, many birds use nest boxes during the win-

An example of a pole-mounted predator baffle below a bluebird nest box.

Nest Box Tips for Landlords

- Do build or buy sturdily constructed nest boxes that are built from untreated wood (or another weatherproof material) with walls that are at least 3/4 inch thick. See page 157 for a simple bird house plan.
- Do not stain or paint the interior of the box. Stain or paint on the box exterior will help the box last longer. Light colors reflect sunlight and keep box interiors from getting too hot.
- Perches by the entry hole are unnecessary and may actually encourage competitors and predators.
- The box roof should be slanted and extend out several inches over the entry hole to keep out the weather.
- Nest boxes should have an access door for monitoring. Access doors that swing upward to open on the side or front of the box are easiest to use and safest for birds.
- The box should have holes for ventilation at the top of the vertical walls. Drainage holes in the floor will permit excess moisture to escape.
- Mount boxes on poles away from nearby trees and structures.
- Place a pole-mounted predator baffle beneath the nest box to keep snakes and mammals from gaining access to the nest.

ter months as nighttime roosts. A loose feather, insect parts, berry seeds, or a few droppings are classic evidence of roosting activity.

During breeding season, your regular visits will help you know when nest building begins and when eggs are laid, and will give you an idea about how soon the eggs will hatch and the babies leave the nest. Bird nests are vulnerable

Top: A daily bird notes diary. Bottom: A checklist for sightings.

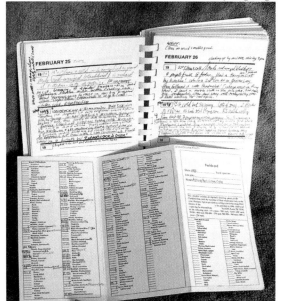

to a variety of dangers, including harsh weather and predators such as cats, raccoons, snakes, and even birds, as well as nest-site competitors. These dangers are greatly reduced when nest boxes are monitored because the birds' landlord (you) can take steps to protect the nest.

On my trips to check each of our 10 nest boxes, I keep a small notebook with me to record my observations. Each nest box has its own name and number in my notebook, along with the date of each visit and a note about what I've found. When nesting starts in a box I note the date, what materials are used to construct the nest, and the date that the first egg was laid. Once the clutch is complete and the female begins incubating the eggs, I can estimate the hatching date. This usually takes about 14 days. Another 14 to 21 days later, I know the young birds will be ready to leave the nest.

Peeking Inside

When checking a nest box, approach quietly. During the breeding season, you may scare the female off the nest temporarily when you open the box. Don't worry. If you keep your visit brief, she'll be back to the nest soon. I visit nest boxes

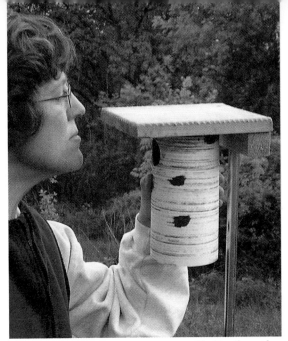
Checking the nest box.

in the late morning on sunny days, when the adult birds are likely to be away finding food. I open the box, quickly count the eggs or young, close the box and move away before pausing to record my notes. It's a myth that opening a nest box or checking the young will cause the adults to abandon the nest. In fact, over time many cavity-nesting birds that use nest boxes grow quite accustomed to regular visits.

One final note on nest monitoring. As fledging time approaches for the young birds—normally about two weeks after the eggs hatch—you should curtail your box visits to avoid causing a premature nest departure.

When Things Go Wrong

You open your nest box, and you find broken or missing eggs and the nest in disarray. What happened? The bad news is: A predator has raided your nest, and, in the natural order of things, the eggs or nestlings have been eaten. The good news: There are steps that you can take to avoid such an event in the future.

It's important to protect your nest boxes so predators cannot easily access them. For many landlords the best option is to mount the housing on galvanized metal poles with pole-mounted predator baffles installed beneath the boxes. An added advantage to pole-mounting (as opposed to mounting on a fencepost or tree) is

that the housing can be moved to a new location fairly easily.

Follow the steps outlined on page 148 for nest box placement, mounting, and baffling. You may also wish to consult one of the publications listed in the Resources section for specific strategies for dealing with nest box predators and pests.

Creating Bird Habitat

To make your backyard or garden a haven for birds, all you need to do is think like a bird. Look around your yard. Where is the food, the water? Where are the places to hide from predators or to shelter in bad weather? Is nesting habitat available?

An ideal bird habitat can be created in a tiny, urban garden just as it can be created in a large, rural setting. Birds love varied habitats; so when you are planning your yard, landscape, or gardens, resist the urge to plant matching plants in straight lines. Instead, let your imagination go wild—literally. Give the edges of beds or gardens natural curves. Scatter trees, shrubs, and vines in clumps or islands around the area you are designing. On the edges of your property, try to create natural transitions from the grass of your yard to the tops of your trees with short- and medium-height plants that provide food and shelter for birds.

Edible Habitat

Birds have evolved over millions of years right alongside the native plants with which they share the planet. These same native plants can work for you in your bird-friendly habitat plan. Your local nursery, nature center, or native plant society should be able to recommend plant species that are native to your region. Native plants not only provide food in the form of fruits and nuts, but birds may also eat the plants' buds, leaves, nectar, and sap, as well as the insects that live on the plants. When choosing your native plants, select a wide variety of species, sizes, shapes, and seasonality. Planting only one or two plant species will minimize the number of birds your habitat will attract. Consult the Bird-Friendly Plants chart on page 162 for suggested plant families.

Water

Birds need water all year long for drinking and bathing. The best way to offer water to birds is in a shallow birdbath with about 2 inches of water in it. I've always had good luck attracting birds to water in my yard when the bath was on or near the ground and when the water had some motion to it.

The sight and sound of moving water are highly attractive to birds. You can add motion to any birdbath or water feature with a mister, dripper, or a recirculating pump. Misters and drippers attach to your garden hose and let out a small amount of water that disturbs the surface of the bath; these ripples are eye-catchingly attractive to birds. Recirculating pumps, which require electricity, recycle the water from the main bath through a pump and filter, and then back to the bath. In winter, add a small, electric birdbath heater to keep the water open and available to birds.

If you already have a water garden or water feature, consider making part of it accessible to birds. This can be accomplished by placing a flat rock shelf on or near the water's surface, or by allowing recirculating water to trickle over an exposed flat rock. Our backyard water garden is ringed with American goldfinches almost every day all year-round. They use a large, flat piece of slate that gets splashed by our small waterfall as a place to grab a quick drink.

A male scarlet tanager bathes in a water feature.

Water is a universal attractant for birds—species that might otherwise never visit your yard, feeders, or birdhouses will visit a clean and alluring birdbath or water feature.

Shelter

When they need to rest, hide from danger, or get out of the weather, birds seek deep cover in the form of thick vegetation, vine tangles, dense evergreens, or brushy areas. These bits of habitat may not be first on a landscaper's list of backyard beautifying accents, but to a bird they are vital havens. Even a brush pile in a corner of your property can offer enough shelter during a storm to help sparrows, cardinals, and other backyard birds survive.

Look at your bird habitat, and observe where the birds go just before a storm or at dusk. These are the places in which they shelter themselves. Consider adding more such habitat, and your yard will be even more attractive to birds.

Places to Nest

The majority of North American birds do not use nest boxes. Most build their nests in places that are hidden from view—in trees, bushes, or in secluded spots on or near the ground. Birds—such as phoebes, barn swallows, and Carolina wrens—are bold enough to build nests on porch ledges, in garages, and in barns. House finches and mourning doves are known for building their nests in hanging flower baskets, but these sites won't satisfy most of our birds.

The places where birds choose to nest are similar to the places they choose to roost and shelter—in thick vegetation and deep cover out of view of passing predators. In providing a nesting habitat for birds, the key is diversity. As you read through the species profiles in this book, notice the habitat features that each species prefers. Then factor this information into your habitat plans.

Helping Other Nesting Birds

There are many things you can do to help non-cavity nesters—all those birds that build

Allow lawn edges to grow wild; bird species thrive in transition or edge habitat.

open-cup nests and will never use one of our nest boxes. The most important thing is to offer variety in your landscaping or backyard habitat. A backyard that is mostly lawn with a tree or two staked out in the middle will not be nearly as appealing as a yard featuring a variety of plant types, including grasses, perennial plants, shrubs, bushes, trees, and other natural elements. The more your landscape looks like nature, the more attractive it will be for birds.

Places for You

As you plan for your bird-friendly habitat, you'll also want to incorporate elements that you can use and enjoy, such as a water garden, benches, shady relaxation spots, and perhaps a location for your feeding station. Remember, the whole point of attracting birds to your property is so that you can enjoy them while they enjoy your offerings. Plan with your favorite viewing spots in mind, and you'll be rewarded with year-round free (and natural) entertainment.

Tips for Helping Nesting Birds

- Consider letting a portion of your yard grow up into a weedy patch for sparrows, finches, and towhees to enjoy.
- Offer a basket of nesting material, such as 2- to 3-inch pieces of natural fibers (yarn, pet or human hair, stiff dry grasses, and the like).
- Keep pets, especially cats, from roaming freely in your yard during nesting season.
- Try to limit or eliminate the use of lawn and garden chemicals in and around the parts of your property being used by nesting birds.
- Trim hedges, shrubs, and trees in early spring before nesting season, or in late fall, after nesting season. This way you'll avoid disturbing nesting birds, which are often so secretive that you are unaware of the nest until you stumble onto it.

How to Use This Book

Hello! *and welcome to the fun, friendly, and exciting word of bird watching. Birding is America's fastest-growing hobby and requires little more than some basic tools—binoculars and a field guide—and an interest in the fascinating world of birds. The primary purpose of this book is to start you down the path to a greater understanding and enjoyment of this engaging pastime. To that end, we've chosen the content carefully to provide you, the reader, with the ideal blend of information and detail on many of the most commonly encountered birds of your state. If we've done our job right, this will not be the last bird book you buy.*

At the heart of this book is a set of profiles of your state's 100 most commonly encountered birds. These are the birds that you're most likely to see and hear regularly. *But remember*—birds have wings and they tend to use them, so you'll certainly see and hear many other species as your bird-watching experience grows. For this reason we suggest that you augment this book with a good field guide to help you identify those unfamiliar species you encounter.

Each species profile features a beautiful photograph of the bird, typically an adult male in breeding plumage since this is the most identifiable version of many birds. Please note that adult females, winter-plumage adults, and young birds can look very different. We describe these plumage differences in the profile, but space constraints prevent us from showing images of all these variations. Once again, a good field guide (see the Resources section on page 166 for suggestions) will be useful in identifying any mystery birds you encounter.

We cover all the interesting and useful natural history information about each of the 100 birds—appearance, sounds, behavior, nesting, feeding, range, and migration—and we even tell you where to go and what to do in order to encounter a particular bird in the "Backyard and Beyond" section.

The profiles in the main body of the book are organized *taxonomically*—this means that related species are grouped by bird family using the same general order that ornithologists use to list and classify birds. See the facing page to find a convenient alphabetic listing. In the 100 species profiles, we've used a series of symbols to provide instant insight into the lives of these birds. Here is a key to what each of these icons represents:

 Will use a birdhouse for nesting or roosting.

 Can be attracted to bird feeders.

 Will visit birdbaths or water features for bathing and drinking.

 Has a song or call and can be identified by its vocalizations or sounds.

 A migrant species, seen primarily during spring or fall migration.

Also, turn to pages 7 through 32 to read more about the natural history and ecology of your state and its bird life. We focus on bird watching by season—the specific birds you're likely to encounter and how to attract them—by feeding and by offering the appropriate bird-friendly habitat. This section also describes the many migrants that pass through in spring and fall. As an extra bonus, we briefly describe the "Ten Must-See Birds" for your state. We also include a summary of the "Ten Best Bird-Watching Spots."

At the end of this book you will find a resources list for bird watching (feeding and planting charts, answers to frequently asked questions, birdhouse plans, bird books, field and audio guides, and more) to help you enjoy this hobby more.

Happy bird watching!

—*Bill Thompson, III*

100 Most Commonly Encountered Birds

Pied-billed Grebe

Podilymbus podiceps

Spring/Summer
Year-Round
Winter

Most North American grebes either breed far to the north or in the West, but the stocky little pied-billed grebe also breeds through much of the eastern United States. You can find this frequent diver in varied wetlands, including ponds, lakes, and marshes that have a thick cover of cattails or other vegetation. Pied-billed grebes most often are seen singly or in twos or threes. They don't often vocalize, except during breeding season when they call out a series of penetrating, barking notes.

All About

In general, pied-billed grebes occur in sheltered, lush wetlands. This bird is smallish but has a big head, stocky neck, and a thick bill that differs from the more pointed bills of horned and eared grebes. During breeding season, the bill (which is pale in winter) becomes distinctively adorned with a thick, black band that wraps around an otherwise horn-colored bill. Breeding pied-billed grebes also have black throats, but at other times their soft-brown necks and bodies contrast with whitish throats and puffy, whitish undertails.

Habitat & Range

Pied-billed grebes nest in well-vegetated lakes, ponds, and pockets of marsh. You may find them in brackish water in winter, but they prefer freshwater habitats. The numbers of pied-billed grebes dwindle in the North and swell in the South during winter and migration, when many northern nesters abandon their frigid habitats for warmer, more productive wintering areas.

Feeding

Pied-billed grebes are frequently seen diving for food or diving to evade predators or observers. Their wide-lobed feet push them beneath the water's surface in search of small fish, amphibians, and a wide variety of aquatic invertebrates, including crayfish and insects. They also eat some plant matter.

Nesting

Mates call to each other as part of their courtship. Together, they build a nest that is basically a mound of matted vegetation. This mound is fastened to nearby plants and may float or rise from the shallows. The female lays four to six eggs, with the pair sharing the three-week incubation period. Both parents feed the young, which can fly by two months of age.

Backyard & Beyond

Scan marsh edges and ponds to find pied-billed grebes; they are rarely spotted in flight. They have a tendency to appear as if by magic and to disappear just as fast, often leaving a ring of ripples on the water's surface as the only evidence of their presence.

Double-crested Cormorant

Phalacrocorax auritus

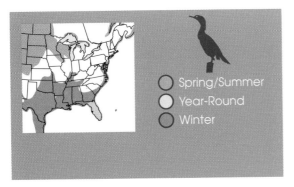

○ Spring/Summer
○ Year-Round
○ Winter

Often, the somewhat snakelike black neck and head is all that betrays the presence of a swimming double-crested cormorant. They are most numerous during the breeding season in spring and summer. In fall, long lines of cormorants can be seen migrating southward. A few may linger all winter in ice-free waters. Double-crested cormorants declined earlier in the twentieth century due to disturbance and hunting at nesting grounds, followed by DDT and other pesticide contamination. Protection, wetland conservation, and the DDT ban have helped these birds recover.

All About

With practice, birders can easily distinguish a distant, flying double-crested cormorant from a pelican, goose, heron, or other large bird by its all-dark form, thick and somewhat wavy neck, longish tail, and slow wingbeats. The cormorant's bright orange throat, bill, and lores stand out on its otherwise black body. Even its heavy webbed feet are blackish. Immatures are dull brown with whitish necks and chests. The double-crested cormorant is named for its pair of head crest plumes that are most visible during breeding season and rarely seen otherwise.

Habitat & Range

Most double-crested cormorant populations are migratory, and these birds turn up at rivers, marshes, swamps, large lakes, bays, and along the coast. Because they travel widely during the day, don't be surprised to see cormorants flying over inland habitats in loose formation. Double-crested cormorants breed in western Alaska, central Canada, and down both coasts of the United States; they winter along the coast and well inland throughout the eastern United States.

Feeding

Double-crested cormorants are very adaptable, seeking a wide variety of fish, and also crustaceans, amphibians, and other aquatic animals. Their webbed feet propel them under water after their aquatic prey, and much of their feeding is done not far beneath the surface.

Nesting

Double-crested cormorants nest in colonies in trees, on cliffs, and on islands. Females build much of the platform nest, while males provide the many sticks and other materials. Females usually lay three or four eggs, which both parents incubate for about a month. Young leave the nest 21 to 30 days after hatching, but are not fully on their own until after two months.

Backyard & Beyond

Watch for the "periscope" heads of partially submerged cormorants and try not to confuse them with those of the more dagger-billed loons, which have slimmer, straighter bills and at least some light coloration on the head. After long swims, cormorants often sun themselves on dead trees and shorelines, holding out their wings to dry.

Common Loon

Gavia immer

- ○ Spring/Summer
- ○ Year-Round
- ○ Winter

The common loon is one of the best-known North American water birds. Its high yodeling cry echoes across large, remote northern lakes evoking unspoiled wilderness to the listener. Once heard, the loon's wailing tremolo is hard to forget.

All About

The common loon is a large, long diving bird that rides low in the water. In profile the loon's massive head and bill help to separate it visually from other waterfowl. In breeding plumage it has a black head, bill, and neck band. Its throat and breast are white and its back is checkered in black and white; this nondescript plumage may render the loon unfamiliar to some bird watchers. In winter plumage the common loon is a dull gray-and-white. In flight the common loon appears dark above, white below.

Habitat & Range

Common loons breed on remote lakes as far north as the treeless tundra and as far south as New England and northern Michigan, Wisconsin, and Minnesota. In recent decades, the species has declined due to human disturbance, pollution, and habitat loss. Though most common loons spend winter on the ocean, some linger on large inland rivers, lakes, and reservoirs. They can be encountered on large bodies of water during spring or fall migration; huge concentrations occur on protected bays in the Great Lakes.

Feeding

A foraging common loon swims along with its head underwater scanning for schools of small fish, its primary food. It catches fish by diving in pursuit, powered by strong webbed feet. Once caught in the loon's bill a fish cannot escape. The loon's tongue and the roof of its mouth have small, inward-pointing barbules that enhance its grip. Fish are swallowed headfirst. Other foods include small crustaceans and aquatic plant matter.

Nesting

Common loons nest on remote lakes where both mates build a mound of aquatic plant matter for their one or two eggs on land but near the water. Both birds share the incubation duties, which can last a month. After hatching, young loons may leave the nest within a day and are able to swim and dive immediately, but they may hitch a ride on a parent's back. They are able to fly after about 10 weeks, at which point they become independent from the parents.

Backyard & Beyond

Loons are partial to large bodies of water because they need the "runway" space for take-off and landing. They are heavy-bodied birds that must run across the water's surface to build up speed for flight. Loons spend much of the non-breeding season alone, so scanning the surface of a lake or reservoir is a good way to spot a distant swimming loon.

Great Blue Heron

Ardea herodias

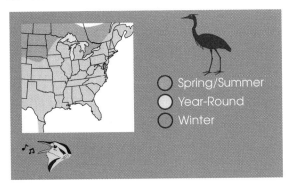

○ Spring/Summer
○ Year-Round
○ Winter

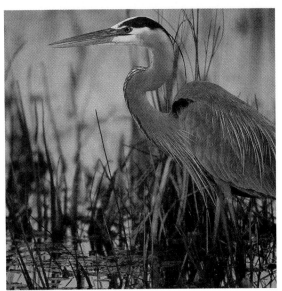

Northvia America's largest and most widespread heron is found, at one time or another, virtually wherever water and small aquatic creatures are found. Although the best known of our dozen heron species, the great blue heron is not always called by its correct name. Many non-birders call it a crane or a stork, but the heron can be instantly distinguished from these other large, long-legged birds by its folded-back neck in flight and the S-shaped curvature of its neck at rest.

All About

Adult great blue herons have a black stripe running from the eye to the back of the neck; immature birds have a blackish cap. During the breeding season the heron's plumage is enhanced by long plume feathers on the head, neck, and back. The great blue heron's croaking *ccrraaaaaaaank* call is often heard as it takes flight.

Habitat & Range

Found across the United States, southern Canada, and up the Pacific coast to Alaska, the great blue heron ventures where few other herons dare. Many eastern birds migrate to the South or to the tropics—as far south as northwestern South America—in winter. However, many great blues spend the winter in the Midwest, wherever there is ice-free water.

Feeding

Great blue herons seek a variety of prey in a range of wet habitats. Fish are a mainstay, but amphibians, reptiles, birds, small mammals, and invertebrates feature on the menu, as well. Feeding strategy varies: They may hunt alongside each other, wading slowly up to their bellies in water, or may stand alone for long periods, waiting to thrust their bills at unsuspecting prey. Great blue herons sometimes stalk rodents in dry fields or haunt beaches and docks in search of live or discarded sea life.

Nesting

Great blue herons nest in large colonies, often in tall trees away from human disturbance. They will nest in the company of other water birds, in areas with water beneath nesting trees, probably to thwart predators. Each year, great blue heron pairs form bonds through a series of posing displays, including stretching, preening, crest raising, circling in flight, and twig shaking. Males provide sticks, which females place in the large platform nest. Females usually lay three to five eggs, which they incubate for almost a month. Both parents feed the young, which take flight 2 to 2 1/2 months after hatching.

Backyard & Beyond

Despite their large size, great blue herons sometimes turn up at small backyard ponds seeking fish and frogs. They are far more frequent in marshes, swamps, rivers, lakes, and reservoirs.

Green Heron

Butorides virescens

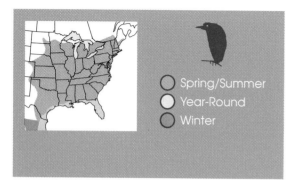

- ○ Spring/Summer
- ◑ Year-Round
- ○ Winter

The green heron isn't exactly green, but it's the most greenish of the North American herons. Perhaps a better name would have been "squat heron" or "little heron" or "common pond heron." The bird was known until recently as the "green-backed heron," and this is an apt moniker since the adults have blackish green backs.*

All About

The least bittern is our smallest heron, but the green heron is the smallest *easily seen* heron. While a green heron will sometimes stretch its neck out to peer at approaching birders or predators, its head is usually held close to the body, giving the bird a squat look. Identification of adults is straightforward: The back and crown are blackish with a green tinge, the neck and face are dark chestnut, and the belly is gray. Yellow legs flush to bright orange during breeding season. Young birds are brown streaked, and care should be taken not to mistake them for bitterns. Subadults are a mixture of brown and streaky and rusty necked. The piercing *KEEE-OWK* call will draw attention to birds flushed out to the open that might otherwise be missed.

Habitat & Range

In spring and summer, look for green herons along wooded streams and ponds, around lakes, at drainage ditches, and in marshes, often near woody cover. In winter, green herons move south from northern nesting areas, spending the winter in Florida and the Gulf States and south-ward into the tropics. Green herons also nest throughout the West Indies and in Central America south to Panama.

Feeding

Like stock-still balls of rust and greenish feathers, green herons wait patiently by the water's edge for fish, frogs, crayfish, various insects, and other small prey. They also slowly walk through the water and wait for prey to show. They have even been known to drop small baits, such as fish food pellets, bits of bread (from people feeding park ducks), or flower petals into the water to attract curious fish and other potential prey.

Nesting

Green herons nest in pairs or small clusters, but avoid large colonies. They nest in trees or shrubs that may either be near or fairly far from water and feeding areas. Three to seven eggs are laid in a stick platform nest primarily built by the female. Both parents incubate the eggs for about three weeks; both then feed their young, which can fly by three weeks of age.

Backyard & Beyond

Green herons may visit backyard ponds to investigate the goldfish or frogs. They also frequently fly over neighborhoods en route to golf course ponds, streams, lakes, or drainage ditches. Green herons are frequently overlooked until startled into flight.

Canada Goose

Branta canadensis

- ○ Spring/Summer
- ○ Year-Round
- ○ Winter

The Canada goose enjoys an almost iconic status with human observers (though large, nonmigratory flocks can wear out their welcome). Their huge, V-shaped flights mark the passing of seasons, their honking is reminiscent of wilderness itself, and their strong family bonds (they mate for life) endear them to us. Many non-bird watchers mistakenly call this bird the Canadian goose.

All About

The Canada goose's black neck and white cheek strap are unmistakable. In flight, Canadas beat their wings deeply and slowly and show a black-and-white tail. Their familiar call is a deep, two-syllable *ha-ronk* and is given by mated pairs as well as flocking birds. Canadas also give a variety of softer cackling calls to each other, especially when they are on the ground. More than a dozen different subspecies exist in North America, and their sizes vary from 25 to 45 inches in length.

Habitat & Range

The Canada goose is a habitat generalist when it comes to water, settling in lakes, bays, rivers, and city parks and ponds. The species has enjoyed unprecedented success in living with or near humans, and today it nests all across the upper two-thirds of North America. Some re-established populations of Canada goose are year-round, nonmigratory residents, though many birds nesting in northern North America migrate to the southern United States in winter.

Spring migration begins early, and many females are incubating by mid-March.

Feeding

Aquatic plants, grasses, grains, and seeds are the Canada's primary foods. To reach submerged food, it will tip its tail in the air and extend its neck below the water's surface. Flocks leave roosting areas in the morning to forage in nearby fields, meadows, and marshes. Urban populations often live on handouts of cracked corn near city park lakes and golf course ponds.

Nesting

Located on a high spot near water, the nest is a small mound made of surrounding sticks and vegetation and lined with down plucked from the female. Half a dozen or more eggs are laid and incubated by the female for nearly a month while the male stands guard and brings her food. Within two days of hatching, young goslings are herded by their parents to the nearest water. Families stay together until the following breeding season, though young birds become self-sufficient in about two months.

Backyard & Beyond

Some housing developments and golf courses find them (and their droppings) a nuisance. To best see Canadas, visit a wildlife refuge where large flocks congregate during winter and during spring and fall migration. Watching hundreds of loudly honking Canadas is quite a spectacle.

Wood Duck

Aix sponsa

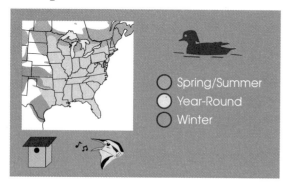

○ Spring/Summer
○ Year-Round
○ Winter

The up-slurred WHEEEP *of the wood duck is a familiar sound to anyone frequenting areas where woodland and fresh water mix. Patience and a bit of stealth will reward the birder seeking a good look at these cagey, dazzling ducks. Across much of the Midwest, wood ducks abound, finding ample habitat and welcoming nest boxes.*

All About

The male wood duck takes its colorful plumage to an extreme. In breeding plumage, it has a green crown and black face offset by white slashes reaching up from its white throat. The bill looks painted, a bright red-orange with black and white touches. Breast and undertail are chestnut, while the sides are adorned with vertical white and blackish slashes followed by a panel of butterscotch yellow. The male's back is metallic green. These colors fade during summer, as the birds molt into *eclipse*, or nonbreeding, plumage, but the bright bill and eye and face pattern remain. Both male and female have backward-facing crests that give them a helmeted look. The female wood duck is easy to identify, not only because of her head shape, but also because of her white, tear-shaped eye rings. Otherwise, females are grayish brown and generously flecked with whitish spots on their sides.

Habitat & Range

The perfect setting for wood ducks combines tranquil fresh water with plenty of trees—bottomland swamps, riverside forests, and tree-lined ponds and lakes. Wood ducks are permanent residents in much of the Midwest and South, except in the Appalachians, where populations withdraw during the cold months. Northern populations, from southern Canada through the Northeast, retreat south in winter.

Feeding

Wood ducks eat a variety of seeds and some fruits from aquatic and forest plants, including acorns. Sometimes, they eat grain. Insects and other small animals supplement their diet; though, for recently fledged birds, these are a mainstay.

Nesting

Wood ducks are cavity nesters, setting up house in holes high in mature or dead trees. They also nest down low in nest boxes. The nest is simply an accumulation of down placed on the cavity floor, where the female incubates her 8 to 15 pale eggs between $3^1/2$ and 5 weeks. Chicks usually tumble out of their nest the day after hatching. Females accompany them for about six weeks, and they can fly at about two months of age.

Backyard & Beyond

If you live near fresh water, you may see wood ducks fly over your property. If your property includes a pond or wetland, you may attract wood ducks with a nesting box, which ideally would be set in the water on a pole fitted with a pole-mounted, predator baffle.

Mallard

Anas platyrhynchos

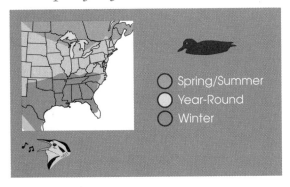

- Spring/Summer
- Year-Round
- Winter

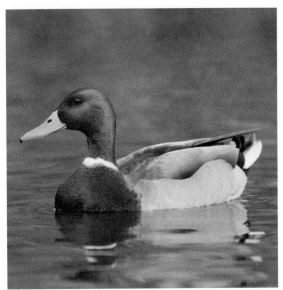

Of all the North American duck species, there's one that nearly everyone knows—the mallard. Abundant all across the continent, the mallard is known to interbreed commonly with black ducks and other wild duck species, as well as with domesticated ducks. Large numbers of semi-tame mallards exist on city park ponds, golf courses, and reservoirs, getting by on handouts from humans.

All About

The male mallard's green head and yellow bill are easily recognizable, but female mallards—with their overall dark brown coloration—can be confused with black ducks, mottled ducks, and other female ducks. Look for her orange and black bill and listen for the loud, raucous *quack, quack-quack, quack-quack* call, given only by female mallards. Mallards are fairly large ducks with a 23-inch body length.

Habitat & Range

Like other dabbling ducks, mallards prefer shallow bodies of fresh water at all times of year, including marshes, flooded woodlots, ponds, and swamps. They can be found year-round across most of the United States, but a large number of mallards breed in the far North and spend the winter in the Southeast.

Feeding

Mallards feed by scooping up seeds and plant material from the water's surface, by tipping up—tails in the air—to reach submerged plants, and by grazing for waste grain in agricultural fields. They eat everything from seeds and vegetation to insects, small fish, crawfish, and frogs.

Nesting

Mallards pair up well before the spring breeding season. The hen mallard chooses the nest site, usually in or near thick vegetation on the ground. She then builds a small bowl out of nearby plant material and lines it with her own down. Between 7 and 12 eggs are laid and incubated by the hen for a month. Like other ducks, mallard ducklings leave the nest within hours after hatching and follow their mother to the nearest water. Though ducklings feed themselves right away, it's nearly two months before they are able to fly. Predators take a heavy toll on nests and young, especially in parks where natural predators are augmented by domestic pets.

Backyard & Beyond

If you want to feed the mallards in your local park, don't bother with stale bread, which holds little nutritional value for birds. Instead, offer some cracked corn. This inexpensive food is available at most stores selling birdseed and is relished by mallards. When you've got a hungry flock of panhandling mallards nearby, take time to look at the birds' fine plumage. Look, too, for wild ducks of other species that may be "hanging out" with the local flock of tame mallards, as well as for the many interesting hybrids that result from the mallard's promiscuous nature.

Blue-winged Teal

Anas discors

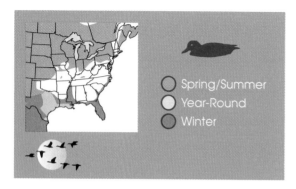

- ○ Spring/Summer
- ○ Year-Round
- ○ Winter

A fast-flying, small (14 inches long) duck, the blue-winged teal shows the blue shoulder patch for which it is named only when the wings are extended. Blue-wingeds fly in tight flocks and seem to be wary as they pass repeatedly over a body of water before landing. However, they are not as skittish as other ducks when approached by humans, perhaps because they know they can explode off the water and straight into the air in seconds.

All About

Males have a blue-gray head and a distinctive white face crescent and hip patch, making them easy to identify even from a distance. Females are a warm, gray-brown overall with a slight echo of the males' white face crescent. Identifying them is made somewhat easier by the fact that blue-winged teal pairs form in early winter and stay together through spring migration.

Habitat & Range

Blue-winged teal breed throughout the northeastern, central, and western United States. Most blue-winged teal spend the winter south of the United States, as far as South America. They are considered fair-weather ducks by many bird watchers because they stay far to the south until spring is in full force. Perhaps it is their later spring arrival and their earlier fall departure that has earned them the nicknames "summer teal" and "August teal." Their preferred habitats—at all seasons—are shallow, freshwater marshes and ponds.

Feeding

Teal feed on seeds and plant matter gleaned from the water's surface or by swimming with their heads submerged to find snails, aquatic insects, and crustaceans. Unlike other dabbling ducks, blue-wingeds do not "tip up" to feed on submerged vegetation.

Nesting

Like many other ducks, blue-winged teal nest on the ground in a spot concealed by thick vegetation. The female builds a shallow, basket-shaped nest out of dried grasses lined with her down. A clutch of nine or more eggs is laid and incubated by the hen for slightly more than three weeks. Teal ducklings leave the nest almost immediately and are able to feed themselves right away, but it will be six weeks before they are fully flighted.

Backyard & Beyond

The blue-winged's preference for shallow water means that it can show up almost anywhere—from farm or city ponds to marshes, mudflats, and sewage settling pools. If you see a flock of small ducks flying pell-mell, twisting and turning as one, chances are they are blue-winged teal. You can clinch the identification by looking for the male teal's white face crescent, or for the flash of blue, white, and green in the wings.

Ring-necked Duck
Aythya collaris

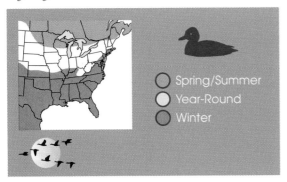

○ Spring/Summer
● Year-Round
○ Winter

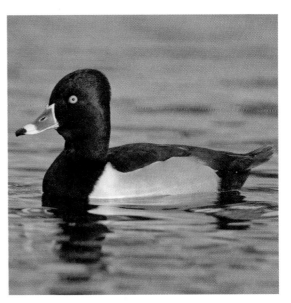

The ring-necked duck is fairly common all across the United States and Canada and a common migrant through the Midwest. Flocks of ringnecks frequent marshes, swamps, and sheltered and wooded corners of lakes. These birds are often found in areas where the only other regularly sighted ducks are wood ducks and mallards (in interior areas). Ringnecks are also found on open water and areas with a wider diversity of ducks.

All About
Closely related and superficially similar to the greater and lesser scaups, this diving bird has a few embellishments that easily set it apart from the scaup. Like the scaup, the male ringneck is blackish—in most light—on its head, chest, and back. However, even at a distance, the adult male ring-necked duck has a vertical white comma that edges its gray sides. Its bill is three-toned: The tip is black, followed by a white band, then much gray, then a white border where the bill meets the head. Like the scaup, the female ringneck is more somber in coloration and markings, but she has a noticeably dark crown compared with the rest of her head. She sports a white eye ring, and usually has a clearly three-toned bill. As with the red-bellied woodpecker, the ring-necked duck's name was poorly chosen by "dead-bird-in-the-hand" early ornithologists: Only in rare circumstances will you see its namesake rusty collar.

Habitat & Range
Most ring-necked ducks winter in the United States, below the northern tier of states, and south into central Mexico. Others winter in the West Indies, and a few are found as far south as Panama. Unlike scaup, ring-necked ducks frequent small or smallish bodies of water, and they rarely enter salt water. Summer finds them nesting in Canada, Alaska, and a good number of northern U.S. states in freshwater wetlands, usually surrounded by forest.

Feeding
Ring-necked ducks dive for their supper, snipping roots and stems of plants, eating seeds, insects, and mollusks. Like other waterfowl, their recently hatched young eat mostly insects.

Nesting
The female ring-necked duck usually lays between 8 and 10 eggs in a nest of grasses or other plants clipped from nearby. She incubates the eggs for almost a month. After they hatch, she accompanies her chicks until they can fly, shortly before two months of age.

Backyard & Beyond
Early in the morning or in well-protected areas, you may catch close-up looks at ring-necked ducks on small ponds or lakes. Even at a distance, though, the gray, white, and black markings on the male's sides help identify these birds as they dive underwater and pop back up to the surface.

Lesser Scaup

Aythya affinis

Spring/Summer
Year-Round
Winter

We have two scaup species in North America— greater and lesser scaup—both are medium-sized, black-and-white ducks, and they can be difficult to tell apart. The lesser scaup is by far the more commonly encountered of the two, especially on inland bodies of water. Both species are named for their characteristic skawwp! call, but the similarities don't end there. Both scaup species are excellent swimmers and divers, both have drab brownish mates, and both show lots of white in the wing in flight.

All About

Older field guides suggest that greater and lesser scaup can be identified based upon head color, but this is very unreliable in poor light. Separating scaup species in the field is most accurately done based on head shape—lessers have a thinner head with more of a peak on top, while greaters have a rounder head and larger bill. Female scaup are brownish gray overall with a white ring around the base of the bill. Hens can be identified based on the males with which they associate because the two scaup species are rarely seen in mixed flocks. All scaup show a blue-gray bill with a black tip—an important clue to separate the scaup from the superficially similar ring-necked duck, which has a white ring on its bill.

Habitat & Range

Lesser scaup are one of most common wintering ducks on inland bodies of water, with flocks sometimes numbering in the thousands. They are very late migrants in both spring and fall migration, arriving on the breeding grounds as late as mid-May and not leaving until just before the winter freeze-up.

Feeding

Specialists in diving for their food, lesser scaup eat snails, mussels, small clams, fish, and aquatic insects. They also rely on plant matter and seeds for food, especially in fall and winter.

Nesting

Preferring to nest in thick vegetation on dry ground or islands near water, the female lesser scaup does nearly all of the hard work. The nest is a scrape lined with dry grass and lots of the hen's down into which 8 to 10 eggs are laid. Hen scaup incubate their eggs for longer than three weeks before hatching. Hatchlings leave the nest within a day of emerging and are able to feed themselves immediately. Within two weeks they are diving for food, and two months later they are fully flighted.

Backyard & Beyond

Lesser scaup can be found on almost any open (ice-free) body of water in the continental United States in winter, but they are especially abundant along the Gulf and southern Atlantic coasts. Look for flocks of black-and-white ducks actively diving and bobbing to the surface of a pond, lake, or reservoir.

Ruddy Duck

Oxyura jamaicensis

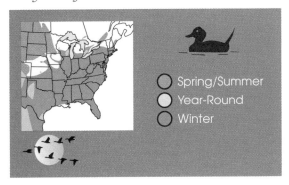

- Spring/Summer
- Year-Round
- Winter

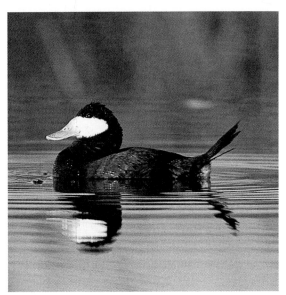

This little dark duck is a familiar sight on marshes, bays, and ponds across North America where it often gathers in sizeable flocks in winter. Perhaps because they are rarely hunted they are among our least "spooky" ducks and thus can often be viewed from close range.

All About

Named for the ruddy-orange color of the breeding male, the ruddy duck is a compact-bodied bird with a big head. The long spiky tail is often held up at an angle, hence its alternate name, "stiff-tailed duck." Breeding males are a lovely blend of colors with rusty body, black head, white cheeks, and blue bill. Females and juveniles are drab gray-brown overall with a contrasting white face stripe. Males retain their white cheeks in winter plumage. In all plumages ruddy ducks are dark-capped and pale-cheeked. Ruddies are swift flyers with rapid wingbeats.

Habitat & Range

During the nesting season, most ruddy ducks are on small marshy lakes and wetlands of the western prairies and the interior West. They winter along the entire U.S. coast and across the eastern U.S., as far north as there is ice-free water. Ruddies migrate at night in small flocks and spend daylight hours during migration resting or sleeping on the water. Because many of North America's ruddy ducks use the prairie pothole region of the western Great Plains, drought years can have a devastating effect on this species.

Feeding

A diving feeder, the ruddy duck uses its large bill stir up food items from the bottom of a pond or lake. Aquatic insect larvae, invertebrates, seeds and plant matter make up the diet, nearly all captured as the ruddy strains the stirred-up mud through its bill. In summer the diet is primarily insect larvae while the winter diet may rely more heavily on seeds.

Nesting

The female weaves a platform nest out of cattails and grasses in thick vegetation suspended just inches above the water. She may also weave a partial roof overhead. She lays between five and ten eggs and incubates them for nearly about 25 days, during which time the male takes his leave and the female assumes all parental duties. Ducklings leave the nest a day after hatching and are able to swim and feed themselves immediately, though the female still cares for them. Young attain flight after seven weeks.

Backyard & Beyond

Look for ruddy ducks on marshy ponds and shallow lakes, along large rivers, and on reservoirs during their prolonged spring and fall migration. In spring, males perform amusing courtship displays with lots of head bobbing, tail spreading, and unusual posturing.

Common Merganser

Mergus merganser

Spring/Summer
Year-Round
Winter

Mergansers are the only North American ducks that are primarily fish eaters; the common merganser is our largest, most boldly marked one. Like our two other mergansers, the common has a serrated bill enabling it to catch and grasp the fish it captures on underwater dives. This adaptation is why the mergansers are often called "saw-bills."

All About
The clean white body, dark green head, and bright-orange bill of the male common merganser are unmistakable identification clues, even at a great distance. The common merganser has the least obvious crest of any of the mergansers, but its large size and bold coloration separate it from the hooded and red-breasted mergansers. Female commons have a dark-brown head and a gray body with a white belly, but share the same bright orange bill color as the male. In flight, common mergansers appear slender and cleanly marked, showing lots of white.

Habitat & Range
Common mergansers breed near northern lakes and rivers that are surrounded by mature forests. Their breeding range covers much of Canada and tiny bits of northern Minnesota, Wisconsin, Michigan, and northern New England. Wintering birds will remain as far north as possible wherever clear, ice-free water is available. During most winters, this bird is the most-common merganser found across the Midwest on deep lakes, rivers, and reservoirs.

Feeding
Doing most of its feeding at morning and dusk, a common merganser will swim along with its head submerged (much like a loon), looking for fish. It pursues fish by diving and swimming after them; common mergansers have been observed swallowing foot-long fish head-first! They also consume mussels, crayfish, shrimp, and salamanders. When dive-feeding in deep water, they may stay under for 30 seconds or more.

Nesting
Common mergansers are cavity nesters, usually choosing a hole in a large tree near water. They will use nest boxes in proper habitat and successful adult females return to nest at the same site in successive years. A lining of wood chips and down is the only improvement made to a cavity and into this nest the female lays between six to twelve eggs. She incubates the eggs for a month or more before they hatch. Young mergansers leap from the cavity a day or so after hatching and follow their mother to the water. They can feed themselves immediately but do not attain flight for at least two months.

Backyard & Beyond
Look for common mergansers on lakes, rivers, and reservoirs from the onset of fall migration in September through spring migration ending in early April. In Europe common mergansers (called "goosanders" there) have increased significantly thanks to the availability of nest boxes.

Turkey Vulture

Cathartes aura

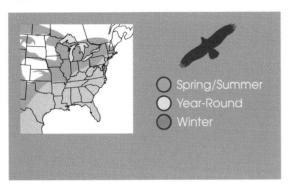

○ Spring/Summer
○ Year-Round
○ Winter

Catharsis—a cleansing or purification—is the root of the turkey vulture's Latin name. It refers to this bird's invaluable service in ridding the landscape of animal carcasses—a necessity in the age of superhighways. The highway system, with its continual supply of shoulder fare, may have contributed to the turkey vulture's northward breeding range expansion.

All About

The tilting flight, with wings held in a shallow "V", immediately distinguishes a turkey vulture from most other large, dark birds in flight. At close range, the underwings appear two-toned, with the flight feathers having a reflective, pewter sheen. The small, naked head is red; the bill bone-white. On the ground, a turkey vulture appears to be all wing—a long blackish trapezoid, topped by a tiny red head. Hoarse hisses are their only sounds. Nestlings produce a continuous breathy roar when cornered in the nest.

Habitat & Range

Ranging widely as they search for food, turkey vultures prefer farmland pastures where carcasses might be found, and with nearby forests where they find nesting and roosting spots. Communal roosters, they may be seen warming themselves with wings spread open to the sun. Turkey vultures are migratory in the northern parts of their range, mingling with resident birds in the southern United States, some traveling as far south as Amazonia before returning in early spring.

Feeding

Powerful olfactory senses help the turkey vulture locate carcasses, and they may circle in groups, narrowing down the scent source, before spotting it. This allows them to find carrion in deep woods. One circling vulture brings sharp-eyed companions from miles around, and they share their plunder, rising with heavy flaps from roadsides when disturbed. Its bare head allows the vulture to reach into larger carcasses without fouling its feathers.

Nesting

Turkey vultures hide their nests on rock ledges, in hollow logs, under boulders, or in unused animal burrows. The female lays two eggs, which she and her mate incubate for around 28 days. The young are in the nest cavity and its vicinity for about 12 weeks, making first flights as early as 60 days of age. After a few weeks of exercising and being fed in the nest vicinity, they appear to be independent upon their first extended flight.

Backyard & Beyond

Turkey vultures have learned to exploit factory farms, especially chicken farms, for the inevitable carcasses they produce. They are closely attuned to spring calving and lambing times. Rather than being seen as harbingers of death, turkey vultures might be considered for their great beauty in flight and as a vital cleanup crew.

Cooper's Hawk

Accipiter cooperii

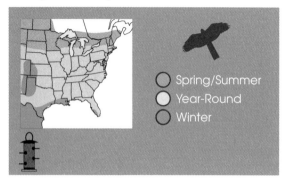

- ○ Spring/Summer
- ○ Year-Round
- ○ Winter

ooper's hawks often perch in inconspicuous places, shooting through the branches or dropping from trees to nab unsuspecting prey. A flurry of fearful birds and a gray flash may mark the arrival of a Cooper's hawk to your backyard. Cooper's hawks are medium-sized hawks and formidable hunters that are usually seen singly except during migration, when they pass by in varying numbers at hawk-watching spots.

All About

Care must be taken to differentiate the Cooper's hawk from the similar sharp-shinned hawk. Adults of both species have similar markings, as do their brown-backed immatures and that of the northern goshawk (larger birds rarely seen south of Virginia, Indiana, and Missouri). Size is often not a trustworthy identification tool in the field—proportions and tail edges are more telling. Compared with the sharp-shinned hawk, the Cooper's has a proportionately larger head and neck and a rounded (not notched) or square-tipped tail (as does the sharp-shinned). Perched, adult Cooper's hawks often show a contrast between a blackish crown and gray nape and back. In flight, its head protrudes well beyond its often straight-held wings, and its tail usually looks rounded. Sharp-shinned hawks look like a capital "T" in flight, their shorter heads almost even with the leading edge of their wings.

Habitat & Range

In many areas, Cooper's hawks are uncommon nesters. Far-northern birds generally winter to the south. You can look for Cooper's hawks in any type of forest, along forest edges, and in woods near watercourses. But don't be surprised if you find one elsewhere, particularly in winter and fall. They seem to be adapting to suburban life, nesting near backyards or in city parks. During spring and fall, migrating Cooper's hawks gravitate toward ridges and coasts.

Feeding

These midsized hawks generally feed on midsized birds, including robins, flickers, and pigeons, but they also eat small mammals, including chipmunks and squirrels. Insects and reptiles sometimes feature on the menu.

Nesting

Cooper's hawks place their bulky stick nests high on horizontal branches in large trees, sometimes building them atop another large bird or squirrel nest. The female lays three to five eggs and incubates them for about five weeks. The male brings food, but the female feeds it to the young, which usually take flight about four or five weeks after hatching.

Backyard & Beyond

Cooper's hawks are attracted to what bird feeders attract—keeping intact natural predator and prey interactions, even in the suburbs. They will not scare birds from your feeders for long and, when successful, Cooper's hawks are usually weeding out the less-fit birds.

Red-tailed Hawk

Buteo jamaicensis

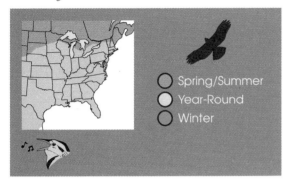

○ Spring/Summer
○ Year-Round
○ Winter

This bird is the large raptor people most often see doing "lazy circles in the sky." The red-tailed hawk inhabits open terrain across the continent and south to Central America. It thrives in habitats opened up by human activities, such as farming or forest clearing. They are also the large raptor most commonly seen perched along roadways and power lines.

All About

Red-tailed hawks occur across the continent in quite a variety of plumage colorations. In the East, however, count on a few easy field marks to help identify adult birds: the reddish-orange tail, a dark-streaked belly band, and a white chest. This hat trick of field marks can easily be seen in many soaring redtails, as well as in perched birds. Additionally, two chocolate-colored bars adorn the leading edge of the underwing. Overall, soaring red-tailed hawks are bulkier and more formidable in general appearance than slimmer red-shouldered hawks and broad-winged hawks, which have shorter tails. Red-tailed hawks younger than two years old lack the telltale reddish tail, but they still exhibit the belly band and white chest.

Habitat & Range

Look for red-tailed hawks along highway edges, over farm fields and forest clearings, and in almost any other open habitat with at least some telephone poles or trees on which they can perch and scan for prey. From tundra to tropical forests, the red-tailed hawk is a formidable pred-ator. They breed as far south as Panama and on various Caribbean islands, thus the species name *jamaicensis*. For nesting, they usually avoid areas with a lot of human activity, even though they nest near New York City's Central Park and pass through suburbs during migration.

Feeding

Many farmers appreciate seeing red-tailed hawks flap over their acreage, as they eat many voles, mice, rats, rabbits, squirrels, and other small mammals. Other prey can include a variety of birds and reptiles. Red-tailed hawks may glide down from a perch to grab prey, dive down, or hover and then drop on prey.

Nesting

Nests are usually found in tall trees, although these birds will nest on cliffs and sometimes even buildings. Both mates build the large stick nest, which they line with softer materials. The female usually lays two or three eggs, which both parents incubate for about a month. The male hunts for food, passing it to his mate, who feeds their young. Nestlings fly after about 10 weeks.

Backyard & Beyond

You may hear the red-tailed hawk's blood-curdling cry around its nesting grounds. Because they range widely and some populations migrate short or long distances, you may see red-tailed hawks soaring or gliding over your home.

Northern Harrier

Circus cyaneus

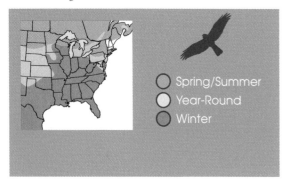

- ○ Spring/Summer
- ○ Year-Round
- ○ Winter

The slender, low-flying form of the northern harrier is associated with grasslands and marshes across most of North America during one season or another. Young birds, adult females, and adult males are very different in appearance and size—an unusual trait among raptors.

All About

The northern harrier's key field mark is a large white rump patch, but its shape—long slender wings and long tail—is also distinctive. First-year juveniles sport a rich chocolate brown on their back and wings accompanied by an unstreaked, rust-colored breast. Adult females, which can be twice as large as males, are the same colors as juveniles but have a heavily streaked breast and belly. Adult males are pale gray below and slate gray above, and are sometimes referred to by bird watchers as "gray ghosts." A ring of feathers surrounding the face form a facial disc, an owl-like adaptation that channels sound to the ears.

Habitat & Range

Present year-round in grassland habitat across the northern two-thirds of North America, the northern harrier is considered a locally common species. Their winter range includes most of the U.S. with the exception of high-mountain habitat in the East. Prairies, marshy grass- lands, wetlands, and old hayfields are home to the harrier. Unlike many other raptors, harriers will migrate and forage in rainy or snowy weather.

Feeding

Voles, mice, rats, shrews, rabbits, and other small mammals are the primary prey of the northern harrier, but small birds, snakes, other reptiles, and insects are also eaten. Harriers glide very low over grassy habitat, watching and listening for movement below them, and then wheeling to turn, hover, and pounce when prey is located.

Nesting

Harrier nests are built out of grasses, weed stems, and sticks placed on the ground, or on top of a platform built in cattails or other vegetation and suspended over water. The nests are always in dense vegetation and built primarily by the female. She lays a clutch of three to seven eggs and incubates them for about 30 days. The male delivers food to the female during incubation and after hatching, but she takes over when the chicks are about two weeks old. Five weeks after hatching the young harriers can fly.

Backyard & Beyond

Harriers prefer grasslands, rough meadows, and grassy marshes (the harrier was formerly called the marsh hawk) for foraging, though they can also be seen along grassy dunes, old strip mines, and airport fields. Look for a large bird with a small head flying low over the ground, wheeling and teetering like a vulture. When the white rump patch flashes, you'll know you've got your harrier.

Bald Eagle

Haliaeetus leucocephalus

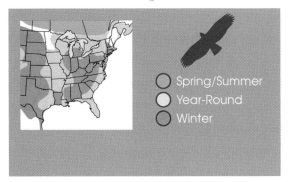

○ Spring/Summer
○ Year-Round
○ Winter

The bald eagle barely edged out the wild turkey when our founding fathers were voting on a national symbol. Skilled fishing bird, scavenger, and pirate, the bald eagle is an opportunistic raptor that's been given a second chance thanks to improved conservation and bans on DDT, which dramatically impaired the birds' breeding and sent their population into steep decline in the decades following World War II.

All About

There is no confusing the adult bald eagle, with its huge size and gleaming white head and tail. Adult plumage is not attained until after the third year. Until then, immature birds are dark brown with varying degrees of white mottling on their backs, wings, bellies, and, in older birds, heads. Depending upon age, the large bill is blackish or accented in the bright yellow seen in adults. Immatures and adults have strong, bright yellow talons.

Habitat & Range

Water plays a strong role where bald eagles hunt and nest. In the process of rebounding in many areas, bald eagles now nest in most states, where they are often local nesters tied to specific sites. They are particularly common from Florida to coastal South Carolina and around the Great Lakes, but the largest breeding populations are in Alaska and western Canada. During winter, bald eagles often congregate at wetland areas, rivers, and dams, where fishing or carrion feeding is particularly productive.

Feeding

Bald eagles hunt from perches or swoop down after sighting prey while soaring. Although fish are preferred prey (frequently grappled from the water in the eagle's mighty talons), eagles also eat a wide variety of other foods, depending upon individual, time of year, and location. Carrion—particularly dead fish, birds, and mammals—plays an important dietary role. Many live animals are also caught: muskrats, reptiles, amphibians, crustaceans, and birds—as large as great blue herons—have been documented. Bald eagles also steal fish from ospreys and other birds.

Nesting

Bald eagles nest high in large trees in huge, bulky stick nests that are often used again over the years. Both mates collect sticks, and nest building may take several months. The female usually lays two eggs, which she and her mate incubate for just over a month. Once the first chick hatches, both parents incubate and *brood*, or cover, the eggs and hatchlings. Both parents feed their young, which leave the nest between 8 to 14 weeks after hatching.

Backyard & Beyond

Recently, bald eagles have started nesting in closer proximity to human development, thanks to protection from disturbance. If you see a large, dark raptor soaring slowly in the sky, with flat wings, look for the other clues to the bald eagle's identity.

Osprey

Pandion haliaetus

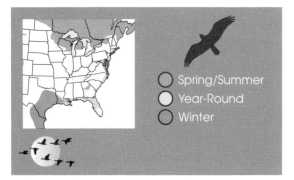

○ Spring/Summer
● Year-Round
○ Winter

The bold chocolate and white "fish hawk," so familiar to boaters and fishermen, is happy to exploit artificial nesting platforms, from power poles to those built specifically for it. Though osprey populations declined by 90 percent from the 1950s to the 1970s (poisoned by persistent organochlorides), they have made a heartening rebound in recent decades.

All About

Chocolate-brown above and pure white below, the osprey is armed with long, pale green legs and grappling-hook talons for seizing fish. Fierce yellow eyes are ringed in black, making the bird look as though it is wearing aviator's goggles. A banded gray tail and ragged crest complete this gangly bird's unusual look. Females have streaked upper breasts and are larger than males. When disturbed, ospreys give a series of high, piercing, chicklike peeps and thin screams.

Habitat & Range

One of the most widespread species, the osprey inhabits rivers, lakes, and coastlines throughout much of the United States. It is still reclaiming territory in the interior United States, helped by osprey reintroduction programs. Lacking body down, ospreys must migrate to stay warm and to find sufficient food in unfrozen waters, traveling down both coasts of Mexico and Central America.

Feeding

The only North American raptor to feed exclusively on fish, the osprey soars and hovers over shallow, clear waters of estuaries, marshes, lakes, and rivers, searching for fish. Spotting prey, it folds its wings and plunges, feet first, often completely beneath the surface. Unique cylindrical, recurved talons and horny spikes on the soles of its feet hold the fish securely until the osprey reaches a "carving block," usually a dead snag, where it can eat. Fish are always carried with the head facing into the wind, and are sometimes eaten as a snack on migration, far from water.

Nesting

The huge stick nests ospreys build are a familiar site on channel markers, dead trees, and artificial nesting platforms along shorelines. Nesting pairs add sticks yearly until the nests assume enormous proportions. In the soft, grass-lined center the female lays two to three eggs, which she and her mate incubate for around 37 days. The male provides all the female's food during this time. Chicks stay in the nest for about 55 days, taking short flights, and are fed on or near the nest for around two weeks after first attaining flight.

Backyard & Beyond

Though artificial nesting platforms have had a positive influence on osprey populations, they are by no means out of danger. Overfishing, pesticide contamination, and persecution on Latin American wintering grounds (where they are shot by the hundreds at fish farms) continue to limit populations.

American Kestrel

Falco sparverius

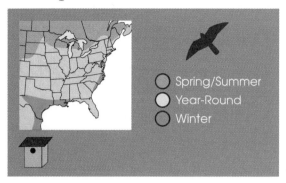

○ Spring/Summer
● Year-Round
○ Winter

North America's smallest falcon is also the most familiar to many, hovering over farm fields and air strips, perching on telephone poles and wires, and nesting in boxes put out by concerned landowners, who welcome these insect and rodent eaters. In some regions, kestrel numbers have fallen in recent decades, probably due to large-scale landscape changes, as farm areas have reverted to forest and as cities and suburbs have stretched out to once-rural areas.

All About

In flight, the kestrel has sharp-looking, pointed wings and a slender, long tail. In comparison to the merlin and peregrine falcons, it is slim. Sharp-shinned and Cooper's hawks also have long tails, but their wings are broad, not pointed. While soaring, the kestrel's wings look more rounded and the tail fans. Adult males are brightly colored, with blue-gray wings and crown, rufous tail, and a rusty back embellished with black barring. Black spots speckle the underparts. Both sexes have two vertical stripes on the face and a black spot on the back of the neck. Adult females lack the male's blue-gray wings, have barred tails, and—instead of black spots—sport rusty lines of spots on their underparts.

Habitat & Range

The American kestrel is not strictly a farm bird, although many farms provide the ideal habitat for them. They also nest and hunt in open urban areas, open forest, clearings, and even deserts. They are truly American in the New World sense, nesting from Alaska to southern Argentina. In the North, numbers dwindle in winter, when northern birds move south *en masse* to winter in warmer areas.

Feeding

Grasshoppers and other large insects are important prey to kestrels, but voles, mice, and other rodents also play a part in their diet, as do small birds, reptiles, and other small animals.

Nesting

American kestrels are cavity nesters. Females usually lay their four to six eggs in a tree hole or other cavity, sometimes in a crevice in a building or cliff, or in a nest box. Both parents share the month-long incubation duties. Young fly about a month after hatching, and parents feed them until about two weeks after they leave the nest.

Backyard & Beyond

Provision of nest boxes in rural areas has helped American kestrel populations, and this is one potential way to attract kestrels to your property if you live in an open area. Kestrels also pass through suburban areas during migration. They may frequent open suburbs rich in grasshoppers and such prey as small birds and lizards. They will use snags placed in the middle of grassy meadows as hunting and eating perches.

Wild Turkey

Meleagris gallopavo

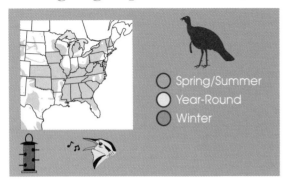

○ Spring/Summer
○ Year-Round
○ Winter

When restocking programs abandoned using farm-raised birds and turned to releasing wild-caught birds in the 1940s, the repopulation of wild turkeys into their former haunts took off. Today, the large dark forms of wild turkeys are a familiar sight along many highways, and the birds even come to backyard feeders.

All About

A tall, strong-legged bird, the wild turkey's feathers are iridescent with dark bronze, shot with hints of copper and acid green. Displaying in spring, the male erects its plumage in the strut posture, its enormous tail fanned, wings drooping, and wattles ablaze. A "beard" of wiry, barbless feathers sprouts from the center of his breast. Hens are visibly smaller and paler than gobblers, with a brown cast to their plumage and without distensible wattles. Along with the male's explosive gobble, turkeys employ a great variety of calls, including yelps and hollow *putt* sounds, in their intraflock communication.

Habitat & Range

Dense deciduous forests—either uplands or bottomlands—with some clearings are ideal turkey habitats. The nuts from oaks and other nut trees make up an important component of their diet. Some exploit agricultural fields for spilled grain. Wild turkeys are nonmigratory and may fast for more than a week in severe weather.

Feeding

The wild turkey's strong legs and feet help it scratch its way across the forest floor, raking away debris to uncover acorns, tree seeds, and invertebrates. Turkeys pluck buds and fruits as they walk or clamber through branches, and they strip grasses of their seeds by running stems through their bills. Young poults take a number of insects and invertebrates.

Nesting

Gobblers display—gobbling and strutting—in early spring to attract visiting hens. After mating, the hen lays about a dozen eggs in a feather-lined bowl in the ground at the foot of a tree or under brush. She incubates them alone for about 26 days. When all chicks have hatched and imprinted on the hen (from one to three days later), they leave the nest, following her every move. She feeds them for the first few days; after that they pick up their own food. She broods them on the ground until they are able to join her in a roost tree at night; she still shelters them with spread wings on the roost.

Backyard & Beyond

Wild turkeys may, in some rural and suburban situations, be attracted into yards with cracked corn spread on the ground. A small flock can consume as much as 50 pounds per week. Watching their fascinating social behavior and courtship behavior is a rich reward. Rotate feeding areas to prevent the spread of disease.

American Coot

Fulica americana

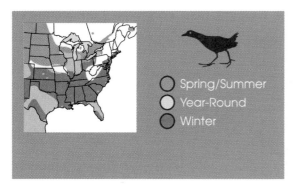

○ Spring/Summer
○ Year-Round
○ Winter

What looks like a duck and acts like a duck, but is not a duck? It's the American coot, of course. Coots are duck-like in many ways, but they are actually members of the rail family and are the most common (and most commonly seen) of all the rails. Like ducks, coots are excellent swimmers and use this ability to find and eat aquatic vegetation. However, coots are reluctant and awkward fliers—they must run, pattering across the water's surface and flapping madly to lift their heavy bodies into the air.

All About

Chunky and almost all black with a contrasting white bill and red eyes and forehead patch, the coot is hard to mistake for anything else. The common moorhen and purple gallinule are similar in shape, but both are more colorful (the gallinule much more so) and less common than coots. Coots swim using the lobed toes on their powerful feet, and when swimming they bob their heads back and forth with a "funky chicken" motion. Coots are raucous, loud birds that utter a variety of grunts, cackles, and croaks.

Habitat & Range

American coots are widespread across North America, especially in winter when they can be found in huge flocks on large bodies of water. They breed throughout the central and western portions of the continent, and they are year-round residents in parts of the Midwest and South. During the breeding season, coots prefer ponds, lakes, and marshes of almost any size, provided that they have large stands of tall reeds, such as cattails.

Feeding

Finding most of their food on or below the surface of the water, coots dabble, swim, and dive when foraging. They are equally at home on land, grazing on the grass of city parks and golf courses. Their diet is largely vegetarian with the main menu items being duckweed, algae, and various pondweeds and sedges.

Nesting

The female coot builds a floating, basket-shaped platform of vegetation with a lined cup to hold the eggs. She lays up to a dozen eggs and incubates them for about 23 days. Young coots have shiny, bald, red heads and golden down, an adaptation that is thought to trigger feeding by the parents. Babies leave the nest after a day or so and are able to find food on their own shortly thereafter.

Backyard & Beyond

Though they may not be a backyard bird, coots should be easy to find in nearby parks and on golf course water hazards. In winter, look for flocks of coots on almost any body of water, from reservoirs to sewage ponds.

Killdeer
Charadrius vociferus

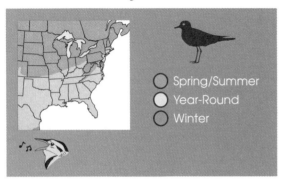

○ Spring/Summer
○ Year-Round
○ Winter

The killdeer is a large, double-banded plover that screams its name across farm fields and other grass- and dirt-covered habitats. If you see an orange-tailed, stripe-winged bird calling KILL-DEEE, KILL-DEEE, you can rest assured that it's this plover. Despite their lousy-tasting flesh, many killdeer were shot during the late 1800s, along with a wide range of other shorebirds. These species are now protected from harm by federal and state laws.

All About
On its white breast, two black bands stand out. Other plovers—such as the smaller but similar semipalmated plover—have only one band or none at all. Otherwise, killdeer are wet-sand brown above and clear white below, with white around the front of the face and eye. The killdeer is one of our largest and longest-tailed plovers, so even mixed with a few other species on a mudflat, they stand out, especially when you spot those two breast bands. Much of the tail is orange, except the tip, which is black punctuated with white dabs.

Habitat & Range
Unlike most other plovers, killdeer often forage or nest far from water. You may find them on ball fields and airport runways, on turf, in pastures, and in farm fields, as well as on mudflats. They are found throughout North America, but northern birds head south for the winter.

Feeding
A farmer's friend, the killdeer spends its foraging time searching for beetles, grasshoppers, caterpillars, and other insects. Crayfish, centipedes, spiders, and other invertebrates are also eaten, as well as some seeds.

Nesting
A simple scrape in the dirt or gravel (including gravel-covered roofs) will do for a killdeer pair, although they sometimes add embellishments, such as a lining of pebbles, grass, or other small materials. Females lay three to five blotched eggs, which both parents incubate for just less than a month. Nesting in exposed habitats, killdeer rely on camouflage and deception to keep their eggs and chicks safe. If an intruder approaches the nest, an adult killdeer may feign injury—dragging a wing as if it is broken and exposing its bright tail—then lure the person or predator away from the nest. Adults watch over their hatchlings, little puffballs that can run around and find food by themselves shortly after hatching. They can fly before they reach one month old.

Backyard & Beyond
Killdeer are attracted to large areas of grass as well as to short-cropped fields, so you may see them on your property if it's relatively treeless and large. Their cries carry long distances, so you may also hear killdeer passing by or calling from nearby nesting grounds.

Lesser Yellowlegs

Tringa flavipes

○ Spring/Summer
○ Year-Round
○ Winter

Lesser yellowlegs is a tall shorebird commonly seen in a variety of saltwater and freshwater situations. It winters in the Gulf States and along southern seacoasts, both east and west, so wherever you live in North America you stand a chance of seeing this species at some time during the year. Lessers often travel in large flocks and may be found together with greater yellowlegs.

All About

True to its name, this bird has bright yellow legs, which really stand out against its dark back and speckled underparts. The sexes are alike. When alarmed, it will take flight with a loud *tu* or *tu-tu* call, trailing its long yellow legs behind. The only species the lesser yellowlegs is likely to be confused with is the equally common greater yellowlegs, a nearly identical, but larger, close relative. In flight, both show white on the rump. The smaller lesser yellowlegs has a shorter, straighter bill than the greater, and overall it has a much more delicate appearance.

Habitat & Range

During migrations, the lesser yellowlegs is more likely than the greater yellowlegs to visit fresh water. It occurs widely and may stop at small ponds or wetlands, temporary rainwater puddles, marshes and mudflats, and flooded fields.

Feeding

Lesser yellowlegs feed in shallow water where they find their prey—aquatic insects, snails, small fish, and crustaceans—on or just beneath the water's surface. They sometimes swing their heads back and forth underwater in an effort to stir up food. On land, the lesser yellowlegs may snatch up terrestrial insects and worms from the ground, or pick flying insects out of the air.

Nesting

Breeding at the edge of the northern tundra, lesser yellowlegs nest in natural clearings with small clusters of vegetation. The nest is merely a scrape in the ground, softened with a few fallen leaves and placed next to a fallen log or under a low shrub, usually within 200 yards of a water source. Nesting starts as early as May, with the male calling loudly from the top of a tree or other elevated perch. The female lays three to four eggs, and both parents share the 18- to 20-day incubation. Within hours of hatching, the young are able to leave the nest. As soon as the chicks are self-sufficient—as early as July—the adults leave for the south. The youngsters start south a few weeks later.

Backyard & Beyond

Any marsh or wetland in your neighborhood might host lesser yellowlegs during migration. Look for lesser yellowlegs in spring from April through June, and in fall from July through September. You should be able to find it easily at mudflats and marshes, mingling with other shorebirds.

Spotted Sandpiper

Actitis macularia

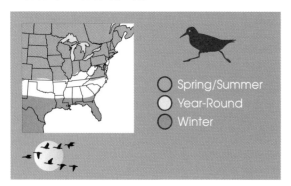

○ Spring/Summer
○ Year-Round
○ Winter

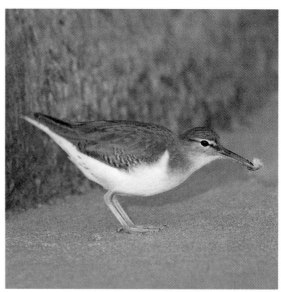

The spotted sandpiper is one of the easiest sandpipers to identify. Not only are its markings distinctive, but so are its mannerisms—the bird signals itself to birders by almost constantly bobbing its posterior. An inland nester across much of northern North America, the spotted sandpiper frequents waterways from creeks and streams to marshes, reservoirs, and mudflats during migration, and shoreline areas during winter.

All About

The wood-thrushlike breast spotting of breeding adult spotted sandpipers sets them apart from other sandpipers, but you can also easily identify spotless immatures (as shown in the photo) and non-breeders. For one thing, the spotted sandpiper's tail and rear end constantly bob up and down as the bird walks or pauses; this is true even in birds that have just left the nest. Also, look for a white crescent on the sides, which curls around the bend of the bird's folded wing, inching toward the back. Spotted sandpipers are about the length of a wood thrush and smaller than a robin—in other words, they are not the tiniest sandpipers, but they are rather small. Breeding individuals have bright orange bills; otherwise, spotted sandpipers have pale pinkish or orangish bills and legs.

Habitat & Range

Spotted sandpipers nest in freshwater habitats, both in forested and open settings across much of North America, except in the far South, where a good number winter. Find them at pools where rainwater collects, along lakeshores, and at streams, rivers, or marshes. Many winter far to the south, from Mexico and Central America to as far south as northern Chile and Argentina.

Feeding

As would be expected of a bird that frequents a mixture of habitats, the spotted sandpiper captures a variety of prey in diverse ways. Insects, crabs, worms, small fish, and other creatures may be picked from the water or shore, caught in quick flights, or chased.

Nesting

Parental care in spotted sandpipers differs from that in many other birds. Female spotted sandpipers often pair up with more than one male, laying two or more clutches of eggs. Both parents build the nest, a depression in the ground usually sheltered by some plant cover and lined with plants or moss. There the female usually lays four eggs, which may be incubated by the male or by both parents for about three weeks. The nestlings teeter as soon as they hatch and can almost immediately scamper from the nest. Usually the male watches over the young, which can fly when they are about 18 days old.

Backyard & Beyond

Any park or backyard with a large pond, stream, or lake is likely to host a spotted sandpiper at one time or another.

American Woodcock

Scolopax minor

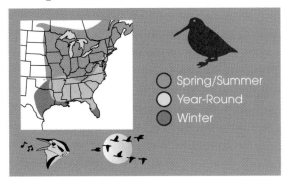

○ Spring/Summer
○ Year-Round
○ Winter

The male American woodcock's courtship display is one of Nature's most unusual and it may be performing it in or near your backyard on early spring evenings. Its nocturnal habits, amazing sky dancing, and camouflage coloration make it one of the most fascinating, weird, and mysterious North American birds.

All About

The American woodcock is a short, stocky shorebird with a long, straight bill and large eyes set far back on the head. This eye position gives it rearward vision, allowing it to watch for danger even when it is probing the ground for earthworms. The woodcock's plumage is a mixture of dark earth tones that hide it perfectly in its preferred woodland habitat. Males find a small clearing from which they repeatedly give a loud, nasal *peent!* call to announce themselves prior to launching into their impressive courtship display. They spiral upward for twenty or more seconds, wings whistling with each flap, then plummet to earth uttering a whistling twitter. Males perform this display before dawn and after dusk, hoping to attract watching females to mate.

Habitat & Range

During the spring and summer, woodcocks can be found in wet woodlands and swampy thickets all across the eastern half of the United States and southern Canada. At night they forage and display in open habitats such as old fields, meadows, and wetland edges.

Feeding

The tip of the woodcock's bill is sensitive and flexible—ideally suited to probing for earthworms and subterranean insects. When it senses an earthworm, the woodcock opens the tip of the upper mandible like a flexible tweezer to grasp the worm and pull it out. Other foods taken include spiders, snails, and some grass seeds.

Nesting

Several males may be displaying in one place while one or more females watch. A female will choose a male, mate with him, and leave. Males have no role in caring for the young. The nest is a simple scrape on the ground lined with and surrounded by dead leaves. Usual clutch size is four eggs and incubation lasts about three weeks. Downy hatchlings leave the nest almost immediately and are tended by the female for a few days until they can feed on their own. They are fully flighted and independent after five weeks.

Backyard & Beyond

On an early spring night at dusk, visit an old meadow surrounded by woods and listen for the low nasal call of the male woodcock and the whistling wings as he ascends for his display flight. If you look toward the western horizon, you may see his silhouette as he dances in the night sky.

Bonaparte's Gull

Larus philadelphia

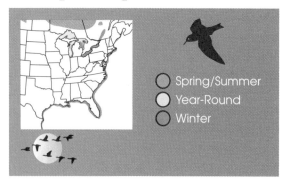

- ○ Spring/Summer
- ○ Year-Round
- ○ Winter

Though it breeds in the coniferous forests of the far North, the Bonaparte's gull is a common winter visitor across much of the U.S. Its small size and lilting ternlike flight separate it visually from other common winter gulls. This species is not named for famed French general Napolean Bonaparte, but for his cousin, French zoologist Charles Lucien Bonaparte.

All About

Between April and August, adult Bonaparte's gulls are in breeding plumage with a black hood and bill and a broken white eye ring. But it is the winter plumage (worn from September through March) that is most familiar to bird watchers. The only remnant of the dark hood is a dark ear spot behind the eye—giving the impressions that the bird is wearing earphones. The legs remain pink and the thin, straight bill remains black all year. In flight, the winter adult appears light overall with the wingtips outlined in black. First-winter birds show a faint black "M" pattern across the backs of their wings.

Habitat & Range

Bonaparte's gulls nest far to the north from east-central Canada into Alaska. Though they spend winters primarily on the ocean coasts, including the Gulf of Mexico, many birds linger inland, moving southward only if a freeze closes all bodies of water. They congregate in huge flocks at dam spillways, reservoirs, sewage lagoons, coastal estuaries, and along rivers, especially where food is abundant.

Feeding

Insects are a primary food during the breeding season, but Bonaparte's gulls also eat small fish, crustaceans, and grasshoppers. They forage while flying and can plunge into the water for a fish, pluck a morsel from the water's surface, or hawk insects in flight with equal skill. In winter you may often seen Bonies foraging among flocks of mergansers, grebes, or cormorants, seizing small fish and other items stirred up by these diving birds.

Nesting

Unlike any other North American gull, the Bonaparte's gull frequently builds its nest in trees, usually in a conifer adjacent to water. They may nest in small, loose colonies. The pair builds the nest of sticks lined with lichen or moss. Three or four eggs are laid and the shared incubation duties last about 24 days. Both parents care for the young until they are ready to undertake fall migration with the adults as early as late July.

Backyard & Beyond

Almost any large, ice-free body of water in winter can host a flock of Bonaparte's gulls. Bonies are usually found in single-species flocks—they rarely associate with other, larger gull species. Though they may be found hawking insects at sewage ponds, don't look for them at garbage dumps with other gulls.

Ring-billed Gull

Larus delawarensis

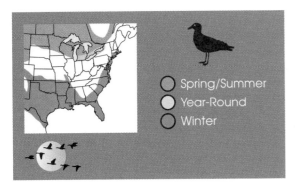

○ Spring/Summer
○ Year-Round
○ Winter

This gull might almost be called the inland gull. Though found in coastal areas like most gulls, it is also the most numerous and widespread gull away from the seacoasts, sometimes found in huge flocks. At first glance it looks like a slightly smaller version of the herring gull, but it has a personality all its own.

All About

The ring-billed gull is a medium-sized (19 inches long) gull, and in adult plumage it has a light gray back and wings on a pure white body. Its wing tips are black with white spots, and it has a black ring near the end of its yellow bill. Males and females look alike. Young ring-billed gulls take three years to mature, during which time their bodies and wings are varying shades of mottled brown and gray, with a white tail that has a prominent, black terminal band. These gulls are smaller, lighter, and more graceful-looking than similarly patterned herring gulls, and they have a more buoyant appearance in flight.

Habitat and Range

In addition to the beaches and bays of the seacoasts, ring-billed gulls may be found at large inland lakes and rivers, in newly plowed fields and pastures, and at sod farms, garbage dumps, and parking lots throughout their range.

Feeding

Ring-billed gulls are omnivorous, thriving on whatever food is on hand. Fish are a favorite item, but insects and earthworms are high on the list, along with grains, refuse, and even small rodents. They will eat the eggs of other species, and they are not averse to taking handouts from humans at parking lots and picnic grounds. (French fries, caught in midair, are popular. Ketchup is optional.)

Nesting

After a courtship routine by the male (which includes bowing, throat-puffing, and a ceremonial walk around the female, enlivened by many odd gesticulations), the mated pair will build its nest on the ground in a fairly open area near water. The ring-billed is colonial, so there are usually lots of similar nests nearby. Both sexes build the flimsy nest of grasses, sticks, and moss; and both take turns incubating the two to four eggs for up to four weeks until hatching. The downy young are tended by their parents in the general vicinity of the nest until they attain flight at about five weeks of age.

Backyard & Beyond

Look for ring-billed gulls in large, open fields after spring or autumn rainstorms, or watch for them anywhere there is an infestation of large insects, such as grasshoppers or locusts. If there is a landfill or dam nearby, it may attract gulls from a wide surrounding area and can make for productive gull watching.

Herring Gull

Larus argentatus

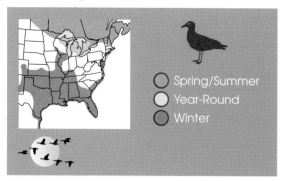

○ Spring/Summer
○ Year-Round
○ Winter

This is the bird that most people think of when they hear the term seagull. *Large, abundant, and widespread, the herring gull is an imposing bird—and, in its adult plumage, it is certainly beautiful. Picture a dozen or more sitting on a pier with ocean waves lapping below, and you have a perfect coastal postcard scene.*

All About

Measuring up to 26 inches in length, the adult herring gull has silver-gray wings tipped in black and white, a dazzling white body, bold yellow bill, and pink legs. Males and females are alike, and they are considerably larger than similar-looking ring-billed gulls. Immature herring gulls wear varying shades of brown or gray-brown and are not fully mature until their fourth year. All ages join in making the yelping or trumpeting calls, which are a constant fact of life throughout the herring gull's entire range.

Habitat & Range

Herring gulls are birds of shorelines, major lakes and rivers, garbage dumps, and, occasionally, farmlands—especially recently tilled fields. Their population, once confined to the northern states, has been spreading southward for decades. They nest across Canada and are found year-round throughout the Great Lakes. Winter flocks may be found along major rivers.

Feeding

Herring gulls eat almost anything, which is one reason for their success. Fish, along with all manner of other seafood, are a staple of the herring gull diet, but they also eat the eggs and chicks of other bird species (they can decimate a tern colony if given the opportunity), all kinds of garbage, large insects and grubs, and even carrion. They are smart and have learned to drop clams onto rocks or pavement to open them. They are quite willing to steal food from other birds. In the gull world, there is no such thing as a guilty conscience.

Nesting

Herring gulls nest on the ground, preferably in the lee of a rock or some other natural feature. Both sexes help scrape out a site and line it with grass, weeds, and feathers. Many nests contain a ball of some kind—whiffle ball, tennis ball—which may be a courtship gift from the male. The usual clutch is three eggs, and both parents share the month-long incubation. The young, downy and active from the start, depend on their parents at least until they fly at about 50 days of age.

Backyard & Beyond

Check the range map above to see when herring gulls might be expected in your area, and then visit the nearest beach! These birds also hang out at sewage outlets, dams, or anywhere that human activity may generate a reliable food supply.

Mourning Dove

Zenaida macroura

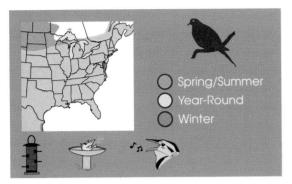

○ Spring/Summer
○ Year-Round
○ Winter

Whether you regard them as songbirds or living skeet targets, if you feed birds, you probably have mourning doves as constant companions. These tapered, graceful brown and pinkish birds wholeheartedly embrace human alterations of the natural landscape, finding their greatest abundance in agricultural and suburban areas. Doves love water, but may foul birdbaths by sitting around the rim, tails in.

All About

The mournful *oooahh, oooh, ooh, ooh* song of the mourning dove echos from power lines and treetops in early spring. Mourning doves travel in flocks, breaking rank only to nest and raise young. Males defend their mates as a kind of mobile territory, defending her and the immediate nest site—but not much else—from other birds.

Habitat & Range

The only habitat shunned by mourning doves is deep, contiguous forest. They are most common in agricultural areas with hedgerows and shelterbelts. They are also abundant in suburban areas as well, where visits to feeding stations are an integral part of their daily routines. Mourning doves migrate, especially far northern populations, but some individuals are resident year-round.

Feeding

Streamlined, fast, and powerful flyers, mourning doves travel in flocks, descending to feed on a great variety of grains and weed seeds that they peck from the ground. They are often seen in ranks on power lines over farm fields. A capacious crop allows mourning doves to gorge—sometimes to the point of being misshapen—and then digest their stored food later when resting.

Nesting

Mourning doves may mate and nest in any month of the year, but males begin to tune up their songs in late winter. They have a production-line breeding mode, following one brood with another as often as six times in a season. The twig nest platform, placed in a wide variety of tree species, but frequently in a pine, is often flimsy enough so that eggs show through from beneath. Two eggs are incubated by both members of the pair, and they hatch in 14 days. Young doves are fed first on crop milk, a secretion unique to the pigeon family, and later on regurgitated seeds. Young remain in the nest for another 15 days but may fledge much earlier. The male feeds them until about day 30, while the female re-nests. Immature birds are visibly smaller and have fine, buff feather edges overall.

Backyard & Beyond

Mourning doves take any seeds that might be offered at feeders, preferring sunflower seeds, cracked corn, millet, milo, and other grains found in seed mixes. They become adept at emptying hopper feeders into their ample crops, and then sitting for long periods afterward to digest their food.

Rock Pigeon

Columba livia

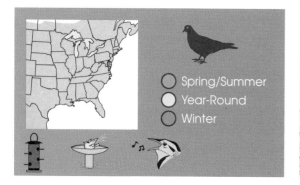

- ◯ Spring/Summer
- ◯ Year-Round
- ◯ Winter

Originating in northern Europe, Africa, and India, rock pigeons—largely gone from their former wild haunts—have spread to cities and towns worldwide thanks to their domestication some five thousand years ago. Evidence of this domestication lies in their highly variable coloration; a flock may contain birds in every color from pure white to reddish to solid black.

All About

A substantial bird with a small head, deep chest, powerful wings, and a square tail, the rock pigeon is built for flight. Wild-type birds are slate-blue with a white rump, black terminal tail band, and two black bars on the secondary wing feathers. Pinkish green iridescence adorns the neck. Pigeons have short, reddish legs and a short, straight bill. Their song is a series of soft, resonant coos—*ooh-ga-rooogh*—and a harsh *Woogh!* serves as an alarm call. Pigeons can be found in flocks except when tending young.

Habitat & Range

It is rare to find rock pigeons in natural habitats, though there are still some cliff-nesting populations in North America. Most consider tall buildings, with their myriad ledges, to be ideal nesting grounds and are happy to take foods, such as bread and popcorn, from city sidewalks. Pigeons are nonmigratory, though their celebrated homing skills are exploited by pigeon racing clubs across the world.

Feeding

Walking and pecking with rapidly bobbing heads, pigeons find their preferred food—grains, seeds, and some fruits—on the ground. Urban birds have highly developed scavenging skills, raiding trashcans and fast food litter for high-carbohydrate fare, such as bread.

Nesting

It's easy to watch pigeons display and even mate; the male's spinning, bowing, and cooing may be conducted underfoot on city sidewalks. Pigeons mate for life, guarding females zealously. They may lay eggs and raise young anytime. Building ledges, highway overpasses, barns, bridges, and other structures may be selected as the site on which to build a stick-and-grass nest and lay two eggs. Both male and female incubate for about 18 days. The rubbery, black-skinned squabs stay in the nest for a variable period of 25 to 45 days. Fat at fledging, they may be forced to fend entirely for themselves upon leaving the nest.

Backyard & Beyond

Thanks to the flocking habit of pigeons, most feeder operators are less than delighted when they descend. The most effective deterrents seem to be sturdy feeders enclosed by wire caging that excludes pigeons while admitting smaller birds. Some people opt to spread food at a distance to keep pigeons from overwhelming seed feeders. Pigeons will eat anything that might be offered, but millet and cracked corn are special favorites.

Yellow-billed Cuckoo

Coccyzus americanus

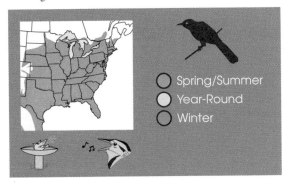

○ Spring/Summer
○ Year-Round
○ Winter

The yellow-billed cuckoo is a furtive, skulking bird of thickets and brushy woodland edges and, though it is fairly large, its retiring habits make it far more easily heard than seen. It often hides deep within the foliage and, when perching in the open, it tends to remain very still. The yellow-billed cuckoo makes a unique repetitive clucking sound that is a sure clue to identification.

All About

Slender and long-tailed, the yellow-billed cuckoo has a plain brown back and creamy white breast. The underside of the tail shows a pattern of bold white spots against a black background, and bright rufous wing patches are visible in flight. The lower part of the bill is yellow. Male and female yellow-billed cuckoos look alike. The only other species they are likely to be confused with is the related black-billed cuckoo, which lacks the rufous wing color and has a black bill, among other differences.

Habitat & Range

Yellow-billed cuckoos inhabit deciduous woodland edges, thickets and tangles along watercourses or roadsides, willow groves, and overgrown orchards. Yellow-billed cuckoos are not generally found in deep interior woodlands, as they prefer some kind of "edge" to their habitat.

Feeding

Yellow-billed cuckoos eat great numbers of hairy caterpillars and many large insects such as dragonflies, cicadas, grasshoppers, crickets, and beetles. Small fruits are a minor but regular part of their diet in summer. Most yellow-billed cuckoos forage by slowly and methodically exploring branches, twigs, and leaves for hidden insects, but they occasionally may act like flycatchers, darting into the air for a meal on the wing, or hovering to seize a caterpillar at the edge of a leaf.

Nesting

Once paired, cuckoos survey the surrounding area for a leafy and secluded nest site, five to ten feet off the ground. Both help build a loose shell of twigs and stems, lining it with fine grasses. Three to five eggs are laid, and both parents share the incubation and feeding of the young. The entire process, from egg laying to fledging, takes only 17 days, one of the shortest such periods for any bird species.

Backyard & Beyond

If you have mature trees rimming your backyard, you may have an occasional yellow-billed cuckoo stopping by on migration—listen for its patented clucking calls. An old folk name for the yellow-billed cuckoo is "raincrow," because these *kowp-kowp-kowp* calls are so often uttered on hot summer afternoons, when thunderstorms are likely to follow. Knowing the cuckoo's call will be helpful in finding this secretive bird; otherwise, check the thickets and edges of your local woodland or park for a chance to find this species.

Great Horned Owl

Bubo virginianus

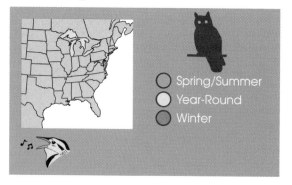

- ○ Spring/Summer
- ○ Year-Round
- ○ Winter

Huge, powerful, and widespread across North America, the great horned is the king of all of our owls. Armed with incredible vision, the great horned sees and pounces on prey, using its powerful talons and bill to dispatch its victim. The deep, hooting call of the great horned—whoo-who-o-o-o-who-who—a staple of movie and television soundtracks, is most often heard in nature just after sunset.

All About
The great horned owl is named for its large size (up to 24 inches tall, with a wingspan of 44 inches) and its long feathered head tufts (horns). A deep rusty brown and buff overall, this owl has large, golden-yellow eyes. Its thick, soft feathers provide excellent insulation from either heat or cold, permitting the great horned to nest as soon as early to midwinter even in regions with harsh winter weather.

Habitat & Range
A nonmigratory bird throughout the Americas, great horned owls can be found as far north as the tree line, and as far south as South America—and in nearly every conceivable habitat and setting. Great horned owls are equally at home in urban and suburban settings, as well as in deep woodlands, grasslands, and deserts.

Feeding
Mammals (rabbits, hares, and large rodents) are the primary prey item of great horned owls. They also eat earthworms, fish, snakes, and even birds as large as great blue herons. They are one of the few predators that will readily kill and consume skunks. Within a great horned owl's territory, it's unusual to find other, smaller owls—they may have been eaten by the resident great horneds. Their primary hunting mode is to perch, watch, and pounce on prey.

Nesting
Great horned owls most often take over an old stick nest built by a hawk, heron, or squirrel, but they will also nest on cliff ledges, in tree cavities, and even on the ground. Two to four eggs are laid and incubation by the female lasts slightly more than a month. The male brings food to his mate on the nest each night. Six weeks or so after hatching, the young owlets venture from the nest to nearby branches. They remain dependent on the adults for many months, but leave the nest area before the next breeding season.

Backyard & Beyond
If you live in or near older woodlands, chances are good that great horned owls are your neighbors. Though there is little you can do to attract great horned owls to your property, listen just after dusk and before dawn for their deep hoots, which carry for great distances. Watch for the great horned's silhouette at dusk along woodland edges, especially in treetops and on power poles.

Barred Owl

Strix varia

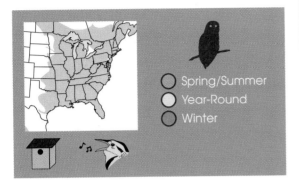

- ○ Spring/Summer
- ○ Year-Round
- ○ Winter

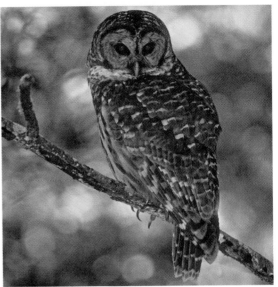

Who cooks for you? Who cooks for you all? *The wild hoots of the barred owl echo through swampy, deciduous woodlands throughout the eastern United States. Its dark, liquid eyes give it a deceptively gentle look, but this owl is a top-of-the-line predator, taking everything from fish to rabbits. Though it does some daylight hunting, most of the barred owl's foraging takes place at night.*

All About

A rounded, earless outline, smoky gray-brown plumage that is heavily mottled and barred with white, broad brown streaks on a white belly, and dark eyes distinguish the barred owl. Its bill and feet are yellow. Its familiar eight-hoot call gives way to raucous and sometimes frightening caterwauling in breeding season. This species is more apt to call in daylight than any other; it may call all day during overcast conditions.

Habitat & Range

Like its famous endangered cousin the spotted owl, the barred owl prefers old forest, probably in part because the large nesting cavities it requires occur in trees of ample girth. It is commonly associated with lowlands, but occupies upland sites as well. The barred owl does not migrate, but may wander in harsh winters.

Feeding

Anything it can kill is fair game for this medium-large owl. Small mammals, as small as mice and up to the size of rabbits, make up at least half the barred owl's diet. It makes acrobatic strikes after squirrels, sometimes turning completely over in flight. Birds, amphibians, reptiles, insects, and other invertebrates compose the rest of its diet.

Nesting

Most barred owls select large nest cavities, such as those formed when a large branch breaks off of a hollow tree. They will also use a hollow in a broken tree trunk, as well as the nests of other raptors or squirrels. Two to three eggs are incubated by the female alone. They hatch from 28 to 33 days later. The male feeds the family for the first two weeks of the chicks' life, after which the female leaves them and helps bring in food. Young owls, clothed in buff-colored down, begin venturing onto branches when they are around five weeks old, before they can fly. They give a hideous, rasping screech as a location call and may be found and observed discreetly from a safe distance. Fledglings are fed by their parents until early autumn, when they strike out to find new territory.

Backyard & Beyond

Surprisingly enough, the barred owl will accept nest boxes, because tree cavities large enough to contain them are hard to find. Plans for a wood duck nest box with a seven-inch entrance hole should accommodate them. This should be mounted as high as possible in a large tree.

Eastern Screech-Owl

Megascops asio

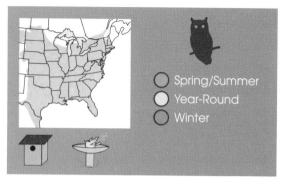

- Spring/Summer
- Year-Round
- Winter

Eastern screech-owls are very acclimated to humans, but their nocturnal habits and cryptic coloration keep us from seeing them regularly. Even when perched in full view in daylight, screech-owls have a remarkable ability to conceal themselves. Found commonly in cities and towns, the screech-owl's success may be due not only to its secretive nature, but also to its ability to take a wide variety of small prey.

All About

A small bird (8½ inches long), the eastern screech-owl occurs in two color variations: reddish and gray, with gray being more common. The screech-owl's plumage appears very bark-like. When a "screech" sits with its body elongated and ear tufts extended, it looks like a broken branch stub. This bird's name is misleading; a screech is rarely voiced. The call most bird watchers hear is a series of descending, whinnying whistles and tremolos on a single note.

Habitat & Range

A nonmigratory, resident bird throughout the eastern United States, the screech-owl is found wherever woodlands are mature enough to have cavities. Unlike many other owl species, the screech-owl is commonly found in urban parks and suburban backyards.

Feeding

Eastern screech-owls will eat almost anything— from mice and voles to moths, earthworms, crawfish, frogs, and fish. In spring and summer, they prey upon small and medium-sized songbirds, but during winter small mammals are more common prey. Screech-owls perch in a tree, waiting and watching for potential prey, most of which is captured with the owl's feet in flight or by pouncing on the ground.

Nesting

Screech-owls nest in natural cavities and will readily use nest boxes. They begin nesting early, from mid-December in the South to late March in the North. Two to six eggs are laid and a month-long incubation period ensues. The female incubates the eggs and broods the young owlets, while the male delivers all the food. Owlets remain in the nest for a month before venturing into nearby trees. They remain dependent on their parents for two months.

Backyard & Beyond

You may very well already have eastern screech-owls in or near your backyard. Spend some time outside at night—especially when the moon is full—listening for the screech-owl's wavering calls. Check natural tree cavities during the day for roosting or nesting owls—they may be peering out of the hole. You can attract screech-owls with an owl nest box. Boxes should be about 12 to 14 inches deep with an internal floor size of 7×7 inches and a 2³/4-inch diameter entry. Place the box above 10 feet high in a shady spot on a tree trunk wider than the box's width.

Whip-poor-will
Caprimulgus vociferus

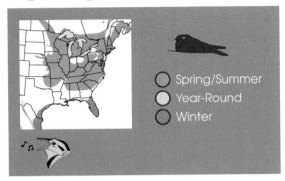

- Spring/Summer
- Year-Round
- Winter

Imagine sleeping all day and flying around the woods singing all night. That's the life of the whip-poor-will. Like its relatives the common nighthawk and chuck-will's widow, the "whip" is most active at night and is often heard calling out its name repeatedly—whip-poor-WILL! whip-poor-WILL! In fact, they have been known to give this call continuously, more than a thousand times in a row. Because of its nocturnal habits and coloration, many bird watchers never get a good look at a whip-poor-will.

All About
The whip-poor-will's body is just under 10 inches in length, and its wingspan is 19 inches—nearly 7 inches shorter than that of the chuck-will's-widow. The whip-poor-will's plumage is a subtle mix of charcoal gray, buff, black, and white. In flight, it shows prominent white corners on the tail. The large, dark eyes of the whip-poor-will are designed to function in the low-light conditions of dawn and dusk.

Habitat & Range
Whip-poor-wills prefer mixed woodlands with little underbrush, open farmlands, brushy fields, and rural roadways. These habitats all lend themselves to the pursuit of flying insects. Whips spend the winter in Florida, around the Gulf Coast, and into Mexico and Central America. They return each spring as early as March. In southern portions of the Midwest, the whip-poor-will is replaced by the closely related chuck-will's-widow.

Feeding
The whip-poor-will is an insect specialist, perching and watching for passing prey, which it pursues in silent flight. Stiff bristle feathers line its wide-opening bill and funnel flying insects into its mouth as it flies along. Primary food items include mosquitoes, moths, beetles, and grasshoppers. Most foraging is done in the half-light of dusk and dawn, and on brightly moonlit nights.

Nesting
A ground nester, the whip-poor-will builds no nest. As early as mid-April, two eggs are laid in a concealed spot on the ground and incubated by both sexes for about 20 days. After hatching, the young birds remain with the parents for two weeks, with both parents sharing the brooding. Young whips are able move around on the ground within a few days after hatching; they are able to fly at about 16 days old. This early mobility helps young whip-poor-wills avoid predators.

Backyard & Beyond
Whip-poor-wills are declining in some parts of their range due to the effects of pesticides and the loss of breeding habitats. If you are close to a calling whip-poor-will, listen for the *cluck* sound that it makes just prior to the *whip*. Perhaps the best way to see whip-poor-wills is to watch for them at dusk as they make their silent, batlike forays after insects along woodland edges and over meadows.

Common Nighthawk

Chordeiles minor

- ○ Spring/Summer
- ○ Year-Round
- ○ Winter

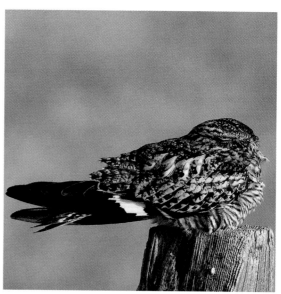

Peent! *is the nasal flight call of the common nighthawk, a familiar sound in cities and towns, though it is usually mistaken for an insect call. This call accompanies the batlike flight of the nighthawk as it courses through the sky, hawking insects. Despite its name, the nighthawk is not a hawk and is active both day and night.*

All About

The common nighthawk is a long-winged, dark bird with characteristic white wing slashes. Its distinctive bounding flight can be used to identify it from a distance as it forages over fields, towns, and woods. Nighthawks belong to the goatsucker family, a name based on the old myth that they drank milk from livestock at night.

Habitat & Range

A common breeding bird throughout North America, nighthawks can be seen in flight over almost any habitat. In cities and towns, nighthawks are attracted to the insects around streetlamps. Beginning in late July, nighthawks can be seen at dusk in large migratory flocks, sometimes numbering dozens of birds. Nighthawks winter in South America, returning to the southern United States by early April.

Feeding

A specialist in catching flying insects, the common nighthawk's mouth opens wide to capture its prey. The nighthawk sees its prey—most often flying ants, beetles, moths, and mayflies—and pursues and catches it. When a nighthawk needs water, it swoops low over a lake or river and skims a drink from the surface.

Nesting

Historically, nighthawk nests were found on the ground in grasslands and in open patches of soil, gravel, or sand. The nest is a shallow depression near a log or stone that helps to shade and conceal it. Now, nighthawk nests are more commonly found on gravel roads or on flat, gravel-covered rooftops in urban areas. The female selects the nest site, lays two eggs, and handles the 18-day incubation. Young nighthawks are brooded by the female for 15 days, protecting them from sun and weather. The male feeds both his mate and the young in the nest. After 20 days, the young birds are able to fly, and the male then takes over their care while the female starts a second nest.

Backyard & Beyond

Nighthawks have good success nesting on gravel roofs, but not so on roofs lined with rubber or foam, materials that pool water and retain heat. Watch and listen for nighthawks in the sky at dawn and dusk. You may hear their *peent!* before you see them. During courtship, male nighthawks perform a diving display near females, swooping swiftly toward the ground. As the male comes out of the dive, he flares his flight feathers, creating a booming sound much like a large truck shifting gears.

Chimney Swift

Chaetura pelagica

Spring/Summer
Year-Round
Winter

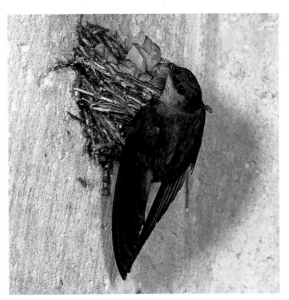

Known by bird watchers as "the flying cigar," the chimney swift is a familiar sight in the sky over cities and towns during the spring, summer, and fall. Its nickname aptly describes the swift's elongated flight silhouette. The twittering calls of chimney swifts are one of the most common bird sounds of summer. The chimney swift is named for its preferred nesting and roosting site—the inside of chimneys. This species spends much of its life on the wing, stopping only to sleep and nest.

All About

Chimney swifts are a dark charcoal-gray overall with a small black bill, eyes, and tiny feet. Indeed their feet are almost useless for walking, but are perfect for clinging to the inside of a chimney. The chimney swift is nearly all wing—with a 5-inch long body and a 14-inch wingspan. Four hundred years ago, all chimney swifts nested in hollow trees and caves, but the arrival of European settlers and their stone chimneys soon provided abundant nesting sites. Today most chimney swifts nest in chimneys and other human structures, such as unused smokestacks and abandoned buildings.

Habitat & Range

Widespread and common across the eastern half of the United States and southern Canada, the chimney swift is found wherever there are suitable nest sites. Fall migratory flocks of swifts are a magnificent spectacle as they form a swirling, chattering cloud descending to roost in a large chimney at dusk. In winter, this tiny bird migrates to South America, returning again in March to the southern United States.

Feeding

An all-insect diet is captured and consumed on the wing. Swifts often are seen flying high in the sky when foraging.

Nesting

A pair of swifts chooses a nest site—usually a chimney. The nest is a half-saucer shape made of sticks held together and made to adhere to the wall of cavity by the birds' saliva. Swifts break small twigs off trees, grabbing them with their feet as they fly past a tree. Two to five eggs are laid, and both parents share incubation (15 days) and brooding duties until the young swifts fledge at about 19 days after hatching.

Backyard & Beyond

Allowing chimney swifts to nest in your older, unused chimney is really easy—just let the swifts find it. They pose no danger and, if not for the sounds of hungry nestlings during a two-week period, you might not know they are there. If hosting swifts is not your cup of tea, check around your town or region for chimneys being used by swifts. Watch for them entering or leaving the large brick chimneys on schools and old factories. Modern chimneys with metal caps and flues are impossible for swifts to use.

Ruby-throated Hummingbird

Archilochus colubris

Spring/Summer
Year-Round
Winter

The only breeding hummingbird east of the Great Plains, the rubythroat enlivens many gardens and yards with its presence. Males are fiercely combative and will defend a single nectar source against all comers. Spectacular pendulum flights, constant chittering, the low hum of beating wings, and the occasional smack of tiny bodies colliding are familiar to anyone lucky enough to have rubythroats at their nectar feeders.

All About

Seen in direct sunlight, the male's ruby throat patch dazzles. Both male and female are iridescent green above. The female's underparts are white, and she sports white spots on her rounded tail. Males appear smaller and darker overall, with grayish-olive underparts and a slightly forked, all dark tail. A squeaky *chip* is uttered constantly while feeding. Males sing a seldom heard, monotonous song from exposed perches at daybreak.

Habitat & Range

Rubythroats prefer mixed deciduous woodlands with clearings, where wildflowers and abundant small insects can be found. They're fairly common in forested areas across the entire eastern United States, falling off abruptly at the Great Plains. Virtually all rubythroats leave for the winter, many making the arduous nonstop flight across the Gulf of Mexico on fat reserves alone. Rubythroats winter in Central America.

Feeding

Though they are usually regarded as wholly nectivorous, rubythroats take a great number of small insects, which they catch by gleaning or in aerial pursuit. They may even rob spider webs of their catch. They are strongly attracted to red or orange flowers, but rubythroats will take nectar from flowers of any color. They hover and probe rapidly, often perching to feed.

Nesting

Once a male rubythroat has mated, his investment in the offspring is over. The female constructs a walnut-sized, thick-walled cup of plant down and spider silk, bound tightly with elastic spider web and encrusted with lichens. This well-insulated nest protects the two lentil-sized eggs when she must leave to forage. The young hatch after about 13 days and remain in the nest for about 21 days. The female regurgitates small insects and nectar into their crops. They are fed for at least a week or longer after fledging.

Backyard & Beyond

Attract rubythroats with a 1:4 solution of white table sugar (sucrose) and water. Wash feeders with hot soapy water every few days and replace the solution. Boiling the solution briefly helps it keep longer. Artificial coloring in the solution is unnecessary (feeders have ample red parts). To thwart a bullying male, hang several feeders within a few feet of each other. He'll be unable to defend them all.

Belted Kingfisher

Ceryle alcyon

Spring/Summer
Year-Round
Winter

The belted kingfisher is a bird many recognize but few know well. Kingfishers take wariness to new extremes, uttering a loud rattle of alarm and swooping off at the slightest disturbance. The belted kingfisher's piercing rattle call, usually given as it takes flight, is more often heard than this wary bird is seen. They are a thrilling presence on streams, rivers, lakes, and marshes—wherever clear water and small fish abound.

All About

Almost comical in proportion, the belted kingfisher has an oversized crested head and a heavy spearlike bill, but diminutive feet. It cannot walk, but only shuffle, and it relies entirely on flight for most of its locomotion. Slate-blue upperparts, a stark-white collar and underparts, and a bluish breast band complete the ensemble. The female wears a "bra"—another rufous breast band below the blue one.

Habitat & Range

Because it is a sight hunter, the belted kingfisher seeks out clear water. Most often found along clear running streams, lakes, and ponds, it will also hunt drainage ditches and marshes. Nesting requires an exposed earthen bank. Kingfishers are migratory in northern latitudes. Though they can survive winter temperatures, they require open water year-round; thus, southern birds may migrate only as far as they must to find open water.

Feeding

Most of its hunting is done from a perch, but the belted kingfisher also hunts on the wing. Suspended in midair like an angel, it hovers, seemingly weightless, over a riffle. Spotting a minnow, it closes its wings and plunges bill-first into the water. It carries the fish in its bill to a sturdy perch (usually a dead snag or partially submerged branch), where it subdues its prey by whacking its head against the perch with sideways flips of its bill. The fish is then swallowed head first. Belted kingfishers also take crayfish and (to a much lesser extent) amphibians, reptiles, small mammals, and young birds.

Nesting

Kingfishers occasionally are forced to commute, if they are unable to find a dry earthen bank near their chosen feeding territory. They may use sand and gravel pits, landfills, or road cuts. This species excavates, digging rapidly with tiny feet straight into the bank, creating a round entrance hole and an upward-sloping tunnel that may extend as much as six feet into the bank. A chamber at the end holds five to eight eggs, which both male and female incubate for about 22 days. Young stay in the burrow for up to 29 days and are fed by their parents for three more weeks.

Backyard & Beyond

Any clear body of water, including backyard ponds with plump goldfish, can host a hunting kingfisher.

Red-headed Woodpecker

Melanerpes erythrocephalus

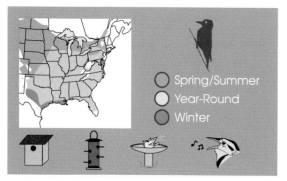

○ Spring/Summer
○ Year-Round
○ Winter

A striking combination of red, black, and white, the red-headed woodpecker is our most easily identifiable woodpecker and a favorite of many bird watchers. Though the species was first described in 1758, Native Americans had long used skins of the red-headed woodpecker as a battle ornament. Sadly, the red-headed has suffered population declines throughout its range, but it remains locally common in the proper habitat.

All About

The red-headed woodpecker could be called the red-*hooded* woodpecker because the red on adult birds forms a complete hood. Some mistakenly refer to the red-bellied woodpecker (which has a Mohawk stripe of red) as a red-headed woodpecker. The red-head's black back and tail are set off by a bright white breast and belly and an all-white patch of secondary (inner) wing feathers. The effect of these contrasting colors is stunning in flight. Red-heads give a variety of *churr-churr* calls as well as a loud, throaty *Queeah!*

Habitat & Range

Prior to the 1900s, red-headed woodpeckers were common in cities and towns. Today, red-heads are sparingly distributed across most of the eastern United States, usually in woods with mature oaks or beeches, in isolated woodlots along rivers, or in dead trees along flooded river bottoms and beaver ponds. Habitats affected by humans—strip mines, clear cuts, tree plantations, and farmlands—may attract red-headed woodpeckers as long as there are scattered, standing trees.

Feeding

Red-heads have the most varied diet of all woodpeckers, but they seem especially attached to acorns and beechnuts. They are excellent flycatchers and are known to eat grasshoppers, fruits, corn, eggs, mice, and even bird nestlings. When nuts and insects are plentiful, red-heads will cache them for later consumption, hiding food items in bark crevices and knotholes. At bird feeders, red-heads eat sunflower seeds, peanuts, and suet, but they are particularly attracted to cracked corn.

Nesting

Avid excavators of nesting and roosting holes, red-heads thus provide homes for many other cavity-nesting creatures. Nest holes are almost always in dead trees or dead portions of living trees, though wooden telephone poles are also used. Five eggs is the normal clutch, and both parents share in the two-week incubation duties. Young birds spend three weeks in the nest cavity before fledging, and they emerge with gray, not red, heads.

Backyard & Beyond

Red-headed woodpeckers are very aggressive and can out-compete European starlings for nest cavities. Look for red-heads in large stands of trees (especially oaks) with little vegetation below them, as in a park or golf course. Reliable locations for seeing red-headed woodpeckers are becoming noteworthy as the species declines.

Red-bellied Woodpecker

Melanerpes carolinus

Spring/Summer
Year-Round
Winter

The red-bellied woodpecker is so common, vocal, and eye-catching that it might be elected "most familiar woodpecker" in a vote of bird watchers in the eastern United States. Although occasionally misidentified as a red-headed woodpecker because of the male redbelly's bill-to-nape stripe of bright red, the red-bellied woodpecker actually is quite different in appearance—and much more common—than the real red-headed woodpecker, which sports an all-red head.

All About

A medium-sized (9¼ inches long) woodpecker with a stout, chisel-shaped bill and a zebra pattern of black-and-white horizontal strips on the back, the red-bellied woodpecker is named for a feature we rarely see—a light wash of pink or red on its belly. Hitching up tree trunks with the aid of its strong feet and stiff tail, the bird's red belly is almost always obscured. Adult males have a solid strip of red from the top of the bill and head and down the back of the neck (the nape). Females have a red nape, but are brownish on the top of the head. The redbelly's loud, rich call sounds like *qurrrr*, and its longer version is more rattling and harsher—*chrr, chrr, chrchrchrchr*.

Habitat & Range

A year-round resident across the eastern United States, the redbelly is an adaptable bird, found wherever there are mature trees. They do not migrate, though some northern birds may move southward in winter.

Feeding

The redbelly is an expert at excavating insects from trees using its bill as a chisel and its long, barbed tongue to extract food items. It will also eat berries, fruits, nuts, tree sap, salamanders, mice, and even small nestling birds. At bird-feeding stations, redbellies relish peanuts, suet, sunflower seeds, and cracked corn.

Nesting

The male redbelly begins courtship by drumming (a rapid pounding with the bill) on a tree trunk or branch to attract the female's attention. Both male and female excavate the nest cavity, which is usually located in a dead tree below an overhanging branch. The 8- to 12-inch deep cavity will accommodate four eggs. Incubation duties are shared and last about 12 days. Nestlings are fed in the nest cavity by both parents for almost a month before they fledge; afterward, they remain near the nest and are fed by the parents for several more weeks. Nest hole competition from European starlings can be fierce and usually results in the redbellies being evicted and forced to excavate a new nest elsewhere.

Backyard & Beyond

Peanuts and suet are the redbelly's favored foods, but you can also offer apple halves stuck on a tree stub, sunflower bits, and grape jelly (in a small dish). Listen for the redbelly's loud, ringing calls and watch for its swooping flight.

Downy Woodpecker

Picoides pubescens

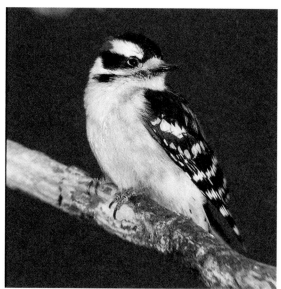

Downy woodpeckers are a favorite of backyard bird watchers because they are often the first woodpeckers to visit bird feeders. Common in any habitat with trees, downies are as equally at home in backyards as they are in remote woods. In all seasons, downy woodpeckers give a rattling whinny that descends in tone. They also utter a sharp pik! call regularly while foraging.

All About

The downy is the smallest ($6^3/4$ inches long), most common, and most widespread woodpecker. Its black-and-white plumage is similar to that of the larger ($9^1/4$ inches long) hairy woodpecker. In both species, the males have a red patch at the back of the head. Downy woodpeckers have an all-white breast and belly and a white stripe down the middle of the back. The wings and tail are black with spots of white.

Habitat & Range

A common resident of woodlands throughout North America, the downy is a habitat generalist—found anywhere there are trees or woody plants on which to find food. Though their population appears stable, downies suffer from nest site competition and from the removal of dead trees, which they need for nesting and feeding.

Feeding

Downy woodpeckers use their stiff tails and strong, clawed feet to propel themselves along tree branches or trunks. As they move along, downies probe and chisel at the tree's bark, searching for insects, insect eggs, ants, and spiders. They also eat fruits, such as sumac and poison ivy. At bird feeders, sunflower seeds and bits, suet, peanuts, and peanut butter are favorite foods.

Nesting

Like all woodpeckers, downies are cavity nesters. Each spring they excavate a new nest hole in the dead stub or trunk of a tree—usually one that is already rotting. The nest hole is placed underneath an overhanging branch higher than 12 feet above the ground. Excavation can take as long as two weeks—even with the male and female participating. Clutch size is usually four to five white eggs, with both sexes incubating. Hatching occurs at 12 days, and both parents feed the young for about three weeks until they fledge.

Backyard & Beyond

Telling the downy and hairy woodpecker apart can be difficult. A way to remember which is which is: *Downy is dinky; hairy is huge.* Downies have a small body, small head, and a small, thin bill. Hairies have a big body, a big head, and a large, chisellike bill. Though downies rarely nest in nest boxes, they readily use them for nighttime roosting, especially in harsh weather. Leave a dead tree or large dead branch on a tree in your yard (in a safe location), and you will be much more likely to attract woodpeckers.

Hairy Woodpecker

Picoides villosus

○ Spring/Summer
○ Year-Round
○ Winter

A familiar visitor to bird feeders, the hairy wood-pecker is named for the long, hairlike white feathers on its back. The hairy looks like a super-sized version of a downy woodpecker, but the best way to tell these two similar species apart is to compare the length of the bill to the length (front-to-back) of the head. The hairy's bill is always longer than the width of its head, and the downy's bill is always shorter than the length of its head. An easier way to remember is: Downy is dinky; hairy is huge.

All About

Hairy woodpeckers are medium-sized wood-peckers (9¼ inches long) with a long, sturdy, chisel-like bill that is used for finding food, for excavating nest holes, and for territorial drum-ming on hollow trees. Males and females look the same with white bellies, a white central back stripe, and distinctly patterned black and white on faces and wings. Adult males, however, have a red patch at the back of the head. Hairies utter a sharp *Peek!* call, as well as a loud ringing rattle on a single pitch.

Habitat & Range

Hairy woodpeckers are year-round residents across North America in mature forests and wherever there are large trees, including suburban backyards, urban parks, and isolated woodlots. They are one of our most widespread woodpeckers with a range extending into Central America.

Feeding

Using their bill, hairy woodpeckers can glean insects from tree bark or excavate them from beneath the bark's surface. Primary diet items include beetles, spiders, moth larvae, and ants, as well as fruits, seeds, and nuts. At bird feeders, hairies readily eat sunflower seeds, peanuts, suet, and cracked corn.

Nesting

It can take up to three weeks for a pair of hairy woodpeckers to excavate their nest cavity in the trunk or dead branch of a living tree. When completed, the nest cavity will have a 2-inch entry hole and will be 4 inches wide and as deep as 16 inches. Into this cozy space, four eggs are laid, and both parents share the roughly two-week incubation period. Less than a month after hatching, young hairies are ready to fledge from the nest, though the parents tend them for sev-eral more weeks. A new nest is excavated each spring, but old cavities are used for roosting at night and in winter.

Backyard & Beyond

If your neighborhood has large shade trees or mature woods, chances are good that you've got hairy woodpeckers nearby. Check large, dead snags and branches for woodpecker holes and listen for the birds' vocalizations and drumming in spring. Offer peanuts, sunflower seeds, or suet (in winter) in hanging feeders to attract hairy woodpeckers to your yard.

Yellow-bellied Sapsucker

Sphyrapicus varius

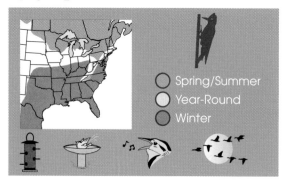

- ○ Spring/Summer
- ○ Year-Round
- ○ Winter

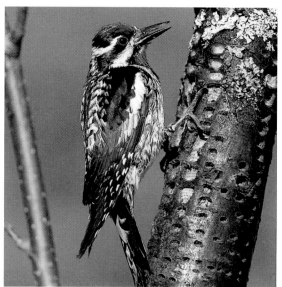

Even non-bird watchers know this bird's name, but *few have ever seen this quiet member of the woodpecker family. Named for its habit of drinking sap running from the holes it drills in trees, the yellow-bellied sapsucker inadvertently provides sap to a host of other creatures, including hummingbirds, warblers, butterflies and other insects, squirrels, and chipmunks.*

All About

The yellow-bellied sapsucker is a medium-sized woodpecker with extensive black-and-white barring over much of its back, wings, and tail. Adults have a brilliant red crown patch and adult males have a red throat patch outlined in black. Females have a white throat. The lemon-yellow belly can be difficult to see on perched birds. Juveniles are very dull-brown versions of the black-and-white adults. Winter and migrant sapsuckers are usually silent, but may give a cat-like, nasal *queeaah* call. In breeding season, sapsuckers are very noisy with lots of calling and staccato drumming.

Habitat & Range

Found in a variety of mixed-woodland habitats, but with a preference for aspen, maple, and fruit trees because of their sap production, the sapsucker will revisit and redrill sap holes from previous seasons and prior years. They breed across the entire breadth of Canada and across the northernmost tier of U.S. states from North Dakota to New England. They migrate to the southeastern quarter of the United States in winter, though some birds venture to Central America and to the Caribbean islands.

Feeding

Sapsuckers drill a line of small holes in the bark of a tree trunk, causing it to ooze sap, which the sapsucker returns to drink later. Insects from sap wells, gleaned from trees or captured in flight, are another important food source, as are fruits, berries, and tree buds. Ruby-throated hummingbirds visit sap wells to drink the sweet sap and eat the insects attracted to it. Suet, suet dough, peanut butter, and fruit are among the foods sapsuckers eat at feeders.

Nesting

Male sapsuckers excavate the nest cavity in a deciduous tree and the female lays up to six eggs on wood chips inside. Both parents share the two weeks of incubation as well as the month-long period of nestling care. After fledging, the adults teach the young for about ten days to forage and drill for sap on their own.

Backyard & Beyond

Because they are mostly silent in winter, you might miss a sapsucker as it sits quietly drilling small sap holes in your backyard. Inspect trees for evidence that a sapsucker has visited: a line of uniform, small holes drilled midway up a tree trunk. If a sapsucker has visited recently you'll see the liquid sap oozing from the holes.

Northern Flicker

Colaptes auratus

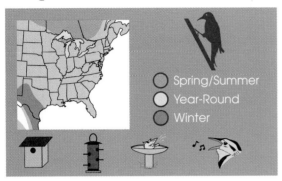

○ Spring/Summer
○ Year-Round
○ Winter

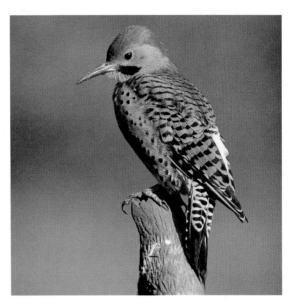

A familiar and fairly large (13 inches long) woodpecker, the northern flicker is a distinctively marked bird that—unlike other woodpeckers—is often seen foraging on the ground. The eastern form of the flicker is known as the yellow-shafted flicker for its bright lemon-yellow underwing and tail color. A red-shafted form of the northern flicker occurs in the West. There are more than 130 different names by which the flicker is known, including high-hole, yellowhammer, and yawkerbird.

All About

The northern flicker is all field marks with its bright yellow wing flashes, white rump, spotted breast, and barred back. It is not easily confused with any other bird. In the East, both sexes have a red crescent on the back of the head, but only males show a black "moustache" mark on the cheek. The flicker has several calls including a single note *kleer*, a short *wickawicka* series, and a monotonous *wickwickwickwick* song. It also communicates by drumming on the resonating surface of a tree, pole, or even metal downspouts and chimney flues.

Habitat & Range

Widespread across North America, the northern flicker is found almost everywhere wooded habitats exist, though open woods and woodland edges are preferred. Flickers in the northern portion of the range migrate southward in winter, while southern birds are nonmigratory.

Feeding

Flickers feed on the ground where they specialize in eating ants. A flicker pokes its long bill into an anthill and uses its long, sticky tongue to extract the ants. They also eat other insects, as well as fruits and seeds. At bird feeders, they will eat suet, peanuts, fruits, and sunflower bits.

Nesting

Excavating a new nest cavity almost every year, flickers perform a much-needed service for many other hole-nesting birds—from chickadees to ducks—that use old flicker nests. Both sexes excavate the nest cavity in a dead tree or branch. The female lays between 5 and 10 eggs; both sexes share the 11-day incubation period. Young flickers leave the nest after about 25 days. Flickers will use nest boxes with an interior floor of 7×7 inches, an interior height of 16 to 24 inches, and a 2$1/2$-inch entry hole. Because excavation is a vital part of courtship, boxes packed full of woodchips are more attractive. Competition for cavities from European starlings is fierce and may be causing a decline in flickers.

Backyard & Beyond

Offering suet, corn, or peanuts and nest boxes in your wooded backyard is one way to attract flickers. Equally important is the presence of ground-dwelling insects (leave those non-threatening anthills alone!) and dead trees or dead branches. A large, dead tree branch placed vertically in your yard may entice a flicker to stop.

Eastern Wood-Pewee

Contopus virens

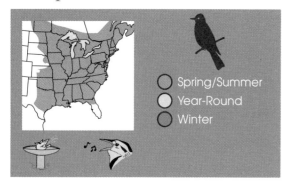

- Spring/Summer
- Year-Round
- Winter

PeeUWEEE? *and* PWEE-eehr *are plaintive sounds familiar to many forest hikers, bikers, and birders. Eastern wood-pewees call their name time after time, but it often takes a little effort to see them—unless you happen to be standing under a branch from which one flaps out, snaps up an insect, and then returns to the same spot.*

All About

Compared with smaller *Empidonax* flycatchers, the eastern wood-pewee is more sturdy, longer-tailed, and longer-winged. It is also generally grayer in appearance, with gray washed across its entire breast (the Acadian flycatcher is mostly whitish below). The wood-pewee lacks the prominent eye ring present in the Acadian and some other *Empidonax* species. Unlike the eastern phoebe, the eastern wood-pewee has two prominent wing bars and a two-toned black-and-orange (not all-black) bill, and it does not pump its tail. It usually feeds higher up than the phoebe, sallying forth from bare branches to grab its prey.

Habitat & Range

Common nesters across the forested eastern United States and southeastern Canada, eastern wood-pewees reach their southern breeding limits from northern Florida west to central Texas. They nest in deciduous forests and mixed deciduous and coniferous forests; they are often active at the forest edge and in clearings.

Feeding

Eastern wood-pewees pick their insect prey from leaves while hovering, but they are most noticeable when they sally forth from an exposed perch to capture flying insects (often the snap of bill meeting bug is audible). After the capture, they often return to the same perch to repeat the entire process—after ingesting their latest meal. They are most active and most vocal early and late in the day.

Nesting

Eastern wood-pewee nests are shallow cups made of weeds, grasses, bark, and other materials; they are placed on tree branches above or well above head level. On the outside, the nest is often festooned with lichens; inside, it is lined with such soft materials as plant fluff, hair, and fine grasses. There, the female usually lays three eggs. She incubates the eggs for just under two weeks. Both the male and the female feed the young, which leave the nest about two weeks after hatching.

Backyard & Beyond

In many areas, eastern wood-pewees are common migrants. It pays to learn this bird's field marks rather than just memorizing its song because wood-pewees don't usually sing while migrating to or from their South American wintering grounds. By "planting" snags—dead trees or large dead tree limbs—in your garden, you can provide hunting perches for migrating wood-pewees and other flycatchers.

Eastern Phoebe

Sayornis phoebe

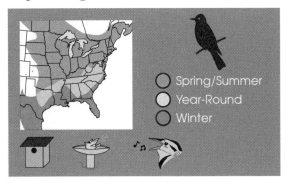

○ Spring/Summer
○ Year-Round
○ Winter

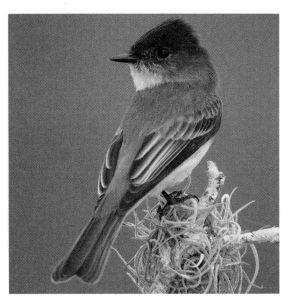

A very adaptable flycatcher, the eastern phoebe often nests on human structures, such as on building ledges, inside barns, under bridges, and in culverts. Nesting in such proximity to humans, phoebes are used to our activity and this apparent tameness allows us to think of them as "our phoebes." Many bird watchers consider the early spring return of the phoebe (and not the American robin) to be the most reliable sign of spring's arrival.

All About

The eastern phoebe, unlike most other flycatchers, is relatively easy to identify. A medium-sized bird that constantly wags its tail, the phoebe also gives a vocal clue to its identity by softly uttering its name—*fee-bee*. Phoebes are a dark, drab gray-brown on the back, with faint wing bars and a light breast and belly, often washed with yellow.

Habitat & Range

Wherever there is a suitable nesting ledge (with abundant flying insects nearby), phoebes may be found. Natural habitats include woodland edges and small streams. Common throughout most of eastern North America during the spring and summer (eastern phoebes breed far into northern Canada), in winter many phoebes migrate to the southern Atlantic Coast and along the Gulf Coast into Mexico.

Feeding

The eastern phoebe is a perch-and-wait hunter, watching for flying insects from an exposed perch and making short flying forays to nab its prey. Phoebes consume vast quantities of flying insects, but will also pluck food items from the ground or vegetation. Wasps, bees, flying ants, moths, and butterflies constitute much of their prey. In fall and winter, when insects are scarce, phoebes will eat small fruits and berries.

Nesting

Phoebes are early nesters throughout the breeding range, and nest building often begins almost immediately after a male attracts a mate to a likely site. Favored natural nest sites include rock ledges and caves, but they also nest in barns or outbuildings, and on handy ledges or sills on house porches. The female builds the cup-shaped nest out of mud, moss, and grass. Four to six eggs are laid and incubated by the female alone, for just over two weeks. Young phoebes, unless disturbed earlier, fledge after about 16 days.

Backyard & Beyond

Bird watchers love phoebes not only because they are common, but also because they are so full of energy and seem willing to make their nests in close proximity to humans. To attract phoebes to your property, place nesting shelves (about 6×8 inches in size) about a foot below the eaves of your house, garage, or outbuilding. Choose a site that is away from human activity and is as safe as possible from predators, such as snakes, raccoons, and cats.

Great Crested Flycatcher

Myiarchus crinitus

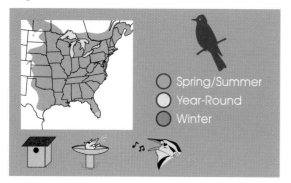

○ Spring/Summer
○ Year-Round
○ Winter

Although one of the largest and most common eastern flycatchers, the great crested is raucous enough that it is usually heard before it is seen. A loud, enthusiastic wheeep! or whit-whit-whit-whit call is most often heard in woodland clearings during the summer months. The great crested is unusual among eastern flycatchers in that it is a cavity nester, relying on old woodpecker holes, hollow trees, and even birdhouses for nest sites. Adding to this bird's preference for the unusual is its habit of using shed snakeskin in its nest construction.

All About

One of our larger flycatchers at 8^1/$_2$ inches tall, the great crested is a pleasing blend of colors with a lemon belly and underwings and a rufous tail, set off by a gray head and olive back. Males and females are alike in appearance, and both will aggressively defend their nesting territory against trespassing birds of almost any species.

Habitat & Range

Great crested flycatchers can be found in open woodlands, forest clearings, and even in wooded city parks throughout eastern North America during the summer months. Winter finds most of them in southern Mexico and southward to South America, though some spend the winter in south Florida. Fall migration starts in late August, with spring migrants returning to the United States as early as late March.

Feeding

Capturing flying insects is the great crested's main foraging mode, but it will also glean insects from vegetation and supplement its diet with small berries and fruits. Butterflies, moths, beetles, and grasshoppers are its most common foods. Great cresteds usually forage high in the treetops or from a high, exposed perch.

Nesting

A cavity nester that cannot excavate its own nest hole, it must rely on finding old woodpecker holes, naturally occurring hollows in trees, or human-supplied nest boxes. After inspecting possible nest sites with her mate, the female begins nest building using an incredible array of material, including animal hair, feathers, pine needles, string, cellophane, and shed snakeskin. Why great cresteds use such a variety of materials is a mystery. Five or more eggs are laid and incubated by the female for about two weeks. Two weeks after hatching, young flycatchers leave the nest.

Backyard & Beyond

Any backyard with large shade trees and adjacent woodland in the eastern United States has the potential to attract nesting great crested flycatchers. To encourage them, leave standing any dead or hollow trees, especially ones with knotholes or existing woodpecker holes. Nest box dimensions should be: interior floor of 6×6 inches, inside height of 12 inches, entry hole of 1^3/$_4$ to 2 inches. Mount at a height of 10 to 20 feet.

Eastern Kingbird

Tyrannus tyrannus

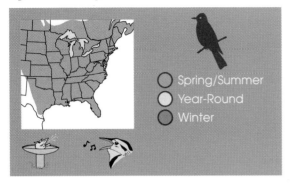

○ Spring/Summer
○ Year-Round
○ Winter

High in the treetops a medium-sized, black-and-white bird flutters out to catch flying insects and aggressively attacks other birds in flight, all the while emitting a sputtery series of sharp notes that sound like the zapping of an electric current. This is the eastern kingbird, whose Latin name translates into "tyrant of tyrants," the most common kingbird found in the East.

All About

The eastern kingbird is an excellent flier, able to catch flying insects and aggressively defend its breeding territory with its aerial mastery. Both sexes are blackish above and white below. The female's chest is grayish. Male kingbirds have a small, red-orange patch of feathers on the crown, though this is rarely seen. A thin, white band on the tail margin clinches the identification.

Habitat & Range

Spending the breeding season in open areas with scattered trees, eastern kingbirds prefer locations near water, probably for the bounty of insects. Fairly common in agricultural areas, pastures, city parks, and suburban neighborhoods with large trees and open understory during summer, most eastern kingbirds migrate to Central and South America in winter. In migration, the kingbird travels in loose flocks, and it is not uncommon to see a dozen or more birds in one tree in spring or fall.

Feeding

The eastern kingbird, or beebird, is an insect eater, specializing in bees, wasps, moths, butterflies, and other large, flying insects. Sit-and-watch hunters, kingbirds find an exposed perch and wait for something edible to fly past. They then sally forth and grab the prey in their bill, returning to the perch to stun and eat the insect. Kingbirds also eat fruits at all seasons, including mulberries, cherries, and elderberries. Fruits make up the bulk of their winter diet in the tropics.

Nesting

The kingbird's nest is placed high in a tree and is a large, loosely woven cup of bark, twigs, and weed stems. Females do all of the nest building and incubation. A typical clutch is two to five eggs with a 15-day incubation period. Hatchling kingbirds spend about 16 days in the nest before fledging, after which they are attended to by both parents for several more weeks.

Backyard & Beyond

Kingbirds can often be seen perching high in a tree or along fences or power lines, hunting for insects. They are very active in their territories in summer, so watch for their fluttery flycatching flights and listen for their loud zapping calls. The old myth that eastern kingbirds prey primarily on honeybees resulted in many of these birds being shot. Studies have now shown that kingbirds eat relatively few honeybees, mostly drones.

Red-eyed Vireo

Vireo olivaceus

Spring/Summer
Year-Round
Winter

Easy to hear and hard to see, the red-eyed vireo is one of the most numerous summer birds of the eastern American woodlands. It arrives in April or early May from its South American wintering grounds, and its song rings out from every wooded tract. Foraging high in the emerging leaves, the vireo sings almost endlessly—one patient listener counted 22,197 songs from the same bird in one summer day!

All About

The red-eyed vireo is about 6 inches long—an olive-backed, white-bellied bird with a gray cap and bold white stripe over its bright red eyes. Males and females are similar. They have sharp, slightly hooked bills designed to catch insect prey. Despite their small size, they are strong fliers; their twice-yearly migration carries them to the Amazon and back. Red-eyeds, like all vireos, are more deliberate in their movements than warblers.

Habitat & Range

Red-eyeds are usually found in open deciduous or mixed woodlands with a strong understory of sapling trees. They sometimes occur in large city parks, orchards, or even wooded suburban backyards.

Feeding

Like many small neotropical migrants, the red-eyed vireo feeds mostly on insects. It gleans its food from the upper branches of tall deciduous trees, singing as it moves slowly along the branches, peering under and around the leaves. Occasionally, it hovers to snatch a bug from an otherwise unreachable surface. In late summer, the red-eyed vireo will supplement its diet with berries of many kinds.

Nesting

The female selects a suitable site, usually 5 to 10 feet off the ground on a horizontal forked twig. She builds a tightly woven nest of fine grasses and strips of grapevine, suspending it below the fork and decorating it with bits of lichen on its outer surfaces. Here she incubates her four eggs for 11 to 14 days. Both parents feed the nestlings for 10 to 12 days until they are ready to fledge. Red-eyed vireos are frequent victims of nest parasitism by cowbirds and only rarely do they fight back by building a floor over the cowbird egg and laying another clutch. Most of the time they simply accept the cowbird chick, to the detriment of their own.

Backyard & Beyond

The best way to find a red-eyed vireo is to learn its song, then listen for it in the spring and summer woods. It is sometimes written as *Here I am, look at me, over here, here I am* sung over and over in a clear sweet voice, usually from high in a tree. Finding the singer will take some persistence and a good pair of binoculars. In fall, silent red-eyed vireos may be spotted in hedgerows and tangles, looking for berries.

Warbling Vireo

Vireo gilvus

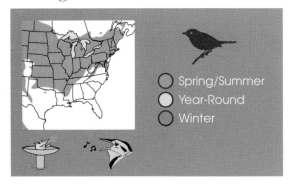

- ○ Spring/Summer
- ○ Year-Round
- ○ Winter

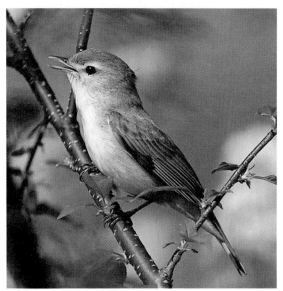

This persistent singer is much more impressive to the ear than to the eye. The warbling vireo is a dull greenish-gray overall, yet it has a vocal repertoire to match the most brilliant of warblers—it's as if the vireo wants to make up for its dull plumage by singing enthusiastically throughout spring and summer. This is one of the few vireos that has benefited from forest fragmentation, and it is far more common now than it was in Colonial times.

All About

A plain little bird, stockier and duller than the equally common red-eyed vireo, the warbling vireo has few obvious field marks. It has a gray-brown back and light belly, offset by yellowish sides, a dark crown, and a white eyebrow line. The warbling vireo's song is described as *If I sees you, I will seize you, and I will squeeze you 'til you squirt!* It is sung repeatedly in a hoarse warble.

Habitat & Range

The warbling vireo's breeding range covers much of the U.S. and western Canada, with the exception of the Southeast and arid regions in the Southwest. It occupies a variety of habitats from mature deciduous forests to urban parks and recovering clear-cuts. In the breeding season, the warbling vireo's habitats of choice are often associated with water; many bird watchers associate this bird's song with large shade trees along streams and rivers. Warbling vireos spend the winter along the western edge of Mexico and Central America.

Feeding

An insect-eating specialist, the warbling vireo gleans moths, caterpillars, beetles, and other insects from foliage as it works its way along the outer branches of a tree. It also captures flying insects during short aerial forays. Large prey items are subdued by whacking them against a tree branch before they are eaten. During fall migration and in winter, warbling vireos eat fruit.

Nesting

The female warbling vireo chooses a nest site, often high in a tall deciduous tree, such as a poplar, maple, or elm. A nest woven of grass, bark strips, and leaves is suspended from a forked branch. The female lays four eggs and both parents share the incubation duties, with the male often singing from the nest—an unusual behavior for a songbird. The young hatch within two weeks, are fed by both parents, and fledge about two weeks later.

Backyard & Beyond

Warbling vireos can be most easily located by listening for their song during spring and summer. Listen for them along wooded waterways, around lakes, and in other places where large shade trees and water are present. Scan the treetops for this plain little songster with the bright, warbling song.

Blue Jay
Cyanocitta cristata

Spring/Summer
Year-Round
Winter

Blue jays are smart, adaptable, and noisy birds. They will often mimic the call of a red-tailed or red-shouldered hawk as they approach a bird feeder, in an apparent attempt to scare other birds away from the food. Sometimes persecuted by humans as nest robbers or bullies at the feeding station, blue jays are one of our most ornate and lovely birds. Bird watchers visiting the United States from abroad are astounded that such a beautiful bird is common in our suburban backyards.

All About
No other eastern bird is blue and crested, making the blue jay almost unmistakable. Males and females are similar. Besides the standard *jay jay* or *jeer jeer* call often used as a scold, blue jays also emit a variety of squeaks, rattles, and croaks, in addition to mimicking other birds' calls. If you hear a sound in the woods that is loud and unmusical, chances are good that it's coming from a blue jay.

Habitat & Range
Blue jays are common in wooded habitats, especially those with oaks. Indeed the blue jay has a special relationship with oaks, burying as many as 5,000 acorns in fall caches for future consumption. Many of these acorns are never retrieved, so jays are credited with helping with forest generation. Resident throughout their range, blue jays in northern latitudes migrate southward in early fall, traveling by daylight in flocks of 10 or more birds, many carrying acorns in their bills.

Feeding
Blue jays will eat almost anything. Grasshoppers and other insects, and acorns and other nuts are their primary foods. Bird eggs or nestlings, mice, frogs, and a variety of human-supplied foods are also eaten. When storing acorns, blue jays will carry as many as five acorns in the throat and bill to the cache site, drop them in a pile, and bury them one at a time. They will return to recover only some of these acorns.

Nesting
Males help gather nesting materials, but females do most of the building in a tree. The twig nest is woven into a cup and lined with wet leaves and rootlets. Suburban blue jays often incorporate string, plastics, and paper (human trash) into nests. The female lays four to six eggs and incubates them for 18 days, followed by about 20 days of nestling care before the young jays fledge.

Backyard & Beyond
A common feeder visitor, blue jays are attracted to suet, peanuts, sunflower seeds, and even dog food. A source of water is highly attractive to blue jays, too. Look for blue jays along woodland edges and listen for their raucous cries, almost always the first clue to their presence.

American Crow

Corvus brachyrhynchos

Spring/Summer
Year-Round
Winter

Noisy, sly, opportunistic, and ubiquitous, the American crow lives among us; yet, comparatively little is known about it. Like other bold, brash corvids (the blue jay being a prime example), the crow is downright sneaky where its personal life is concerned. Few people know that crows may breed cooperatively in groups of up to a dozen birds, helping tend the dominant pair's nest.

All About

An unrelieved glossy black from bill to toenail, crows are armed with a stout, strong bill that acts as a chisel, axe, shovel, or forceps, among other uses. Its distinctive wingbeats appear to row the bird through the sky. Crows are well known for their raucous *caw*. Evidence suggests that crows have different "words" for different situations (assembly, dispersal, mobbing); their language is complex, as is their social behavior. Few people are privileged to hear the crow's song, given by both sexes, which is a long recitation of rattles, coos, growls, and imitations of sounds.

Habitat & Range

Though they are strongly associated with agricultural areas, crows find perfect conditions in cities and suburbs, where they raid pet dishes, bird feeders, and garbage cans. In the northern part of their range, crows are migratory, but all spend the winter within the continental United States. Throughout their range, crows use communal roosts when not breeding, and these can swell to massive proportions by late winter.

Feeding

There's almost nothing edible an American crow will not eat. At roadkills, landfills, and compost piles, crows will load their distensible throat with food and fly heavily off, often caching it under leaves or sod for later enjoyment. Crows forage by walking slowly on the ground—hunting invertebrates and vertebrates alike—and are constantly scanning roadsides and fields as they fly, descending to investigate anything that might be edible.

Nesting

Crows stay in family units composed of a pair and their young from the previous year. These yearlings may help build the nest, incubate, or feed the incubating female or her young. Four or five eggs are laid in the bulky twig nest, which is usually hidden high in a pine. The female incubates for around 17 days, and young fledge at around 36 days of age. Their strangled, nasal calls sometimes betray the nest location.

Backyard & Beyond

Crows are always up to something, and feeding them gives us an opportunity to observe their always-intriguing behavior. To find something a crow might like, open the refrigerator. Freezer-burned meat is a favorite. Cracked or whole corn is irresistible as well. Neighbors may wonder, but crows are well worth watching.

Horned Lark

Eremophila alpestris

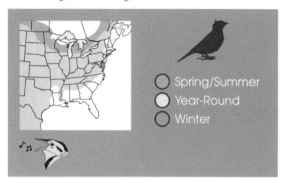

- Spring/Summer
- Year-Round
- Winter

The "horns" on the head of this small bird are not horns at all, but feather tufts that can be raised and lowered. In spite of this conspicuous field mark, horned larks can be surprisingly difficult to see when they are on the ground. Your first clue to their presence may be their high, tinkling call, or when a small flock is startled into flight.

All About

Horned larks are sleek-looking birds of open ground where they are often found in flocks. Males show a yellow face and throat, and a bold black mask or moustache and breast band. The back and wings are a blend of tan and rust. The female's plumage is a paler version of the male's. Their flight style is light and undulating, providing glimpses of the black tail panels, and often accompanied by twittering call notes.

Habitat & Range

Found in all types of wide-open, barren terrain from beaches and dunes to tundra, short-grass prairie, overgrazed fields, gravel roadways, recovering strip mines, and airport runways, the horned lark is widespread across North America. Its population and range have both expanded in the last half-century and the species is now found year-round in nearly every state. Breeding birds from the far North begin fall migration in September.

Feeding

In winter, when horned larks commonly mingle in large flocks with longspurs and snow buntings, seeds are the primary food. During the breeding season and migration, insects are added to the larks' menu. Horned larks forage by walking over the ground, looking for food items. This type of foraging is especially productive in fields where manure has been spread or where the soil has recently been tilled or grain recently harvested.

Nesting

Horned larks may nest very early in spring in the Midwest, but later in the far North. The female chooses the nest site on the ground and digs out a shallow scoop. Into this depression she weaves a nest from grass, rootlets, and other plant material. She lines it with soft materials such as fur or feathers and lays from two to five eggs into it. She alone incubates the eggs for 11 days. Young hatch with a warm down covering and stay in the nest until fledging about 10 days later

Backyard & Beyond

Winter flocks of horned larks can be easier to find than breeding birds. Check in and around agricultural feedlots, in muddy farm fields, active pastures, and anywhere waste grain or seed might be scattered. Scan the ground carefully for the larks' movement—one or more birds may catch your eye as they flutter across the open ground.

Purple Martin

Progne subis

Spring/Summer
Year-Round
Winter

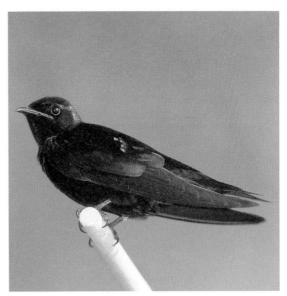

No other North American bird has a closer association with humans than the purple martin. For more than four hundred years, martins in eastern North America have nested in human-supplied housing, at first in hollow gourds offered by Native Americans and today in a variety of specialized housing. Generations of people and martins have grown up together. Even non-bird watchers can appreciate this friendly and familiar bird.

All About

Our largest swallow (at 8 inches), the purple martin is a graceful flyer with a bubbly, liquid song. The adult male has a deep blue body and black wings and tail. Females and youngsters are gray and black with some blue on the back. In flight, martins can be confused with European starlings, but martins have a notched tail and call out almost constantly.

Habitat & Range

Purple martins breed across eastern North America, except for the extreme north. They spend winters in South America but return to the southern United States in mid-January, their arrival eagerly anticipated by their human landlords. Because of their reliance on human-supplied housing, most martins are found around cities, towns, and settlements.

Feeding

Martins eat flying insects almost exclusively, but—contrary to popular opinion and market-ing hype—martins do not eat many mosquitoes. Instead, their diet includes larger flying insects, such as beetles, flies, dragonflies, wasps, butterflies, and moths. In cold, rainy weather, martin landlords often resort to feeding them mealworms and bits of scrambled egg in an effort to keep their beloved birds alive. Some landlords even shoot mealworms into the air with a slingshot just so the martins can catch their food.

Nesting

Martins are rather selective in choosing colony nest sites, but one thing is certain: They like to be with other martins. Research has revealed that they prefer white housing with a large (8×8×8-inch) interior and an 1½-inch entry hole. The housing should be mounted near a human dwelling in an open area. Martins build a loose cup nest inside the cavity out of pine needles and grass, lined with green leaves (which limit parasites). The female lays four to six eggs and does most of the incubation, lasting about 16 days. Both parents feed the nestlings for the month-long period before fledging.

Backyard & Beyond

The most successful martin landlords are those willing to put in the extra effort to care for their tenants with predator-proof housing, elimination of competing house sparrows and starlings, and regular monitoring. Your chances of attracting martins are greatly enhanced if there is an existing colony within a mile of you.

Tree Swallow

Tachycineta bicolor

Spring/Summer
Year-Round
Winter

The lovely tree swallow is making a breeding range expansion in many areas of the U.S. Once limited by the availability of the nesting cavities they require, tree swallows are benefiting greatly from artificial nest boxes erected to attract bluebirds. Their liquid twitters, sharp blue-and-white coloration, and trusting ways make tree swallows a welcome addition to our birdlife.

All About

Long triangular wings, snow-white underparts, and glossy teal-blue upperparts make the tree swallow a beautiful signal of spring. Soaring kitelike, then rising with rapid flaps, they course and dive over meadows and ponds in search of flying insects. Their jingling calls have been likened to the sound of someone shaking paperclips in a glass tumbler. Females are somewhat browner above and a duller blue than males.

Habitat & Range

Tree swallows prefer open fields, preferably near water, for nesting, though they will inhabit upland sites. Marshes also provide the flying insects they require. The tree swallow's breeding range extends across Canada and the northern tier of the U.S. and is expanding southward at a good clip. Tree swallows winter in coastal areas from South Carolina to Florida and along the Gulf Coast into Mexico and Central America. One of our heartiest swallows, the tree swallow often surprisingly shows up early in spring.

Feeding

Eighty percent of a tree swallow's diet is insects; fruits make up the other portion, mainly bayberries that sustain them in adverse winter weather. "Myrtle swallow" would be a more apt name for these birds, as myrtle is another name for bayberry. This ability to eat fruit helps tree swallows survive cold snaps as they make their way northward to breed. During breeding season, insects are caught on the wing in spectacular zigzag flights and are stored in the throat to be fed to nestlings.

Nesting

A foundation of coarse grass leaves and stems is lined with large body feathers, usually white. Tree swallows are mad for feathers in nesting season and can often be induced to take soft white feathers from the hand. The female incubates four to seven eggs for an average of 14 days. Young leave the nest 15 to 25 days later, flying strongly. Second broods are rare.

Backyard & Beyond

Before the advent of artificial nest boxes, tree swallows were limited to old woodpecker holes—a hotly contested resource. A nest box with a 1⁹/₁₆-inch hole, mounted on a predator-proof pole in an open meadow near water, is the best bet for attracting tree swallows. Look for tree swallows hawking insects over ponds, lakes, and rivers during the summer months.

Barn Swallow

Hirundo rustica

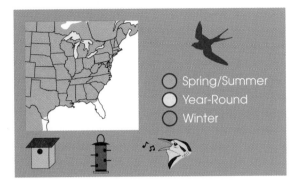

- ○ Spring/Summer
- ○ Year-Round
- ○ Winter

Ⓞne early naturalist estimated that a barn swallow that lived 10 years would fly more than two million miles, enough to travel 87 times around the Earth. This species seems to define what it means to be at home in the air, and it has been compared to an albatross in its ability to stay effortlessly aloft. One of the most familiar and beloved birds in rural America, the barn swallow is welcomed everywhere as a sign of spring.

All About

Glossy blue-black above and orange below, the barn swallow is the only American swallow that has a true "swallow tail," with an elongated outer pair of tail feathers. Males and females are similar, but females are not quite as glossy or highly colored, and the fork in their tails is not quite as pronounced. Like all swallows, they have short legs and rather weak feet used for perching, not walking.

Habitat & Range

A bird of rural areas and farmlands, the barn swallow may be found over any open area, such as pastures, fields, and golf courses, as well as lakes, ponds, and rivers. It has adapted well to humans and is not shy of people, nesting close to settled areas as long as it has open space for feeding. Barn swallows travel in great flocks during migrations, often in company with other swallow species. They arrive in most of their U.S. range in April and leave in early to midfall.

Feeding

Foraging almost entirely on the wing, the barn swallow takes a variety of insect prey, from flies and locusts to moths, grasshoppers, bees, and wasps. Occasionally small berries or seeds are added to the diet, but this is uncommon. Only in bad weather will barn swallows feed on the ground.

Nesting

Nothing says "country" more than a pair of barn swallows zipping in and out of the open doors of a working barn, darting after insects and chattering incessantly. Sometimes two or three pairs will share a favored site. The nest itself is a cup of mud and grass, lined with feathers and placed on a rafter or glued under an eave. Besides barns, barn swallows may use other open buildings, covered porches, or the undersides of bridges or docks. During second nestings, immatures from the first brood help feed and care for their younger siblings.

Backyard & Beyond

During breeding season, you may bring barn swallows into close range by throwing feathers into the air near a flock of soaring birds; the graceful fliers will swoop in to snatch them up for nest linings. Barn swallows also enjoy eating bits of baked eggshells (crumble them first) during breeding season.

Tufted Titmouse

Baeolophus bicolor

Spring/Summer
Year-Round
Winter

From deep mixed woods to old orchards, from city parks to leafy suburban backyards, this friendly and active little bird makes itself at home throughout the year. It is noisy and sociable, quite tame in human company, and fearless among other small birds with which it associates. Its cheerful calls of peter, peter, peter ring out even in midwinter, chasing away the January blahs.

All About

The tufted titmouse is 6^1/$_2$ inches long and dressed primly across its upperparts in gray, with a creamy breast and rusty flanks. A black-button eye stands out against its white cheek, and a crest adorns its head. Its small, sharp bill is black, as are its legs and feet. Titmice are very vocal and, besides their signature *peter* calls, they have a variety of whistled notes—similar to those of the cardinal and Carolina wren. Their harsh, raspy, scolding notes are similar to the chickadee's.

Habitat & Range

The tufted titmouse was originally considered a southern woodland bird, but for the past 50 years it has been expanding its range northward. The species' affinity for bird feeders and nesting boxes has played a part in this expansion. Titmice are nonmigratory and able to survive harsh weather if sufficient food is available.

Feeding

Tufted titmice eat mostly insects and seeds, depending on time of year. Caterpillars are a popular item in summer, but they also take wasps and bees, scale insects, beetles, the larvae of many species, and, in winter, insect eggs. Acorns are a mainstay in fall and winter. At feeders, titmice relish sunflower seeds, suet, suet dough, and peanuts.

Nesting

The natural nesting choice of the tufted titmouse is a tree cavity—an abandoned woodpecker hole, or crack caused by a lightning strike. Other sites include rotted fenceposts, drainage pipes, and nest boxes. The female builds the nest of grass, moss, bark, and leaves, filling up whatever size hole they have adopted. When the main structure is completed, the birds line it with hair—often plucked from a living animal—woodchuck, rabbit, dog, or even a handy human. Five or six eggs are laid, incubated by the female for 12 to 14 days. Both parents feed the young, which fledge at about 15 days. The family group stays together, sometimes into the next year, and year-old birds may help their parents care for the nestlings of the newest brood.

Backyard & Beyond

Tufted titmice sometimes breed in nest boxes, especially those with an entrance hole in the 1^1/$_2$-inch range. In winter they travel in mixed flocks with chickadees, sparrows, woodpeckers, and kinglets. Tufted titmice are easy to locate in woodlands by their noisy scolding calls.

Black-capped Chickadee

Poecile atricapillus

In the southern portions of Ohio, Indiana, Illinois, and Missouri, the resident chickadee is actually the Carolina chickadee (Poecile carolinensis), a slightly smaller but otherwise quite similar cousin of the black-capped chickadee of the northern half of the U.S. Chickadees travel in noisy little bands and draw attention to themselves with their frequent scolding chatter.

All About

Both chickadees have black caps and bibs as well as white cheek patches; gray backs, wings, and tails; and pale underparts with buff-colored flanks. The bill is tiny and dark, and the legs and feet are black. Males and females are alike, and there are no seasonal differences in plumage. In general, black-capped chickadees are larger ($5^{1}/4$ inches long), bigger-headed, with brighter white cheeks. Carolina chickadees are drabber gray overall, smaller ($4^{3}/4$ inches long), with less white in the wings. Vocal clues can be helpful. Black-cappeds sing *fee-bee* (two notes) while Carolinas sing *soo-fee, soo-fay* (four notes). The common *chick-a-dee-dee-dee* call is lower, hoarser, and slower from black-cappeds, and higher and more melodic from Carolinas.

Habitat & Range

The Carolina chickadee is resident (nonmigratory) and through most of its range it is the only chickadee present. It is generally replaced by the black-capped chickadee in the northern half of the Midwestern states. Black-cappeds will occasionally move south in winter. Where the two species overlap they may occasionally interbreed, so identifying individual birds under such circumstances is tricky.

Feeding

Both chickadees have a varied diet. Nearly half of the food taken in the wild consists of insects, such as aphids, ants, moths, and leafhoppers. They also eat spiders, weed seeds, and the seeds and small fruits of many trees and vines. At feeders they are partial to sunflower seeds, suet, and peanuts.

Nesting

Cavity nesters, Carolina and black-capped chickadees seek out natural holes in woodland trees, often adapting old woodpecker holes. They readily accept nesting boxes. The nest (made by the female) is a thick mass of mosses, bark, and grasses, enclosing a cup of soft hair. One side is built up higher than the other and can be pulled down like a flap to cover the young when both parents are away. As many as eight eggs are laid and incubated by the female for 11 to 13 days; both parents then share the feeding of the young until they fledge after two weeks.

Backyard & Beyond

To lure chickadees, offer black-oil sunflower seed in hanging tubes or hopper feeders, suet, or other fats such as "bird pudding." To induce a pair to stay and nest, install one or more nest boxes with entrance holes that are $1^{1}/4$ to $1^{1}/2$ inches in diameter.

White-breasted Nuthatch

Sitta carolinensis

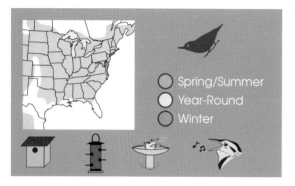

- ○ Spring/Summer
- ○ Year-Round
- ○ Winter

Nuthatches are universally referred to as "upside-down birds," because they forage by probing the bark of tree trunks with their heads downward. During their journeys down the trunk of a tree, they often pause, and then raise their head so that it is parallel to the ground—an absolutely unique posture among birds. The most well-known member of the family is the white-breasted nuthatch, a bird of deciduous woods and well-treed backyards.

All About

At nearly 6 inches in length, the white-breasted nuthatch is the largest of its tribe. Males have gray backs with black caps, white underparts, and a beady black eye on a white face. Females are similar but wear gray, not black, on their heads. White-breasteds are thick-necked and short-tailed, with a stocky appearance. White-breasted nuthatch calls—uttered frequently in all seasons—are a nasal and repetitive *ank-ank*.

Habitat & Range

White-breasted nuthatches prefer deciduous woods, but are also found in large parks and leafy backyards. In northern coniferous woods, and at high elevations along the Appalachian chain, they are replaced by the smaller red-breasted nuthatch, while the brown-headed nuthatch displaces them in the dry pine woods of the South.

Feeding

The white-breasted nuthatch eats both insects and seeds, varying its fare with the seasons. Insects make up nearly 100 percent of their summer diet, with seeds being added in fall and winter. Autumn's extra seeds and nuts are sometimes stashed—or "hatched away"—in tree bark crevices, to be retrieved later—a habit that has given these birds their name. White-breasted nuthatches will come to feeders for sunflower and other seeds, or suet, but they tend to abandon backyard feeders almost entirely in spring and summer when insect prey is plentiful.

Nesting

Nuthatches maintain their pair bond and territory all year long. The nest is placed in a natural cavity, old woodpecker hole, or more rarely a nest box. Built by the female, it is a cup of grasses, bark strips, and twigs and is lined with hair. When the nest is finished, the nuthatches "sweep" the entrance with their bills, rubbing a crushed insect against the wood—the chemicals released may aid in repelling predators. The female incubates a clutch of eight eggs for two weeks. Both parents feed the young for at least two weeks until fledging.

Backyard & Beyond

Nuthatches are irregular feeder visitors, but they like black oil sunflower seeds and suet, peanuts, or peanut butter mix. In woodlands, listen for the nuthatch's nasal calls anytime. Male and female always forage near each other and, in winter, with other species in a mixed flock.

House Wren

Troglodytes aedon

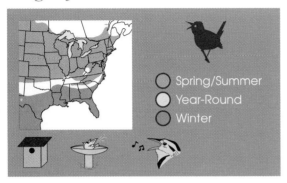

- ○ Spring/Summer
- ○ Year-Round
- ○ Winter

The rich and burbling song of the house wren is surprisingly loud for such a tiny (4 3/4 inches long) bird. House wrens are named for their preference for living in close proximity to humans, often in tiny houses we provide for them. This mostly plain brown bird makes up for its small size and drab coloration by being a fierce competitor for nesting sites.

All About

House wrens are notable for their lack of field marks—the warm-brown upperparts and tail are matched by a grayish breast. Look closely at the house wren, and you'll see a variety of small white and black spots, the only variation in the bird's plumage. Males and females look alike and both have the wrenlike habit of cocking their tails up when perched. The thin, slightly curved bill is ideal for capturing and eating the house wren's insect prey.

Habitat & Range

Spending the summers in thickets and brushy edge habitat adjacent to woodlands, the house wren is a familiar bird in parks, backyards, and gardens, often—but not always—near human settlements. Some house wrens winter in the southernmost states in the United States, but many travel beyond our borders farther south.

Feeding

Insects make up the house wren's diet (grasshoppers, crickets, spiders, and moths are on the menu), but they will also eat snails and caterpillars. Most of their foraging is done in thick vegetation on or near the ground.

Nesting

House wrens nest in a variety of cavities from woodpecker holes to natural cavities and nest boxes. Like Carolina wrens, house wrens will also nest in flowerpots, drainpipes, and other such sites. They are very competitive about nesting sites, often filling all or most available cavities with sticks. The male builds these "dummy" nests, and the female selects one in which to nest. The twig structures are lined with soft materials, such as grass or hair, and the female lays six to eight eggs. She performs the incubation duties, which last from 12 to 14 days. Fledglings leave the nest two or more weeks after hatching. House wrens are known to pierce the eggs of other cavity nesting birds in their territories.

Backyard & Beyond

House wrens will readily accept nest boxes with interior dimensions of 4x4 inches and entry holes of 1 1/4 inches in diameter. Nest boxes placed adjacent to brushy habitat or a wood's edge seem to be most attractive. The house wren's song and scolding calls are heard often wherever they are present. Nest boxes for bluebirds and tree swallows should be placed far from edge habitat, in the open, to avoid conflict and competition from territorial house wrens.

Ruby-crowned Kinglet

Regulus calendula

Spring/Summer
Year-Round
Winter

The appearance of this perky little bird within mixed songbird flocks is a sure sign that fall is on the way. Ruby-crowned kinglets nest in the north and northwest of the continent in mixed coniferous forests. They winter in abundance from the South into Mexico.

All About

After hummingbirds, ruby-crowned and closely related golden-crowned kinglets rate as North America's smallest birds. Like the golden-crowned, the ruby-crowned kinglet is restless, briefly hovering by the tips of branches and constantly flicking its wings—a behavior that sets them apart from larger, longer-tailed warblers. Two other field marks are the bird's wide white eye ring and single, wide wing bar. Otherwise, the ruby-crowned kinglet is a study in olive-drab. Its namesake red crown patch is usually concealed.

Habitat & Range

This bird abounds from northern Maine, New Hampshire, and Vermont west across the upper reaches of the Great Lakes, through central Canada, then south through the western mountain states. Some even nest in a few spots in Arizona and New Mexico. As cold months approach, ruby-crowned kinglets migrate south, spending the winter from southern New England south through the Southeast. In the West, the wintering range extends from the Pacific Northwest south and east across Oklahoma and Texas. Many ruby-crowned kinglets winter in Mexico, but rarely as far south as Guatemala.

During migration and in winter, kinglets are found in a wide variety of habitats, feeding in trees from pines to oaks and in tall shrubs.

Feeding

Much of a ruby-crowned kinglet's life is spent in the relentless pursuit of invertebrates, punctuated here and there in winter by the procurement of a seed or berry. In winter, these birds pick among branches and crags to find dormant spiders and insects and their eggs. In warm months, they feed exclusively on small invertebrates.

Nesting

Surprisingly for such a small bird, the ruby-crowned kinglet may lay up to a dozen small white, brown-speckled eggs—the largest clutch of a North American bird its size. Seven to eight eggs is a more typical clutch, which a female lays and incubates for about two weeks in a tightly bound nest of lichen, moss, spider web, hair, and various plant materials. The nest is usually suspended from a branch close to the trunk and protected from above by overhanging branches. Both parents feed their young, which leave about 16 days after hatching.

Backyard & Beyond

In many parts of the country, October and April are peak months for spotting migrating ruby-crowned kinglets. They may accompany chickadees and titmice that come to your feeders, or be seen with migrating warblers.

Blue-gray Gnatcatcher

Polioptila caerulea

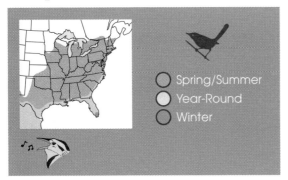

- Spring/Summer
- Year-Round
- Winter

The blue-gray gnatcatcher is the birder's "mini-mockingbird," always in motion and usually talking about it. This graceful, delicate, miniscule bird seems to arrive too early in spring, sallying into swarms of midges from still-budding branches. Its slender, elongated form and flashy black-and-white paneled tail are hard to mistake, though the gnatcatcher often goes unnoticed. It's most likely to be spotted on its early spring migration, for it is a woodland denizen, often hidden by foliage after the trees leaf out.

All About

It's often the gnatcatcher's twangy, whining call—like a miniature banjo being tuned—that alerts us to its presence. Its song is a sputtering, wheezy, petulant-sounding jumble, punctuated by *mews*. The blue-gray gnatcatcher has been recorded mimicking other species, a talent not widely appreciated, perhaps because its high, whispery voice is beyond the hearing register of many bird watchers. A white eye ring and neat black eyeline, blue-gray upperparts, and a long, slender tail edged in white distinguish this elegant bird. Females are similar, but lack the black eyeline.

Habitat & Range

Blue-gray gnatcatchers are strongly associated with oaks in a wide range of habitats, sticking to woodlands dominated by broad-leaved species. They are more often seen along woodland edges than in yards and gardens, except during migration. Gnatcatchers winter in the western coastal scrub of Mexico and Central America.

Feeding

Perching on the outer twigs in the mid- to high canopy, gnatcatchers go out after flying insects or glean the outer foliage for insects and spiders. As they forage, they flick their white outer tail feathers, which is thought to create bursts of light that startles UV-sensitive insects into flight. The bill is a fine black forcep, good for grasping tiny prey.

Nesting

Gnatcatcher nests are often mistaken for those of hummingbirds, being neat, compact cups of silk (often gathered from tent caterpillar nests), plastered with lichens. They are usually saddled on a horizontal limb. It is often possible to witness construction because the male gnatcatcher escorts the nest-building female with much fanfare and conversation. Both male and female incubate four eggs for 13 days, and young birds leave the nest 13 days after hatching. They are still being fed by their parents three weeks after departing the nest but gain independence soon thereafter.

Backyard & Beyond

This species has expanded its range explosively over the past three decades, pioneering into the Northeast and southeastern Canada. However, its range expansion cannot be attributed to feeding stations, as has been postulated for the northward movement of tufted titmice, northern cardinals, and red-bellied woodpeckers. The gnatcatcher relies solely on insects for sustenance.

Eastern Bluebird

Sialia sialis

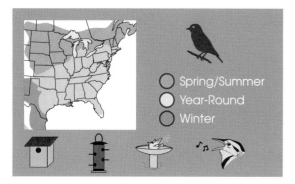

○ Spring/Summer
○ Year-Round
○ Winter

The eastern bluebird is our most famous thrush, even more popular than its cousin, the American robin. Its beauty, its song, and its willingness to live close to us has inspired many poets, songwriters, artists, and bird watchers. You can attract bluebirds to your property if you have a large open lawn, especially if you provide housing. Thanks to a concerted effort by bluebird lovers to provide nest boxes, the eastern bluebird has rebounded from its low population in the 1960s.

All About

The sky-blue back and rusty breast of the male bluebird are echoed in the female's more muted tones. There are three bluebird species in North America, but only the eastern is commonly found in the eastern United States. Bluebirds are often seen perched along fence lines, on wires, or high in trees. They may appear all dark in bright sunlight, so many observers miss seeing them. During spring courtship, paired bluebirds can be seen fluttering their wings near a prospective nesting site, uttering their rich *turalee turalay* song.

Habitat & Range

Bluebirds are resident (nonmigratory) throughout the eastern United States in open habitats, such as pastures, grasslands, parks, and large suburban lawns (especially where bluebird nest boxes are available). The two habitat requirements of bluebirds are large, open, grassy areas for foraging and cavities for roosting and nesting. In harsh winter weather, bluebirds may migrate short distances to find food or shelter.

Feeding

From an elevated perch, bluebirds watch for moving insects and then drop to the ground to pounce on them or to capture flying insects in midair. They eat insects year-round and will shift to fruits and berries when insects are scarce. Bluebirds visit feeders for mealworms, berries, and suet or suet dough.

Nesting

Bluebirds are cavity nesters and will use old woodpecker holes or natural cavities in trees where available. Human-supplied nest boxes are an important resource for the eastern bluebird. The female bluebird builds the nest inside the cavity using bark strips, grass, and hair. She lays four to six eggs and incubates them for 12 to 16 days. Both parents care for the nestlings until fledging occurs after 14 to 18 days.

Backyard & Beyond

If you offer housing, it's important to monitor and manage it to keep non-native house sparrows and starlings from usurping it and to keep predators from accessing the eggs or young. Place the houses (with $1^1/_2$-inch entrance holes) on metal poles with a pole-mounted baffle beneath the house. House location should be in the middle of a large, open, grassy lawn or field. Bluebirds catch insects on the ground in grassy areas, so they are particularly vulnerable to lawn chemicals.

American Robin

Turdus migratorius

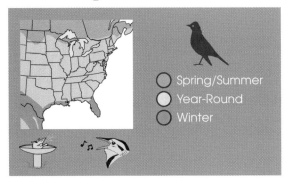

○ Spring/Summer
○ Year-Round
○ Winter

Almost all North Americans have grown up having a fairly intimate acquaintance with a thrush. The American robin, the largest, most widespread, and most abundant North American thrush, has followed the watered lawn—with its plentiful earthworm prey base—westward across the continent. Only parts of Florida, Texas, and the Southwest, where the soil is too sandy to support the introduced common earthworm, lack robins.

All About

The robin's simple yet evocative *cheerily-cheerio* song meshes well with the thunk of basketballs and the drone of lawnmowers in suburban neighborhoods all across North America; yet, they also hide their nests in mountaintop spruce and fir forests, where they are as wary as any hermit thrush. Males sport brick-red breasts and black heads with broken white spectacles and a streaked white throat and lower belly. Females are paler.

Habitat & Range

The robin is primarily a bird of lawns with trees and shrubs, though it also breeds in high mountain forests near clear-cuts or openings. Few other species show its adaptability to diverse habitats, from landscaped parking lot islets to dense, secluded forests. Migration is marked in northern climes, but is less so in southern ones.

Feeding

Running, then standing erect and motionless on a lawn, the robin watches and listens for earthworms and other invertebrates crawling in the grass. A quick stab captures them, sometimes resulting in a tug-of-war with a recalcitrant night crawler. Robins flock in fall to exploit fruiting trees and shrubs, fluttering and giggling as they reach for food.

Nesting

Most bird watchers are familiar with the robin's sturdy mud-and-grass cup, often nestled in an evergreen, a climbing vine, on a horizontal branch, or even on a windowsill. The female incubates three to four eggs for 12 to 14 days. Adults can be seen foraging with bills full of earthworms as soon as the young hatch. Young leave the nest, barely able to flutter, on about the thirteenth day. They are distinguished by their spotted, whitish breasts and reedy, begging calls. The male feeds them for another three weeks, while the female usually starts a second brood.

Backyard & Beyond

By mowing the lawn regularly and planting dense evergreens and fruit-bearing shrubs and trees, we unwittingly provide perfect conditions for robins. Robins seldom visit feeders, but will take bread, chopped raisins, and crumbled moistened dog chow in severe winter weather. Oddly enough, the American robin is the only member of its genus, *Turdus*, that breeds in any numbers in North America. The closely related clay-colored robin, which looks like a washed-out, American robin, breeds sparingly in south Texas.

Wood Thrush

Hylocichla mustelina

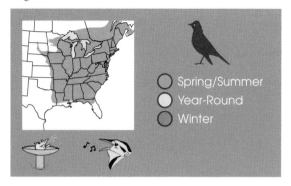

- ○ Spring/Summer
- ○ Year-Round
- ○ Winter

The lilting flutelike song of the wood thrush inspires bird watchers, naturalists, poets, musicians, and humankind in general. Few things are more beautiful than the evening song of the wood thrush as it echoes from deep within the forest. However, this species has suffered severe declines in population during the past thirty years due to loss of habitat, forest fragmentation, and nest parasitism from the brown-headed cowbird.*

All About

This medium-sized (7³/4 inches in length) brown thrush has a bright rufous head and neck, olive-brown back and tail, and a white breast with large dark spots. Erect and robinlike in its posture, the wood thrush sings a multi-pitched and highly variable *eeeolay* song and utters a *whit-whit-whit* call when agitated. Wood thrush males do most of their singing at dawn and dusk, and usually from a midlevel perch in the forest.

Habitat & Range

Wood thrushes only spend their summers with us in eastern North America, arriving as early as April, but departing for the tropics by mid-August or later. Many make the flight across the Gulf of Mexico in both spring and fall. During the breeding season, they can be found in mixed deciduous forests with tall trees and a thick understory. Fragmented forest plots or those with cleared understory (due to deer browsing or human landscaping) are far less attractive to wood thrushes.

Feeding

Feeding much like a robin on the forest floor, the wood thrush sweeps aside leaf litter with its bill to uncover insects, larvae, millipedes, moths, ants, and even salamanders and snails. In fall, wood thrushes will feed in forest edge habitats to take advantage of fruits and berries.

Nesting

The female wood thrush builds a cup-shaped nest out of grasses, leaves, and rootlets, usually held together with mud, in the fork of a tree branch within 20 feet of the ground. She lays three to four eggs and incubates them for about 12 days before they hatch. Young wood thrushes are ready to fledge two weeks later. Wood thrush nests in fragmented forest habitats are more likely to be parasitized by the brown-headed cowbird, which does not build its own nest, but rather lays its eggs in the nests of other songbirds—often at the expense of the host species.

Backyard & Beyond

From spring through fall your best chance of locating a wood thrush is to listen for a male singing from patches of dense forest. Once you hear the song, patiently scan the upper, inner branches of the forest for this rusty-brown master singer. If you live in wooded habitat that is home to wood thrushes, be a good neighbor and keep pets restrained during breeding season.

Veery

Catharus fuscescens

Spring/Summer
Year-Round
Winter

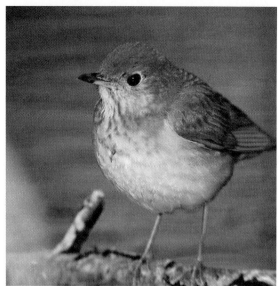

The spiraling, almost unearthly song of the veery captivates most people who hear it. Actually seeing this shade-loving songbird is far more challenging. Although still a common nester in many areas, the veery has declined in many parts of its range, perhaps due to destruction of its winter habitat and, on its nesting grounds, from nest parasitism by cowbirds combined with the paring down of underbrush by surging deer populations.

All About

Of all North American thrushes, the veery shows the greatest contrast between rich rustiness above and plainness below. A "typical" veery has a rusty wash on its breast and cheeks and a head lacking strong markings. Diffuse spotting punctuates the breast's rusty wash, but the remaining underparts are white. Western and Newfoundland birds are darker and more heavily spotted below, but the face is still plain, lacking the distinctive eye rings found on similar Swainson's and hermit thrushes.

Habitat & Range

The veery nests across much of southern Canada, in the western mountains down to Colorado, across the Great Lakes states and throughout the Northeast, as well as in the Appalachians. Favored nesting habitat is moist deciduous forests with plenty of bushy undergrowth. In fall, most veeries migrate across the Gulf of Mexico and western birds apparently migrate through the East before taking this southbound flight. Veeries winter in tropical forests from Colombia to Brazil. Studies indicate that older second-growth forests are far more attractive to nesting veeries than those cut in the last decade or two.

Feeding

The veery spends most of its time on or near the ground, feeding on a mix of berries and insects that it finds by hopping, flycatching, or flipping over dead leaves. Prey includes beetles, snails, ants, wasps, caterpillars, and spiders. Berries and other small fruits are particularly important in late summer and fall. The veery spends more than half the year outside the U.S. and Canada. Its diet during this time is not well documented.

Nesting

A female veery builds a nest on or near the ground. Using dead leaves as a base, she later constructs a cup of small bark bits, weeds, and leaf mold. The female incubates her clutch of four, sometimes three or five, blue-green eggs, which hatch after 12 days. Young leave the nest about 12 days after hatching, and are fed by both parents.

Backyard & Beyond

Migrating veeries put in appearances in backyards, not at feeders but often in berry-bearing shrubs and trees including spicebush, elderberry, dogwood, and blackberry. These birds migrate primarily at night and many die after colliding with tall buildings and communications towers.

Gray Catbird

Dumetella carolinensis

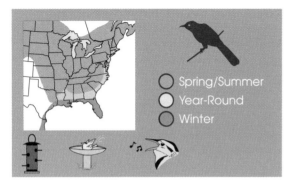

○ Spring/Summer
○ Year-Round
○ Winter

Named for its mewing catlike call, the catbird is actually a multitalented singer that is almost comparable to the mockingbird in its vocal versatility. Able to operate both sides of its syrinx, or vocal organ, independently, it can actually sing two different songs at once, and it's a mimic, too—not a bad resume for an otherwise plain gray bird.

All About

A slim, slate-gray bird about 9 inches long, the catbird is distinguished by a solid black cap and a bright chestnut patch under its tail. Because of its habit of cocking its tail, this patch is often visible. Catbirds are easy to recognize because—no matter what age, sex, or season—they all look the same. Very vocal, the male catbird makes an almost endless array of sounds, one after the other; some are his own and others are "stolen" from other birds or even from frogs, domestic animals, or mechanical devices heard in his travels. You can usually tell a catbird's song from that of other mimics, though, because each phrase is repeated only once, and the telltale *meouw* is thrown in from time to time.

Habitat & Range

In most of its U.S. range, the catbird is migratory, moving southward in winter, away from the coldest weather. Flying at night, migrant catbirds are often victims of collision, striking tall buildings or communication towers with distressing frequency. A few avoid the dangers of migration by remaining in their northern territories, a tactic that works if they are well fed and the season is not overly harsh.

Feeding

Foraging in thickets and brambles, the gray catbird eats mostly insects in spring and summer, adding small fruits as fall approaches. Favored insects include caterpillars, ants, aphids, termites, cicadas, and dragonflies. Among fruits it chooses grapes, cherries, and berries, followed by such late-lingering items as multiflora rosehips, catbrier, privet berries, bittersweet, and mountain ash.

Nesting

Singing from deep within a thicket, the male catbird courts his female in spring. After mating, she builds a bulky cup of twigs, weeds, and leaves, sometimes adding bits of paper or string and then lining it with fine grasses or hair. She incubates her three or four eggs for about two weeks; both parents then feed the nestlings for 10 to 12 days until they fledge. Two broods are common.

Backyard & Beyond

If a catbird remains in your neighborhood during winter it may be attracted by offerings of dried or fresh fruit, suet, doughnuts, peanut hearts, or table scraps. These birds are easily intimidated by other species, so they are more likely to respond to food scattered on the ground than concentrated in a small feeding dish.

Brown Thrasher

Toxostoma rufum

Spring/Summer
Year-Round
Winter

The brown thrasher has a lush resounding voice, and sings a seemingly endless train of melodies—its own and others'—from one end of a spring day to the other, and it may stay hidden in a deep shrub all the while. The brown thrasher is common throughout its range, but not as well known as it ought to be. This mimic is a cheerful and friendly addition to any backyard.

All About

Nearly a foot long, the brown thrasher is a strong and handsome bird, equally at home in woodland edges or shrubby backyards. Its upperparts are bright cinnamon, broken only by two, thin, white wing bars; its white breast is heavily streaked in brown. It has a long tail, a long slightly curved bill, and strong sturdy legs well suited to "thrashing" about on the ground. Beginning birders may confuse a thrasher with one of the thrushes, or perhaps a fox sparrow, but the thrasher is much larger, with a longer bill and tail. The thrasher's song is almost as rich and varied as a mockingbird's, and it is very similar in quality, but where the mocker usually sings its phrases three times each, the thrasher utters his only twice.

Habitat & Range

Often seen on the ground, the brown thrasher is a bird of woodland edges, thickets, hedgerows, brushy riversides and parks, and shrubby backyards. It retreats from the northern reaches of its breeding range to spend the winter in less frigid areas, usually returning sometime in April. In most of the South, it is a year-round bird.

Feeding

More than half the brown thrasher's diet consists of insects—beetles, grasshoppers, cicadas, and caterpillars—most of which it finds on the ground as it rummages with feet and bill among the leaf litter. Brown thrashers also eat fruits, nuts, seeds, and acorns.

Nesting

The male brown thrasher sings vigorously upon first arriving at its breeding grounds, both to establish territory and to attract a mate. The mated pair builds a large, twiggy nest in deep cover, usually quite close to the ground. Both parents incubate four eggs for nearly two weeks. Chicks are fully feathered and ready to fly in just nine days, an adaptation to avoid predators, which are especially dangerous to low-nesting birds. Two and sometimes three broods are raised each year.

Backyard & Beyond

Brown thrashers will visit feeding stations for seeds and grains that are scattered on the ground. Nuts are popular, as are suet mixtures, cornbread, doughnuts, and raisins. Thrashers are not particularly shy of humans, but do require some shrubs or hedges nearby where they can retreat if they feel threatened.

European Starling

Sturnus vulgaris

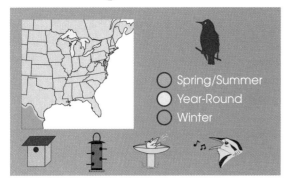

○ Spring/Summer
○ Year-Round
○ Winter

In 1889, there were no European starlings in North America, yet today—just over a century later—we have more than 200 million. Blame a fan of William Shakespeare. In 1890, a flock of a hundred starlings was released in New York's Central Park in an attempt to bring to America all the bird species mentioned in Shakespeare's plays. The adaptable starling soon spread westward in history's greatest avian population explosion.

All About

Glossy black overall, with a yellow bill during breeding season, the starling is one of the most familiar birds—not only because it is so common, but because it almost always lives close to human settlements. In winter, starlings are duller overall, covered with white spots (little stars, or "starlings") and with a blackish bill. In all seasons, starlings are very vocal, displaying an astonishing ability to mimic other bird songs, sirens, voices, barks, or mechanical sounds. In flight, starlings flap their triangular-shaped wings rapidly.

Habitat & Range

Starlings cover the entire North American continent year-round, except for the far North in winter. In fall they form gigantic, noisy flocks roaming in search of food and roosting sites. Every habitat type can host starlings, but they prefer those altered by humans (farmland, urban, and suburban areas) and tend to avoid remote, pristine habitats except where humans are present.

Feeding

Insects, berries, fruits, and seeds are the starling's regular diet, but they are highly adaptable—as willing to eat French fries from a dumpster as they are to find bugs in our lawns or suet at our feeders. The starling's traditional foraging technique is to insert its long, sharp bill into the ground and then open it to expose beetle grubs and other prey.

Nesting

Starlings are cavity nesters that cannot excavate their own holes, so they use existing cavities, such as woodpecker holes, pipes, crevices in buildings, and birdhouses. Sites are often usurped from other, less aggressive cavity nesters, such as bluebirds or purple martins. Once a male has a site, a female will help finish the nest—a messy affair of grass, feathers, paper, and plastic. Between four and six eggs are laid and incubated by both parents for about 12 days. Young starlings leave the nest three weeks later.

Backyard & Beyond

Most Americans can see a starling simply by looking out their window. Many bird watchers consider them a pest at their feeders and birdhouses. To discourage starlings at your feeders, simply remove the foods they prefer: suet, peanuts, bread, and cracked corn. At nest boxes, an entry hole diameter of 1 9/16 inches or less will exclude starlings. Frequent removal of their nesting material will also discourage them.

Cedar Waxwing

Bombycilla cedrorum

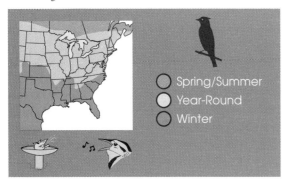

○ Spring/Summer
◐ Year-Round
○ Winter

A beady, insectlike trill first alerts many bird watchers to the presence of cedar waxwings, so completely do they blend into canopy foliage. These wandering fruit-eaters appear and disappear seemingly without rhyme or reason, descending to strip a tree of its fruits, then whirling off to parts unknown. Fermented fruits may cause entire flocks to stagger about on the ground until the intoxication wears off.

All About

"Sleek" is the word most often used to describe the silky fawn plumage of the cedar waxwing. A velvety-black bandit mask hides the eyes, and a bright yellow band tips the gray tail. Older birds have red tips on the secondary wing feather shafts, which look like shiny drops of sealing wax. Cedar waxwings are most often seen in flocks in fall and winter.

Habitat & Range

The cedar waxwing's only real habitat requirement is the presence of fruit-bearing trees and shrubs; thus, it can be found everywhere except grasslands, deserts, and deep interior forests. Thought to be nomadic, the species does make a poorly understood migration that takes it as far south as southern Central America.

Feeding

Cedar waxwings travel in tight flocks to locate and feed on small fruits. They may be completely hidden in leaves as they flutter and pluck fruit, only to explode out with reedy calls and a rush of wings when startled. In late summer, they may be seen in twisting, dodging pursuits of winged insects over water.

Nesting

Though they defend no territory and in some places are semicolonial, cedar waxwings are monogamous. Both sexes help build a bulky, cup-shaped nest in the outer canopy of a tree. Leaves, straw, twigs, and string, often in a trailing mass, comprise the nest. The female lays four eggs and incubates them for 12 days, while the male feeds her. Young are fed on insects for the first two days, then solely on regurgitated fruits, leaving the nest around 15 days later. This fruit-based diet ensures that any parasitic brown-headed cowbirds hatching in their nests do not survive. Large flocks of immature birds (identifiable by their yellowish, streaked bellies) linger near breeding grounds for one or two months after the adults leave.

Backyard & Beyond

Attracting cedar waxwings is best accomplished by planting the trees and shrubs they prefer—serviceberry, hawthorn, firethorn, dogwood, chokecherry, viburnums, native honeysuckles, blueberries, cedars, and others with small fruits. They may also visit birdbaths, especially those with moving water. Worldwide, there are only two other species of waxwing: the Bohemian and Japanese waxwings. Waxwings are related to silky flycatchers, a largely tropical family.

Magnolia Warbler

Dendroica magnolia

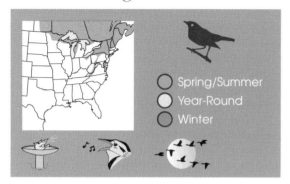

- Spring/Summer
- Year-Round
- Winter

A small and active bird, the magnolia warbler (or "maggie" as some bird watchers call it) is a frequently seen spring migrant because it forages low in shrubby vegetation. The striking magnolia warbler has no particular association with magnolias—it was named in 1810 by early American ornithologist Alexander Wilson when he saw them for the first time in a stand of magnolias in Mississippi.

All About

Magnolia warblers could be the poster bird for bird identification because they have one of everything: a dark mask, white eyeline, gray cap, white wing bars, a black necklace on a contrasting yellow breast, a yellow rump, and white tail panels. As they move about, magnolias almost seem to be trying to show you all of their markings. Adult males in fall plumage are a grayer version of their spring selves, but they retain the yellow breast and white tail panels. Male magnolias sing a highly variable song that sounds like *weeta, weeta, WEETA!* and is more recognizable for its soft delivery than for its rhythmic pattern.

Habitat & Range

During the breeding season, magnolias are found at high elevations or in the far North in young scrubby pine, spruce, fir, and hemlock forests. In migration, magnolias can turn up almost anywhere, but they are most frequently seen in brushy areas with young deciduous trees. Because they are nocturnal migrants, magnolias are frequently seen first thing in the morning,

actively feeding to refuel themselves after a night of travel.

Feeding

Magnolias glean insects, spider eggs, aphids, and beetles from trees and vegetation. As they hop through a sapling, they check the branches, bark, and undersides of leaves for food items. They will also catch insects in midair and will hover briefly to nab an otherwise hard-to-get insect from beneath a hanging leaf.

Nesting

In May and June, magnolia warblers are getting busy with breeding. Both sexes work to build the nest on the male's territory, and the site chosen is usually low and well concealed in a hemlock, spruce, or fir. The female lays three to five eggs and handles the 13-day incubation chores. Young magnolias leave the nest about 10 days after hatching, but the parents will continue to feed them for nearly a month after fledging.

Backyard & Beyond

Magnolias are one of our most common warblers, perhaps due to their preference for habitats with young trees. Finding a maggie in spring is as easy as getting out during the peak spring migration period in late March, April, May, and June. Once the breeding season starts, you'll either need to visit high elevation coniferous forests or head north to the heart of the breeding range.

Yellow-rumped Warbler

Dendroica coronata

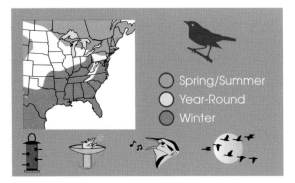

- ○ Spring/Summer
- ○ Year-Round
- ○ Winter

Oone of the best-known warblers in the United States—and easily the most widespread and numerous in winter—the yellow-rumped warbler is a paradox: Its plumage and its habitats are very variable; yet, it is relatively easy to identify whenever you find it. Eastern birds of this species used to be called "myrtle" warblers, while their western counterparts were known as "Audubon's" warblers. They are now all yellow-rumped warblers, despite differences in plumage and habitat. Trendy birders stick to their own favorite name: "butterbutt."

All About

The yellow-rumped warbler is 5 to 6 inches long, with a sharp thin bill and slightly notched tail. In breeding plumage, the eastern male is blue-gray with a white throat and belly, black streaking on the back, a black face patch, two white wing bars, black bib, and yellow spots on the crown, shoulders, and rump. Spring females are browner and duller than their mates. Immatures and fall adults are brown above, with brown-streaked underparts and little or no yellow visible. The one constant in all plumages is the bright yellow rump. That, along with a frequent and distinctive *check!* note, will quickly identify these birds.

Habitat & Range

Breeding in the far North, the eastern race of the yellow-rumped warbler is known in most of the country only as a migrant or winter resident. Migrants can be found in woodlands, hedgerows, thickets, and even along beaches as they stream through in large flocks. Winter birds congregate wherever they can find berries, their principal cold-weather food.

Feeding

In Florida, yellow-rumps are known to drink the juice of broken or fallen oranges, and throughout their winter range they will consume weed seeds large and small. Some yellow-rumps come to backyard feeders where they eat a variety of fare.

Nesting

For nesting, the yellow-rumped warbler selects conifer forests, generally spruce, pine, or cedar. The female builds the nest on a horizontal branch, anywhere from 5 to 50 feet high in the tree, using bark, twigs, weeds, and roots to create an open cup that is then lined with hair and feathers. The female incubates the four or five eggs for 12 to 13 days. When the chicks hatch, both parents feed them for 10 to 12 days until fledging, and then the male feeds them for a time afterward. There are usually two broods per year.

Backyard & Beyond

In winter, yellow-rumped warblers may visit feeders to eat suet, hummingbird nectar, orange halves, or grape jelly. It is possible to lure them with sprigs of bayberry or other wild fruits. Away from home, look for them where natural foods are plentiful, such as in bayberry thickets or stands of wax myrtle.

American Redstart

Setophaga ruticilla

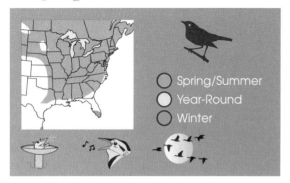

○ Spring/Summer
○ Year-Round
○ Winter

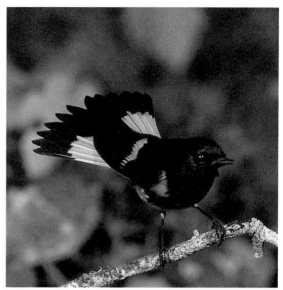

I f you make spishing or pishing noises around a mixed flock of migrating warblers, one of the first birds to pop up for a closer look may be this flashy little bird. The American redstart is a wood warbler that was named after a European member of the thrush family. But the American redstart is a true American original, even if its name derives from elsewhere.

All About

Like Europe's redstarts, the American flashes not red but orange in its tail, as well as on its wings and the sides of its breast. Otherwise, this warbler is black with a white belly. Birders call females and immatures "yellowstarts" because of similarly distinctive flashes of yellow (or in first-spring males yellow-orange) on the tail, wings, and the sides of the breast. Even seasoned birders can be thrown by the redstart's high-pitched, variable song, although some versions are easily recognized, such as *sweet-sweet-sweet-sweet-WHERE.*

Habitat & Range

Within its extensive breeding range across eastern and northern North America, American redstarts nest in a variety of wooded habitats (deciduous or mixed) with an understory of young trees. In mountainous areas, they are common nesters in regrowing forests or at the forest edge. During migration, American redstarts are among the most visible migrating warblers. They primarily winter from Mexico south to northern South America and in the Caribbean, although small numbers winter in

Florida and more rarely in Texas and Louisiana.

Feeding

Spiders, caterpillars, and a wide variety of other small invertebrates wind up between the thin mandibles of the flittering redstart. The birds mostly seek insect prey, which they pick off leaves or capture in midair sallies, but redstarts also sometimes eat berries and seeds.

Nesting

The female redstart twines together grasses and other plant materials and spider webs to make its cup nest, which is placed in young trees, often no higher than 15 feet above the ground. The female usually lays four eggs, which she incubates for about 12 days. Both parents feed their young. Before they are 10 days old, the young leave the nest but are attended by either parent.

Backyard & Beyond

Among the most common migrant warblers, American redstarts frequently turn up in backyard trees during spring and fall. You can increase your odds of finding them at home by planting small native trees or shrubs where these insectivorous birds can seek insects. Shallow birdbaths or pools attract redstarts and other warblers; take care to situate water sources near shady cover that will still allow birds to see approaching cats.

Ovenbird

Seiurus aurocapilla

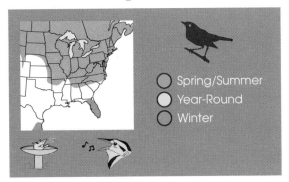

○ Spring/Summer
○ Year-Round
○ Winter

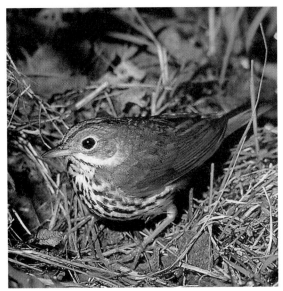

The ovenbird is a warbler that looks like a small speckled thrush. This deep forest bird only thrives where forests remain in large blocks, probably because if clearings are nearby, there are more nest predators and parasitic brown-headed cowbirds. Although spotting the forest-dwelling ovenbird takes patience, the bird's TEAcher-TEAcher-TEAcher-TEAcher *song is distinctive and rings through the woods in spring and summer.*

All About

A good look at the ovenbird's head will help you differentiate it from larger thrushes and same-sized waterthrushes. The wide, white eye ring is the first clue. The waterthrushes lack this, having instead a white stripe (*supercilium*) running from above the eye to the back of the head. Several species of brown-backed thrushes have eye rings that are not as pronounced. These birds are also much larger and have heavier bills than the ovenbird. Thrushes hop and feed, at one moment still, then dashing; the ovenbird walks methodically. The ovenbird has neat "stripes" of spots running down its breast, while the thrushes are more randomly speckled underneath. While not always visible, the ovenbird's black-bordered, orange crown patch is a diagnostic field mark.

Habitat & Range

Ovenbirds nest in mature deciduous or mixed deciduous and pine forests, but they can appear in any habitat during spring and fall migration. Most winter in Mexico, Central America, and on Caribbean islands. Forests that host nesting ovenbirds have a thick layer of dry leaf litter beneath them, providing the birds with feeding and nesting opportunities.

Feeding

The ovenbird quietly chugs along the leafy forest floor, walking and looking for insects, spiders, and other invertebrates (such as earthworms and snails) among the leaves littering the ground.

Nesting

This bird is named for its domed nest, which usually sits on the ground and is so well camouflaged with dead leaves that you can easily walk past without noticing it. Although leaves help conceal the nest, the female ovenbird constructs this structure using grasses, bark, and other materials. There is a side entrance for stealthy exit and entry. Inside, the female lays four or five eggs and incubates them for up to two weeks. Both parents feed the young. They leave the nest after about a week, but they are still fed by the adults for about two weeks afterward.

Backyard & Beyond

If you have a well-treed backyard with ample leaf litter, you may spot a foraging ovenbird walking in your woods during migration. If you hear the ovenbird's loud song, watch for it on a low- to mid-height perch or foraging on the ground.

Common Yellowthroat

Geothlypis trichas

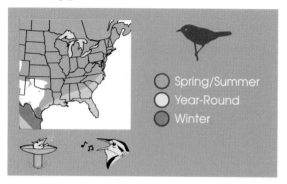

- ○ Spring/Summer
- ○ Year-Round
- ○ Winter

This charming bird may be the most popular warbler in North America. It is certainly one of the most widespread and well known. Its repetitive song, written as witchety-witchety-witch *actually does sound like that, and beginners trying to learn bird songs find that the yellowthroat's is one of the easiest to master.*

All About

Averaging about 5 inches in length, the common yellowthroat packs a lot of personality into a very small frame. Males are olive on top with a lemon-yellow throat and upper breast, white belly, yellow patch under the tail, and a bold black mask across the eyes, thinly bordered in white on top. The female is similar, but lacks the black mask. These are very active little birds and seem to be less timid than most warblers, possibly because they are nearly always low to the ground and therefore relatively easy to view. Their distinctive song continues well into the heat of summer.

Habitat & Range

Only in the dry southwestern states is the common yellowthroat hard to find during the breeding season. Everywhere else this little bird has no trouble locating the moist, shrubby, brushy conditions it needs for nesting. Even a relatively small patch of suitable habitat will do for a single pair, while large areas may host many nests. In winter and on migration, yellowthroats extend their interests to include shrubby backyards, dry woodland edges, and similar sites.

Feeding

Yellowthroats are almost exclusively insect-eaters, though they will add a few small seeds to their diet from time to time. Some favored insects are moths, aphids, leafhoppers, small caterpillars, mayflies, grasshoppers, and grubs. Foraging is done low to the ground, in dense cover.

Nesting

Female yellowthroats build a bulky cup nest quite low to the ground in thick weeds, using grasses, sedges, and other materials taken from the surrounding area. After lining it with fine grasses and hair, she lays three to five eggs and incubates them for 12 days. Her mate will bring her food during this time, and will then help her feed the nestlings for up to 10 days until fledging. The family stays together longer than most warblers, as the adults continue to feed the dependent young. Common yellowthroats are frequent victims of cowbird nest parasitism and do not seem to have an adequate defense against it.

Backyard & Beyond

In breeding season, thickets, hedgerows, marsh edges, and abandoned and overgrown farm fields are good places to look for common yellowthroats. Listen for their *witchety* song from spring through fall. They may be hard to find, but their loud, scolding *chuck* notes will often give them away.

Black-throated Green Warbler

Dendroica virens

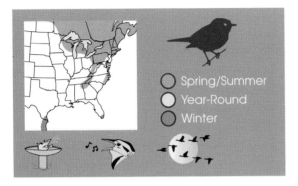

- Spring/Summer
- Year-Round
- Winter

Easy to identify both by sight and by voice, the black-throated green warbler brings spring, summer, and fall cheer to many birders. Listen for its wheezy zoo-zee zoo zoo zee *or* zee zee zee zoo zee *song. Both male and female black-throated greens are colorful and easy to identify.*

All About

This bird often appears in trees high above your head, but even a quick side or belly view reveals important identification clues, such as the bright yellow head framed from below by sharply contrasting black on the breast (and throat in male) and from above by an olive crown. The sides are streaked in black and the birds sport two white wing bars. They also have a yellow bar that runs across their white under-tails, or vents.

Habitat & Range

The black-throated green warbler breeds primarily in coniferous and mixed forests from as far west as British Columbia, east through the Northeast, and down into the Appalachians. A few winter in southern Florida and southern Texas, but most black-throated green warblers migrate to Mexico and Central America for winter. During migration, black-throated green warblers are among the most conspicuous migrant warblers, actively foraging along woodland edges.

Feeding

While nesting, black-throated green warblers eat insects, particularly caterpillars. They capture prey by snatching it from leaves but also by hovering at the tips of branches to locate and grab insects. During migration, poison ivy berries are among the fruits eaten. While on tropical wintering grounds, black-throated greens have been observed feeding on secretions that hang in globules from a commonplace tree called the cecropia.

Nesting

Male and female black-throated green warblers share nest-building duties, making a cup of grassy stems and twigs, spider webs, and bark, which they line with softer materials such as feathers. This construction may take up to eight days and the female seems to choose the nest site, which is frequently between three to nine feet off the ground in a conifer, where two or more branches meet the trunk. Only the female incubates the four (sometimes three or five) eggs, usually for 12 days. The eggs are grayish or whitish drizzled with reddish brown markings. Females feed the young initially, joined after a number of days by the male. Young leave the nest after about 11 days, following one of the parents for about a month.

Backyard & Beyond

This common migrant warbler retains most of its key field marks in its non-breeding plumage. During migration, scour chickadee and titmouse flocks and you may find black-throated green and other warblers in the treetops with these active feeders.

Yellow Warbler

Dendroica petechia

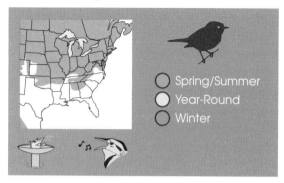

○ Spring/Summer
◐ Year-Round
○ Winter

*O*ne of North America's most familiar and wide-spread wood warblers, the yellow warbler's sweet-sweet-I'm-so-sweet *song can be heard across the continent, from Alaska down to Mexico. In all, there are about forty different subspecies of the yellow warbler. Unlike many other wood warblers, population of the yellow warbler does not seem to be declining.*

All About

To many beginning birders, the yellow warbler is the "ambassador of warblers" because it is often one of the first to be identified, thanks to its colorful plumage, easy field marks, and wide breeding range. Males are bright yellow all over, their underparts streaked with rays of orange. Females are also yellow overall, including their undertails and underwings, but they lack bold streaking. The yellow warbler's song varies somewhat and is not always easily distinguished from that of chestnut-sided warblers.

Habitat & Range

Yellow warblers are often found nesting in small trees or shrubs that grow at the edges of marshes, swamps, streams, lakes, and rivers. They sometimes set up housekeeping in drier deciduous forests, orchards, and thickets as well. On tropical wintering grounds, yellow warblers do not favor dense forest, but prefer partially open landscapes. In North America, the breeding range extends from Alaska through Canada, across the northern half of the U. S., as well as along the southern California coast and parts of Arizona down into

western Mexico. North American birds winter from Mexico into northern South America.

Feeding

Yellow warblers pick prey off leaves and grab flying insects in midair. Midges, caterpillars, spiders, mayflies, moths, and beetles are among the small invertebrates they capture. They also will eat an occasional berry or two.

Nesting

A female yellow warbler usually builds an open cup nest in the fork of a young tree or shrub. The nest is fashioned from weed stalks, grasses, and bark shreds, but lined with finer materials such as plant fluff and hair. She usually lays between four and five greenish, dark-spotted or speckled eggs, which hatch after 12 days of incubation. After hatching, young are fed by both parents before they fly off when they are between 9 to 12 days old. Brown-headed cowbirds often lay their eggs in yellow warbler nests; to thwart this, the yellow warbler sometimes builds a new level onto the nest to cover the cowbird eggs, then lays a new clutch of eggs.

Backyard & Beyond

Large properties backing up to water may host nesting yellow warblers, as long as waterside thickets are preserved. Yellow warblers also appear in backyard gardens during migration. They seem to show a particular preference for foraging in willow trees, so watch and listen for them there.

Rose-breasted Grosbeak

Pheucticus ludovicianus

Spring/Summer
Year-Round
Winter

With its triangular scarlet breast patch and some-what penguinlike pied plumage coloration, the male rose-breasted grosbeak is a North American beauty. This gorgeous songbird remains plentiful in a variety of habitats. The male's robinlike song is breezier and punctuated by a chip sound like a squeaky sneaker that, once learned, gives the bird away every time.

All About

It is hard to mistake a male rose-breasted gros-beak. No other bird has a black head and back, a triangular rose-red breast patch, and clear white belly. Equally striking in flight, the male flashes rose-red under his wings with a wide, rectangular white wing patch. The female has a dramatically difference appearance. Looking like an over-grown brown and white finch, she is streaked below and has a broad white line both above her eye and below her dark ear patch. In fall, imma-ture males look similar but have an orangey wash across the underparts. Especially near the western edge of the breeding range, care should be taken when identifying females and immatures, which strongly resemble those of the closely related black-headed grosbeak, a western species.

Habitat & Range

The rose-breasted grosbeak breeds from far northwestern Canada, throughout the Midwest and Northeast, and at high elevations in the Appalachians. It prefers to nest in open wood-lands or at the forest edge. These requirements are often met in neighborhood parks, along wooded roadsides, and sometimes in suburban neighborhoods. At its wintering grounds in the tropics, this bird also tends to occur in semi-open situations, sometimes with just scat-tered trees.

Feeding

With its versatile, heavy bill, the rose-breasted grosbeak feeds both on vegetable and animal matter. During fall migration, it mostly eats berries and seeds, including sunflower seeds offered at feeders. Insect prey in spring and sum-mer can include beetles (including the Colorado potato beetle), bees, ants, bugs, and caterpillars.

Nesting

A female grosbeak builds her nest in a tree or tall shrub, usually between 5 and 20 feet above the ground. Assisted a·bit by the male, she works twigs, weeds, and leaves into the loosely woven open cup nest, then usually lays four eggs. Both parents incubate for about two weeks, then feed their nestlings, which leave the nest between 9 to 12 days after hatching.

Backyard & Beyond

At the feeder, rose-breasted grosbeaks will eat sunflower and safflower seeds and shelled peanuts. Elderberry, juneberry, raspberry, black-berry, and mulberry are among the shrubs and small trees that can be planted to attract migrant rose-breasted grosbeaks, which also feed on a variety of weed seeds.

Scarlet Tanager

Piranga olivacea

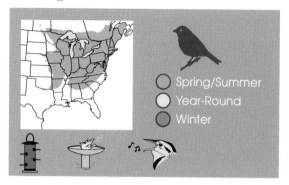

○ Spring/Summer
○ Year-Round
○ Winter

The male scarlet tanager in spring plumage ranks among the most stunningly beautiful birds in North America. One glance at his neon-bright plumage can turn even the most disinterested person into a confirmed bird watcher. Oddly, this dazzling bird's song has been compared to "a robin with a bad cold." A distinctive chick-burr call is often the first clue of a scarlet tanager's presence.

All About

The male scarlet tanager in spring plumage has a solid-red body and jet-black wings and tail, with a black-button eye and bone-gray bill. The female is dull olive above with dark wings and pale yellow underparts. Immatures resemble females, and in late summer the adult males take on the muted olive-yellow plumage. In all plumages, the scarlet tanager's wings are darker than those of the summer tanager. At just 7 inches long, scarlet tanagers are the smallest of the four North American tanager species.

Habitat & Range

Preferring deciduous forests with oaks, maples, and beeches, scarlet tanagers generally inhabit areas farther north (or, in the South, at higher elevations) than summer tanagers. They arrive in April or May and depart by midautumn. Flocks of early migrants are sometimes decimated by sudden late-spring snowfalls or ice storms, which cause them to starve or freeze to death. Sometimes being the early bird is not such a good idea.

Feeding

Basically insectivorous, the scarlet tanager moves quietly about in the upper canopy of deciduous trees in search of prey. Small summer fruits—such as blueberries and mulberries—are also taken, as are fall staples, such as poison ivy berries and sumac fruits. Scarlet tanagers occasionally engage in flycatching, or hovering behavior, to obtain food. Early or late in the season, cold weather may force them to the ground to forage for bugs in sheltered microhabitats.

Nesting

Typically, the scarlet tanager nests in a large, unbroken, wooded tract and high in a deciduous tree—often, but not always—an oak. It will be situated well out from the trunk on a horizontal limb. Made by the female alone, it is shallow and loosely constructed of twigs, rootlets, weeds, and other plant material. Three to five eggs are laid, and the female incubates them for up to two weeks until hatching. Both parents feed the young during the 9- to 14-day nestling period and for two weeks more after fledging occurs.

Backyard & Beyond

Scarlet tanagers are not common at bird feeders, but they do—on occasion—respond to offerings of bread, doughnuts, orange halves, or a peanut butter-cornmeal mixture. They will also eat small fruits and, in fall migration, may be a regular sight along tangled hedgerows overrun by poison ivy or multiflora rose.

Northern Cardinal

Cardinalis cardinalis

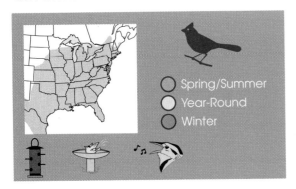

- ○ Spring/Summer
- ◐ Year-Round
- ○ Winter

Cardinals are the familiar and beloved "redbird" found all across the eastern United States. This bird's popularity is such that seven U.S. states and countless sports teams have chosen the cardinal as their official emblem. In spring and summer, cardinal pairs can be found together, often with the male perched high above, singing his what-cheer-cheer-cheer song. In fall and winter, cardinals can be found in large loose flocks, especially during harsh weather.

All About

A black face and a long red crest smartly set off the bright red plumage of the male cardinal. Females are a muted, brownish version of the male. Strongly territorial, mated cardinal pairs will vigorously defend their nesting turf from rivals, even going so far as to attack their own reflections in windows, mistaking the image for another cardinal. One of the cardinal's most notable behaviors is the "courtship kiss" in which a male feeds a bit of food to a female he is wooing.

Habitat & Range

Found in a variety of habitats—from deserts to wetlands to manicured backyards, cardinals prefer an *edge habitat*—a place where woodland and open space meet. They are resident (nonmigratory) and thriving throughout their range, which has expanded northward in recent decades—thanks in part to the availability of food at bird feeders.

Feeding

Cardinals forage on or near the ground. During warm weather, insects, berries, buds, and seeds are their primary diet. Gardeners appreciate cardinals for eating grubs, beetles, caterpillars, and other garden pests. In winter, cardinals shift to a greater reliance on seeds, nuts, and wild fruits. At bird feeders cardinals prefer sunflower seeds, but will also eat mixed seeds, suet, fruits, and peanuts.

Nesting

Female cardinals choose thick cover—vine or rose tangles or shrubs—in which to weave their shallow, cup-shaped nests out of grasses, rootlets, twigs, and bark strips. Into this nest, the female will lay three to five eggs and incubate them for nearly two weeks before they hatch. Both parents feed the youngsters for about 10 days before they fledge. In summer, young cardinals can often be seen following a parent around, begging to be fed. Males will take on this duty while the female starts a second brood.

Backyard & Beyond

You can enjoy cardinals all year long in your backyard by offering them the four things they need to survive: food, water, a place to roost, and a place to nest. A few bird feeders, a chemical-free lawn and garden, and some thick brushy cover will suit their requirements nicely. Watch for cardinals early and late—they are often the first birds active at dawn and the last ones to "turn in" at dusk.

Indigo Bunting

Passerina cyanea

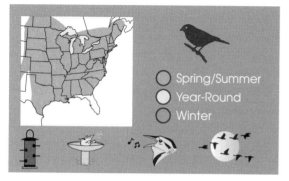

- ○ Spring/Summer
- ○ Year-Round
- ○ Winter

Appearing all black against the light, a male indigo bunting properly lit is an unforgettable sight. A persistent late-season singer, he sings a jingly song comprised of paired notes that are often described as: Fire! Fire! Where? Where? Here! Here! Put it out! Put it out! Much of what we know about celestial navigation in songbirds derives from work with captive indigo buntings at the Cornell Lab of Ornithology.

All About

The breathtaking, all-blue male indigo bunting, with his silvery conical bill, is unmistakable. Females and immatures are a warm cocoa-brown overall. This bunting has a habit of twitching its tail to the side, and its *spit!* note is characteristic. Males change their blue feathers for brown in autumn, which makes for some interestingly mottled specimens. They molt again on the wintering grounds and return in spring, blue once more.

Habitat & Range

This species is common on roadsides and disturbed areas where "trashy" vegetation flourishes. Power line cuts, old fields, landfills, railroads, and hedgerows ring with the songs of indigo buntings, especially as summer reaches its fullest. Indigo buntings are strongly migratory, wintering in Central and northern South America.

Feeding

The indigo bunting takes insects when they are available, especially to feed its nestlings. Weed seeds are its mainstay, supplemented by berries and small fruits. It forages on or near the ground, as well as in low shrubs and trees. Watch for them in autumn, bending grass stems and flicking their tails side to side as they forage in weedy patches.

Nesting

Indigo buntings have a rather loose definition of monogamy, with extra-pair copulations being quite frequent. Males visit females in neighboring territories, and females visit males. Males vary in their tendency to feed young; some are attentive parents, whereas others leave most of the chick rearing to their mates. The nest is bulky but compact, cup-shaped, and constructed of bark strips, grass and weed stems, and skeletonized leaves, all bound with spider webs. It's often low in blackberry, sumac, or other brushy vegetation. These birds nest quite late in the season, reflecting their dependence on late-maturing weed seeds. Three to four eggs are incubated by the female for about 12 days, and the young leave the nest from 8 to 14 days later.

Backyard & Beyond

Lucky is the one who hosts indigo buntings! Spring arrivals are most often first seen feasting on dandelion seeds. Later, black-oil sunflower seeds and millet mixes prove attractive. The growing popularity of "meadows in a can" make for rich feeding grounds for indigo buntings, which flock to coneflower, Mexican hat, cosmos, coreopsis, and especially foxtail grasses.

Eastern Towhee

Pipilo erythrophthalmus

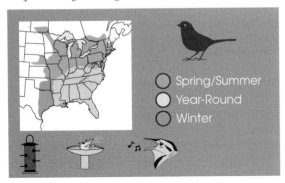

○ Spring/Summer
○ Year-Round
○ Winter

Drink your TEA! *sings the towhee throughout the brushy woodlands of the eastern United States. Formerly called the rufous-sided towhee (a much more descriptive name), this large (8½ inches long) sparrow is boldly patterned and spends nearly all its time on the ground scratching among the leaf litter, looking for food. The name towhee comes from the bird's call, which has also been transcribed as* chewink. *Many people know this bird as the chewink instead of towhee.*

All About

Clean, flashy colors have given the towhee the nickname "Hollywood robin." In flight, the bird's white wing and tail spots are noticeable. Female eastern towhees replace the male's black plumage areas with chocolate brown. Towhees' preference for thick cover and brushy habitat make them harder to see than other common species. The loud scratching of a foraging towhee sounds like a large animal walking through dry leaves; this is often your first clue to a towhee's presence.

Habitat & Range

Widespread across the eastern half of the United States and southern Canada, towhees in the northern part of the range are migratory, but those in the southern half are resident (nonmigratory). During mild winters, towhees may linger until harsh weather forces them to migrate or to seek the cover of wooded valleys and hollows. Brushy woodland thickets and edge habitats are preferred, but towhees are also found in older woodlands and suburban backyards.

Feeding

Towhees eat just about anything found on the woodland floor, including insects, seeds, fruits, and even snails, spiders, and millipedes. They prefer to scratch the ground under feeding stations for mixed seeds, cracked corn, and sunflower seeds (which they crack with their powerful bill).

Nesting

Towhees nest on or near the ground in a well-concealed spot. The female weaves a cup-shaped nest out of rootlets, bark strips, and grass. She also handles all the incubation duty, which typically lasts about 12 days. Normal clutch size is three to four eggs; young towhees fledge in about 10 days. Both towhee parents feed the youngsters, which allows the female to start a second—and sometimes a third—brood.

Backyard & Beyond

Spring is the best time to find an eastern towhee. Male towhees are especially vocal during the breeding season and will leave deep cover to sing from a high perch within their territory. Make your feeders much more attractive to towhees by adding a brush pile nearby to help these shy birds feel more at home. In summer, recently fledged towhees can be confusing and hard to identify with their streaky, gray-brown coloring. Their white tail spots and ground-scratching habits will give them away.

Field Sparrow

Spizella pusilla

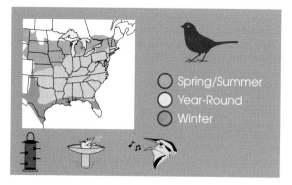

○ Spring/Summer
○ Year-Round
○ Winter

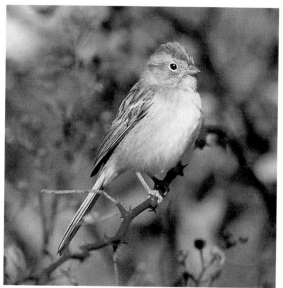

The field sparrow's clear whistled notes on a single tone is an easy bird song to learn and remember. Listen throughout the day, even in summer, for this persistent singer. Its rhythmic pattern resembles a ping-pong ball being dropped onto a table. A subtly beautiful sparrow of farm pastures and shrubby old meadows, the field sparrow is familiar to bird watchers in rural habitats.

All About

The field sparrow is a small bird (5³/4 inches long) with a biggish bill and long tail, but the first field marks most birders notice are the pink bill, plain face, and white ring surrounding the dark eye. Telling the field sparrow apart from chipping or tree sparrows is a matter of noting the field's unmarked buffy-gray breast and indistinct head stripes of brown and gray.

Habitat & Range

As its name suggests, the field sparrow is found in fields, but it prefers brushy, older fields that have the beginnings of reforestation—saplings, small shrubs, and large thick clumps of grass. Field sparrows are found all across the eastern United States, but—unlike many of our migrant songbirds—they may only migrate a few hundred miles to spend the winter. In spring and summer, males do their singing from an exposed perch within their territories.

Feeding

Throughout the year, the field sparrow's diet is grass seeds and other small plant seeds; in spring and summer the diet shifts to insects. Moths, grasshoppers, flies, and other grassland insects make up half of their summer diet, with most of the insects being found on or near the ground. In winter, as flocks of field sparrows forage together, a single bird will perch on top of a tall grass stem, letting its weight bend the stalk to the ground where the seeds can more easily be eaten.

Nesting

In early spring (April to May) field sparrow nests are built on the ground, near a grass clump or small shrub. Later nests (June to July) may be in taller shrubs or vegetation, but the construction is the same—a loosely woven outer cup of grass lined with fine, soft grasses, all built by the female. Three to six eggs are laid and incubated by the female for about 12 days. Like other ground nesters, young field sparrows develop quickly and may leave the nest within a week. Flight is attained in two weeks and independence from the parents two weeks later.

Backyard & Beyond

Within the breeding range, any older farm field should host field sparrows. Look for males perched on top of saplings or fenceposts. Field sparrows will come to cracked corn, mixed seeds, and eggshell bits scattered on the ground beneath bird feeders.

Chipping Sparrow

Spizella passerina

Spring/Summer
Year-Round
Winter

A close look at this natty little bird reveals much to admire in its quiet and confiding ways. As common as it is around dooryards and gardens, we know surprisingly little about the chipping sparrow's mating systems. One Ontario study showed males not to be monogamous, as assumed, but to mate freely.

All About

A rusty beret and bold, white eyeline are the best field marks of this slender little sparrow. Plain gray underparts, a streaked brown back, and a small, all-black bill set off its striking head markings. It is an under-appreciated bird, perhaps because it is so small and unobtrusive. Rather dry, monotonous trills, as well as its signature chipping notes, are the ambient sounds of a chipping sparrow's territory.

Habitat & Range

Before the massive expansion of suburbs, the chipping sparrow was limited to open, grassy coniferous forests and parklike woodlands with shrubby understories. Our suburban habitats have just the right mix of short grass, shrubbery, and conifers that chipping sparrows need, so we enjoy their company on doorsteps and sidewalks. Although northern populations are strongly migratory, southern birds flock up but tend to stay near their breeding grounds.

Feeding

Chipping sparrows forage primarily on or near the ground, feasting on weed and grass seeds and some smaller fruits. They feed insects to the young, however, sometimes flycatching on the wing. Winter flocks of up to 50 birds perch in trees, descending *en masse* to the ground to peck for seeds, then adjourning to treetops before the next feeding bout. At feeding stations, they'll peck on the ground or perch on hopper feeders.

Nesting

Female chipping sparrows weave lovely little nests of thin twigs and weed stems, with a center composed of animal hair. These are often concealed in low trees and shrubs, but are easily located by the shrilling of older nestlings. Females incubate the four eggs for around 12 days, and the young leave the nest about 9 to 12 days later. Streaky, brown, and nondescript, they're fed by their parents for three more weeks before forming juvenile flocks.

Backyard & Beyond

Chipping sparrows eagerly accept mixed seeds and suet dough mixtures offered on or near the ground. They're fond of rolled oats, and live mealworms will be taken straight to the young. They greatly appreciate baked and crushed eggshells strewn on a sidewalk. But it's most fun to offer them human or pet hair clippings. A trip to any salon can net a season's worth, and you may have the pleasure of finding a used nest lined with your own hair—the ultimate vanity piece for the discerning gardener.

White-throated Sparrow

Zonotrichia albicollis

Spring/Summer
Year-Round
Winter

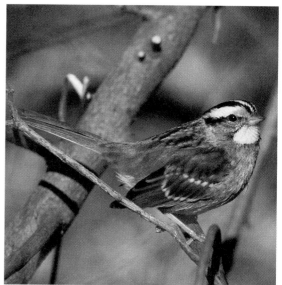

Old Sam Peabody, Peabody, Peabody *is the sweet whistled song of the white-throated sparrow. In Canada, where this species spends the breeding season, the song is transcribed as* Oh sweet Canada, Canada, Canada—*but there's no arguing that the white-throated sparrow's song is easy to recognize. From September to March these northern breeders are with us, in loose flocks with other sparrows, brightening winter days with their cheery sounds.*

All About

The first field mark most bird watchers notice on the white-throated sparrow is not the white throat, but the black-and-white striped head pattern with a yellow spot between the eyes and bill. Even at a distance this striking pattern is obvious. Some white-throated sparrows have tan-striped heads and a tannish throat. These belong to the tan-striped variety of the species, though many ornithologists formerly thought these were young birds not yet in adult plumage. This medium-sized (6¾ inches long) sparrow has a gray breast and a brown, lightly patterned back.

Habitat & Range

Spending most of the summer in the boreal coniferous forests of the far North and New England, the white-throated sparrow spends fall and winter to the south, where it is a regular at bird feeders and in brushy edge habitat. It prefers a habitat with thick underbrush and is found near the edge of the woods, along hedgerows, and in brushy thickets in parks and backyards.

Feeding

White-throated sparrows prefer to feed on the ground. In spring and summer, the white-throated sparrow's diet is focused on insects—ants, grubs, and spiders—that it uncovers as it scratches through the leaf litter, much like a towhee does. In fall the diet shifts to include berries; in winter it includes mostly seeds from grasses. At bird feeders they are attracted to mixed seed, cracked corn, and sunflower or peanut bits offered on the ground or on a platform feeder.

Nesting

White-throated sparrows nest on or near the ground in a well-concealed spot. The cup-shaped nest is built by the female from grass, pine needles, and twigs and lined with soft material, such as rootlets or fur. The female incubates the four to five eggs for about two weeks; the male assists her in feeding the nestlings for the nine days prior to fledging. The young birds rely on the parents for food for about another two weeks.

Backyard & Beyond

Look for white-throated sparrows on the ground beneath your feeders from late fall through early spring. If your feeders are some distance from cover, consider moving them closer to the woods' edge, or add a brush pile nearby to make woodland birds (such as white-throated sparrows) feel more at home.

White-crowned Sparrow

Zonotrichia leucophrys

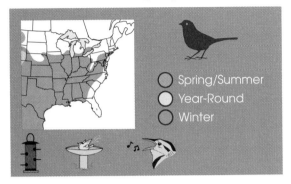

○ Spring/Summer
○ Year-Round
○ Winter

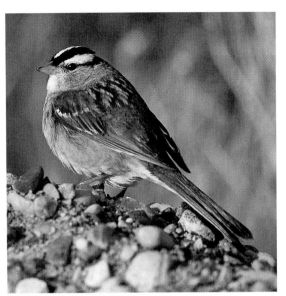

The striking black-and-white stripes on the head of the adult white-crowned sparrow are a field mark that is hard to ignore. Flocks of white-crowned sparrows are fairly common in winter across the Midwest and during spring and fall migrations as the birds travel to and from their breeding range in the far North.

All About

A large sparrow with a badger-striped head, the white-crowned sparrow has a pale gray breast, brown flanks and rump, and two white wing bars on the brown wings. Bill color varies by population from yellow to orange-pink. The white-crowned sparrow's song is a beautiful mix of clear whistled introductory notes, followed by a series of buzzy trills. It can be heard singing on sunny days during winter and prior to spring migration.

Habitat & Range

The white-crowned sparrow breeds in the boreal forest edges, brushy thickets, and scrub of the far North but is also a year-round resident in many parts of the mountainous West. It winters across the southern two-thirds of the U.S. along woodland edges, in brushy fields, hedgerows, and in suburban parks and backyards. In the non-breeding season (September through April) it can often be found in feeding flocks with other sparrow species.

Feeding

The diet of the white-crowned sparrow is composed mainly of plant seeds, which it finds as it forages on the ground. In spring, its diet includes tree buds, fruits, and some insects, especially during breeding season. White crowneds will visit feeding stations, especially if brushy thickets are nearby, preferring to scratch for seed bits on the ground below the feeders.

Nesting

White-crowned sparrows nest on or near the ground, with the females weaving the cup-shaped nest out of grasses, rootlets, twigs, and strips of bark. A grass or animal hair lining holds the four or five eggs as they are laid and helps insulate them during the nearly two-week incubation by the female. Both parents care for the young, which leave the nest within two weeks. In areas where the white-crowned is a year-round resident there may be as many as four broods per year.

Backyard & Beyond

White-crowned sparrow and the closely related white-throated sparrow are common backyard birds in fall and winter across the Midwest. Listen for their high, sweet, whistled songs and their sharp *pink!* call at dawn and dusk from thick brushy habitat. Scatter some mixed seed under your feeders and beneath your shrubs and brush pile to offer these ground feeders something to eat.

Song Sparrow

Melospiza melodia

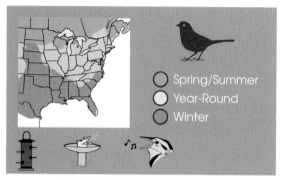

○ Spring/Summer
◉ Year-Round
○ Winter

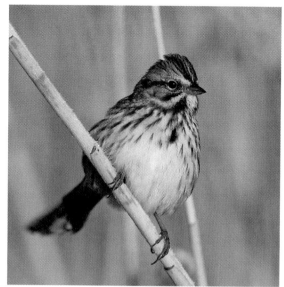

Persistent singing, often year-round, makes this a well-named species. If there's a resident song sparrow in your yard, you'll probably hear its cheery notes at first light—as reliable as, but more pleasant than, a rooster's. One of the best-studied birds in North America, the song sparrow was the subject of Margaret Morse Nice's groundbreaking behavioral study in the 1930s. Much of what we understand about songbird territoriality began with this study.

All About

The classic "little brown job," the song sparrow has a heavily streaked white breast marked with a messy central spot. A grayish, striped face and crown and warm-brown upperparts complete the description. Flight is low and jerky, with the tail twisting distinctively. Three introductory notes leading to a variable jumble of trills and chips distinguish its song. Males and females look similar.

Habitat & Range

Though song sparrows occupy a wide range of habitats, they are most often found in shrubbery near water, from small streams to beach habitats. Song sparrows tend to be migratory in northern climes and year-round residents in the southern United States; this varies by population. The song sparrow is one of the most variable songbirds known. Populations in the Pacific Northwest, for example, are larger, darker, heavier-billed, and virtually unrecognizable compared to southeastern coastal populations.

Feeding

The song sparrow's diet varies seasonally, with insects being its primary prey in spring and summer and with seeds and fruits dominating in fall and winter. Most of the song sparrow's foraging takes place on the ground, where it will scratch and kick about in leaf litter and grasses for weed seeds and insects.

Nesting

The persistent singing of song sparrows is linked to strong territorial behavior; where they are resident year-round, they tend to defend territories year-round. Territory boundaries are quite stable from year to year. Both sexes defend their territory, and they tend to stay with one mate. Females construct a bulky nest of bark strips and weed and grass stems, well hidden deep in a dense shrub. Small, ornamental evergreens are irresistible to song sparrows. The female incubates three to five eggs for about 13 days. Young leave the nest at only 10 days and may be fed by the parents for the next 20 days before they are fully independent.

Backyard & Beyond

Song sparrows readily visit feeders for sunflower seeds, cracked corn, and mixed seeds, preferring to feed on the ground. Peanut butter-based suet mixes are a favorite food, and song sparrows will appear to beg at windows for such fare. They are fond of water and will often nest near a water garden or backyard pond.

Dark-eyed Junco

Junco hyemalis

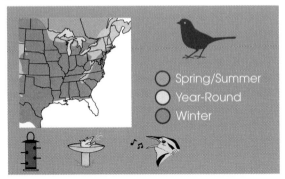

○ Spring/Summer
○ Year-Round
○ Winter

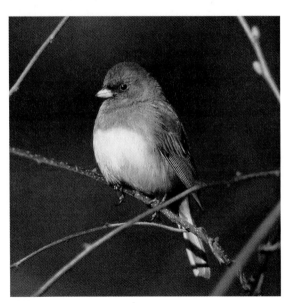

The dark-eyed junco is often called the "snowbird," because it seems to show up at our feeders and in our backyards at the same time as the first snows begin falling over much of the country. But even in the Deep South, this member of the sparrow family is a familiar winter visitor to backyards, gardens, parks, pastures, and feeding stations.

All About

Juncos are medium-sized (6¼ inches long) sparrows, but unlike most sparrows, their plumage lacks streaking. Dark-gray above and white below (or "gray skies above, snow below"), the junco has a conical, pinkish bill and flashes its white outer tail feathers in flight. Male juncos in the East are a darker gray than the brownish-overall females. Western junco forms show a variety of plumage colors, and many of these color forms were considered separate species until recently. Now they are all lumped into a single species: dark-eyed junco. Juncos make a variety of sounds, all of them high-pitched tinkling trills, especially when flushed from cover.

Habitat & Range

Few bird species' ranges cover North America more thoroughly than that of the dark-eyed junco. In winter it can be found in every state. Spring migration begins as early as March and continues through early June. During breeding season, juncos retreat to the far north woods and to coniferous and mixed woodlands at high elevations. Fall migration begins in mid-August through October. Their winter habitat preferences run to brushy edge habitat along woods, fields, and suburban backyards and parks.

Feeding

Juncos find their food on the ground. They are often seen scratching through the leaf litter, grass, or snow when foraging. In spring and summer the junco eats mostly insects, including spiders, caterpillars, ants, grasshoppers, and weevils, but it will also eat berries. In fall and winter the diet shifts to grass and weed seeds, along with birdseed gleaned from the ground beneath feeders.

Nesting

The junco's nest is a simple, open cup of grasses and leaves, loosely woven and lined with finer grasses, fur, or feathers. Nests are normally located on the ground in a concealed spot and built by the female. She incubates her three to five eggs for almost two weeks; the male helps with feeding chores once the young hatch. Within two weeks the young birds leave the nest, and the parents are free to start another brood if the season permits.

Backyard & Beyond

Where there is one junco, there is almost surely a flock. Seek them along the edges of woodlots, old pastures, and in areas with a thick growth of underbrush. Watch for the flashing white in the tail and listen for the juncos' trilling calls.

Eastern Meadowlark

Sturnella magna

O ur two meadowlark species (the second being *western meadowlark*, Sturnella neglecta) *are indistinguishable visually, but their songs are different. The eastern meadowlark's sweet whistled song—* spring of THE year!*—and the western meadowlark's low, descending, whistled and gurgled* Swing low sweet chariot! *are both signs of spring's arrival.*

All About

Familiar birds of rural farm fields, meadows, and grasslands, the eastern and western meadowlarks are known by their distinctive field mark: a bright yellow breast with a "V" of black. Meadowlarks will sing from the ground and in flight, but they often use an elevated perch, such as a fencepost, tree, or power line. In flight, the meadowlark looks chunky and shows white outer tail feathers. A series of shallow, stuttering wingbeats followed by a short glide (sometimes accompanied by a song or chatter) is the typical flight pattern.

Habitat & Range

Eastern meadowlarks prefer grassy meadows, prairies, and pastures with good grass cover. Westerns seem to favor shorter, drier grasslands. Both can also be found along golf courses, in hayfields, and in the grassy margins of airports. As their names suggest, the eastern meadowlark is primarily an eastern bird and the western primarily a western bird, but their ranges overlap significantly in the Midwest. These birds can apparently tell they are different species, because they almost never interbreed.

Feeding

The meadowlark is a ground feeder that searches vegetation in spring and summer for insects, such as crickets, grasshoppers, grubs, and caterpillars. In winter, the diet shifts to seeds, grains, and some fruits. In fall and winter, both meadowlarks often form large single-species flocks, with dozens of birds foraging together in the same field.

Nesting

Meadowlarks nest on the ground in thick grass. The nest is well concealed in a depression on the ground and is woven out of dried grasses. Two to six eggs are laid and incubated for about 14 days. Youngsters fledge about 10 days later. Both parents feed the young. For nesting, meadowlarks seem to prefer grasslands that are cut only once every three to five years. Even so, many meadowlark nests are lost to agricultural activity, predation, and pesticides.

Backyard & Beyond

To find a meadowlark you must locate a suitable habitat, which usually means locating a rural spot with hayfields and pastures. During spring and summer, meadowlarks sing throughout the day, but do so most actively early in the morning. Listen for the slurring whistled song and the sputtering blackbird-like calls. Scan the wires, treetops, and fenceposts for the singing adult bird. Its handsome lemon-yellow-and-black breast should catch your eye.

Brown-headed Cowbird

Molothrus ater

Spring/Summer
Year-Round
Winter

The cowbird's habit of laying its eggs in the nests of other, smaller songbirds makes the brown-headed cowbird a nest parasite. Cowbirds learned this behavior over centuries of following roaming herds of buffalo. The buffalo stirred up insects, the cowbird's main food. But all the movement made it impossible to stop, build a nest, and wait for the young to grow. So the cowbirds did the most convenient thing—laid their eggs in any nest they could find along the way.

All About

The cowbird is a small (7 1/2 inches long) blackbird. Males have a glossy black body and a dark brown head, while females are a dull gray-brown overall. The short, conical bill and pointed wings help to distinguish the brown-headed cowbird from larger blackbirds. The cowbird's song is a series of liquid gurgles followed by a high, thin whistle.

Habitat & Range

Cowbirds are found in a variety of habitats, but they prefer woodland edges, brushy fields, and old pastures, though they are equally at home in city parks and suburban backyards. Forest fragmentation has allowed the cowbird to parasitize the nests of woodland species, such as thrushes and vireos. In winter cowbirds often join flocks of other blackbirds—red-winged blackbirds, grackles, and European starlings—foraging in fields and grasslands and roosting *en masse* in large woodlots.

Feeding

The diet of the cowbird consists of weed and grass seeds, along with insects, especially grasshoppers and beetles. Nearly all food is taken from the ground.

Nesting

Male cowbirds court females with a variety of songs, bows, and sky-pointing displays. When she is ready to lay an egg, she finds a nest that often already contains the eggs of the nest's owner. This "host" nest is most frequently that of a smaller songbird—yellow warblers, song sparrows, red-eyed vireos, and chipping sparrows seem to be frequent victims—and the female cowbird may even remove one of the host's eggs before depositing her own. Hatchling cowbirds are almost always larger than their nestmates, and are able to out-compete them for food, enhancing the cowbird's chances of survival. Some bird species have evolved to recognize cowbird eggs and will build a new nest on top of the old one or will remove the cowbird egg.

Backyard & Beyond

Finding cowbirds is almost never a problem, but limiting their impact on our songbirds can be problematic. One way to discourage cowbirds is to stop offering mixed seed and cracked corn during spring when they show up at bird feeders before many migratory songbirds return. If you see a songbird feeding a fledgling that is larger than itself, the fledgling is likely a cowbird.

Red-winged Blackbird

Agelaius phoeniceus

Spring/Summer
Year-Round
Winter

The red-winged blackbird's name succinctly describes the male's handsome plumage; yet, the females of this ubiquitous species have baffled many a bird watcher. Their streaky brown plumage is confusingly sparrowlike. Studies have shown that one dominant male red-winged blackbird may have many adult females nesting on his territory.

All About

The *conk-a-ree* call of the male red-winged blackbird fills the air over marshes and fields all across North America. As he gives this call, announcing himself loudly to rivals and potential mates alike, he spreads his shoulders just so, showing bright red and yellow epaulets against his black wings. Redwings are medium-sized (8¾ inches long) blackbirds with an all-black body, an orange-red and yellow patch on the shoulder, and a nearly conical black bill. Females are streaky brown overall, but their longer bill helps separate them from the sparrows (which have stouter bills).

Habitat & Range

Wet meadows, cattail marshes, upland grasslands, and pastures are all breeding habitat for red-winged blackbirds. In fall and winter, they may join with other blackbird species to form huge flocks. Northern-nesting redwings migrate (starting in September and October) to the southern U.S., while southern-nesting birds are nonmigratory. Fall blackbird flocks move during the day in oblong, loose clouds of birds. These flocks forage by day in agricultural fields and are often perse-cuted as a nuisance species for the crop damage they inflict. Spring migration begins in mid-February and continues through mid-May.

Feeding

The red-winged blackbird's diet is mostly plant matter—weed seeds, grain, sunflower seeds, and tree seeds—along with some insects, all of which are gleaned from the ground. They will also visit feeding stations for sunflower seeds, cracked corn, peanuts, and suet. Surprisingly, they are able to use a variety of feeder types.

Nesting

Nesting starts early for the red-winged black-bird, with males singing from an exposed perch on their territories as early as February in the South, later in the North. Females choose a nest site on a male's territory and build cup-shaped grass nests that are suspended from vertical supporting vegetation. Mud forms the foundation of the nest and soft grasses are the inner lining. Clutch size is three to four eggs, and the female alone incubates them for 10 to 13 days. Both parents care for the nestlings for about two weeks, until they are ready to leave the nest.

Backyard & Beyond

Red-winged blackbirds are present continent-wide for most of the year. Wet meadows, swamps, and salt marshes are common habitats for these birds, especially in spring and summer. Listen for the male's loud *conk-a-ree* song.

Common Grackle

Quiscalus quiscula

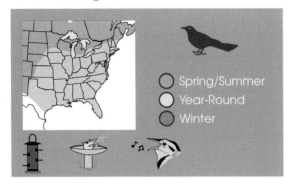

- ○ Spring/Summer
- ○ Year-Round
- ○ Winter

Grackles are large, conspicuous, and noisy birds that are equally at home in a town or country setting. This species benefited greatly from the European settlement of North America as forests were turned into farm fields and new feeding and nesting opportunities emerged for the common grackle. Residential areas and farmland are particularly attractive to grackles.

All About

Nearly half of the common grackle's 12$^{1}/_{2}$-inch length is its tail. The grackle's black plumage is glossy and can show bright purple, bronze, or green highlights, especially on the head. Adult common grackles show a pale yellow eye, contrasting sharply with the dark head. The powerful bill is long and sharply pointed. In flight, grackles hold their long tails in a "V", much like the keel of a boat. Males and females are very similar in appearance. Grackles utter a variety of harsh, metallic tones.

Habitat & Range

Common grackles are found in almost every habitat in eastern North America; though, in winter the population is more concentrated in the eastern and southern United States. Grackles prefer edge habitat and open areas with scattered trees or shrubs. From late summer to early spring, grackles gather in large roosts with other blackbirds. These roosts can contain as many as half a million birds, and are notable both for their noise and their droppings.

Spring migrants may reach breeding territories as early as mid-February. Fall migration begins in September and peaks in October.

Feeding

During breeding season, grackles eat mostly insects, but they are opportunists and will take nestling birds or eggs, small fish, mice, and frogs. In winter the diet shifts to seeds and grain. The impact of foraging winter flocks on crops has earned the common grackle a reputation as an agricultural pest. Most of the grackle's foraging is done on the ground, where the birds toss aside leaves and rubbish to uncover their food.

Nesting

Grackles prefer to nest in dense conifers, close to rich foraging habitat. The large, open-cup nest is built by the female from grass, twigs, and mud and is lined with soft grass. She incubates the four to five eggs for about two weeks. The male joins her in feeding the nestlings an all-insect diet until fledging time arrives about 20 days later.

Backyard & Beyond

Look for long dark lines of migrating common grackles during the day, especially in fall. Migrating flocks can contain thousands of birds and may stretch from horizon to horizon. At feeders grackles relish cracked corn and sunflower seeds most of all. Grackles are also known to take hard, stale pieces of bread and dunk them in a birdbath to soften them up.

Baltimore Oriole

Icterus galbula

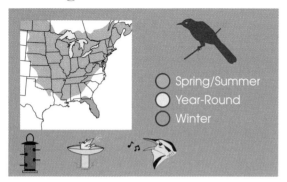

○ Spring/Summer
○ Year-Round
○ Winter

The colorful Baltimore oriole, like many long-distance migrants, leads three flamboyant lives: backyard, park, and forest nester in North America; winter nectar, fruit, and insect-eater in the tropics; and long-distance wanderer while transiting between its two homes. Named for the colonial family that settled Maryland—the family crest of which sported the bird's striking orange and black colors—the Baltimore oriole is one of only two widespread eastern orioles.

All About

At rest and in flight, the male Baltimore oriole is a fireball of citrus orange blazed with black. The bird's head, back, and much of its wings and tail are black. In flight, a bright orange shoulder and white wing bars flash, as do its orange tail corners. The female Baltimore oriole is also colorful, lacking the entirely black head of the male but having vibrant orange-yellow underparts. The Baltimore oriole's unusually rich song and two-note whistle often reveal its presence.

Habitat & Range

The Baltimore oriole breeds in open parklike woodlands, at forest edges—including along waterways—as well as in suburbs and city parks. This bird favors tall, mature deciduous trees, often in very open, widely scattered stands. During migration and on its wintering grounds, it is similarly adaptable, inhabiting forests, hedges, gardens, shade coffee and cacao plantations, and even pastures with scattered trees. Baltimore orioles nest from central Canada, across the southeast of the country, then south through much of the eastern U.S. north of Texas and the southeastern coastal plain. Most of the population winters from Mexico south to northwestern South America and in the northern Lesser Antilles, including Cuba. Some winter in Florida. Each winter, individuals pop up along many other parts of the East Coast and even in southern California.

Feeding

During warm months, Baltimore orioles feed on a wide variety of insects, including caterpillars—at times tearing open tent caterpillar nests. Fruits are also eaten, including some cultivated varieties. In winter, Baltimore orioles eat berries, insects, and nectar, which they extract from flowers with their bristly tongues.

Nesting

A female Baltimore oriole constructs a pendulous nest, sometimes with the help of her mate. Woven of plant fibers, string, and other materials, the nest hangs near the end of a large branch, usually between 20 and 30 feet off the ground. Within the enclosed nest, the female lays four or five bluish or grayish eggs, which are marked with brown and black. She incubates the eggs about two weeks, then both parents feed the nestlings, which leave the nest about two weeks after hatching.

Backyard & Beyond

Halved oranges and sugar water in special feeders often entice Baltimore orioles to visit yards.

House Finch

Carpodacus mexicanus

Spring/Summer
Year-Round
Winter

Bird watchers who rely on an eastern field guide that is more than thirty years old may be forgiven for some confusion. This bird won't be in it! The house finch, native to the West, is a well-established, but recently arrived resident of the eastern United States. Released upon the passage of protective legislation forbidding trade in native wild birds, a small population of the so-called "Hollywood linnets" began breeding on Long Island in 1940, and they have now blanketed the eastern United States with their progeny.

All About

People who feed birds are familiar with the house finches that sometimes cover feeders with fluttering, tweeting flocks. It's easy to see why they were kept as cage birds; the male's cheery, rich song, marked by a few harsh notes, tumbles brightly down the scale. Females are streaky, pale brown birds with white undersides; males have a rich pinkish-red rump, head, and upper breast. By comparison, male purple finches have an overall "dipped in wine" look, with a reddish suffusion to their back and wings, while female purple finches are much more boldly streaked with brown and white than are female house finches.

Habitat & Range

As its name suggests, the house finch prefers nesting and feeding near homes. It's a thoroughly suburban bird in the East, but in its native West, it is found in undisturbed desert habitats as well. This species appears to be developing migratory behavior in the East, with a general movement toward the South in winter.

Feeding

Most of the house finch's diet is vegetarian, and it spends a great deal of time feeding on the ground. Weed seeds, buds, and fruits are its mainstays away from feeding stations.

Nesting

House finch nests are shallow twig platforms with a finely woven inner cup composed of rootlets, grass, feathers, and string. They are tucked into dense ornamental evergreens, hanging baskets, ledges, ivy-covered walls, and other nooks where there is an overhanging structure. Two to five eggs are incubated by the female, while the male feeds her. Young are fed regurgitated seeds and fledge from 12 to 16 days later.

Backyard & Beyond

For most feeding station proprietors, the question is not how to attract house finches, but how to discourage them. Even attractive birds with pleasant songs wear out their welcome when they descend in dozens, monopolizing feeders. Black-oil sunflower seeds are a favorite, closely followed by Niger and mixed seeds. Some people resort to removing perches from tube feeders, thus discouraging house finches, which are poor clingers.

Purple Finch

Carpodacus purpureus

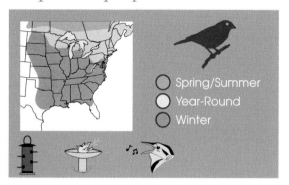

○ Spring/Summer
○ Year-Round
○ Winter

T he male purple finch is a rich raspberry-red (not purple) color and is often confused with the much more common male house finch (which is orange- or brick-red). Purple finches travel in flocks during the non-breeding seasons, and may descend on feeding stations for a few hours or weeks as they roam in search of a winter food source.

All About

"Like it was dipped headfirst in raspberry wine" is how many bird watchers describe the color of the male purple finch, and it's an apt description, because the raspberry color completely encircles the bird's upper body. On the similar male house finch, the red covers only the head, face, and breast. The house finch's back and wings are brown and streaky. Large-headed with a stout bill, the purple finch is hard to miss, often announcing its arrival with a loud *pik!* call. Their song, which is sung beginning in late winter, is a loud, rich warble delivered from a treetop perch. Females are brown-backed with dark brown and white face patterns and dark cheek patches. Their white breasts are boldly streaked with brown.

Habitat & Range

Purple finches breed in a variety of woodland habitats from cool coniferous woods to deciduous forests, orchards, and edge habitat. During migration and in winter, they can be found almost anywhere in the eastern United States from woodland edges to weedy fields and backyard feeding stations. They go wherever food is

available and purple finch "invasions" in winter are often caused by shortages of natural food supplies in the North.

Feeding

Seeds, blossoms, buds, and fruits comprise the purple finch's diet, with some insects also being consumed. Favorite food trees include elms, tulip poplars, maples, sweet gums, sycamores, and ashes. Typical foraging involves a flock of purple finches ranging amid the upper branches, grabbing and eating young buds. Sunflower seed is their preferred food at feeders.

Nesting

Female purple finches do most of the nest building after the pair chooses a site in the outer branches of a large conifer tree. She weaves together bark strips, rootlets, and twigs into a cup and lines it with animal hair and fine grass. Three to seven eggs are deposited and incubated by the female for about two weeks. Both parents feed hatchlings until fledging time, about two weeks later.

Backyard & Beyond

You may have both purple finches and house finches at your feeders, which means you have a great opportunity to learn to tell them apart. Once you see the differences in plumage (on males check the distribution of the red, on females check the facial pattern) you'll find that it's not that hard after all.

Pine Siskin

Carduelis pinus

This slender, streaky little finch is often over-looked—mistaken for a female house finch or a winter-plumaged goldfinch. But a closer look reveals a slender-billed, finely streaked finch adorned with yellow in its wings and tail.

All About

Your first clue to a pine siskin's presence may be its loud, descending *Tzeeeew!* call as a flock drops into your backyard trees. Siskins also give a rising *Zweeeeet!* sound and sing a jumbled twitter of notes similar to a goldfinch's song. Fine brown streaks cover the pine siskin's body, but as the bird moves its yellow wing stripes and tail spots flash— a surprise bit of color on this otherwise drab bird.

Habitat & Range

Across the Midwest and eastern U.S. the pine siskin is a winter visitor. It nests in the conifer-ous forests of the far North and throughout the West, but makes nearly annual appearances throughout eastern North America. During spring and summer, pine siskins are never far from conifers, alders, and the mixed woodlands in which they breed and forage. In winter, siskins often move southward—sometimes in great numbers—in search of food. They forage in weedy fields, hedgerows, pine woods, and at backyard feeding stations.

Feeding

Siskins eat grass and weed seeds, especially wild thistle seeds, plus tree buds, pine seeds, berries, and some insects. Expert clingers, siskins will hang upside down on a catkin clump, pinecone, or weed stem and pry seeds loose with their finely pointed bills. Caterpillars, insect larvae, and spiders are also consumed. At feeders, siskins relish sunflower bits (they are unable to crack open the whole seeds themselves) and thistle (Niger) seed.

Nesting

Male siskins begin courting females in late winter, before reaching their breeding grounds, as the winter feeding flocks are dispersing. Siskins are known to nest in loose colonies in conifer or mixed conifer-deciduous forests. The female builds the cup-shaped nest out of weed stems, grasses, bark strips, vines, and rootlets and lines it with soft material such as animal fur, feathers, thistledown, or moss. She lays three to five eggs and incubates them for about two weeks, during which time the male may bring her food. Both parents feed the nestlings, which leave the nest about 15 days after hatching.

Backyard & Beyond

Add a thistle feeder and seed to your backyard offerings and you'll increase your chances of attracting siskins. Sunflower bits are another attractant, as is a source of open, moving water. Listen for the sharp, zippy calls of siskin flocks as they fly over. And be sure to look carefully at your flocks of drab winter goldfinches—a siskin may be accompanying them.

American Goldfinch

Carduelis tristis

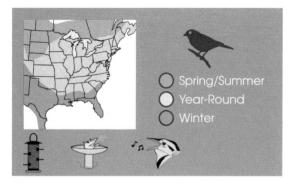

- ○ Spring/Summer
- ○ Year-Round
- ○ Winter

The bright canary-yellow and black plumage of the breeding male American goldfinch has earned this species the nickname "wild canary." It is a familiar visitor to bird feeders at all seasons, especially in winter. The goldfinch's undulating flight is accompanied by a twittering call of perchickoree or potato chip!

All About

American goldfinches appear very different in summer and winter. The male's brilliant yellow body and black cap in summer give way to a drab, olive-brown plumage in winter. Female goldfinches, though never bright yellow, also lose most of their color. Both sexes retain their black wings and tail year-round. The sweet, high-pitched, warbling song of the male is often given in early spring, just as these small (5 inches long) birds are beginning to show their first bright yellow feathers.

Habitat & Range

Weedy fields, brushy woodland edges, and open habitats with scattered shrubs are the American goldfinch's normal habitats. In the breeding season, they prefer weedy fields with thistles and other seed-producing plants. In winter, goldfinches roam in noisy flocks, seeking food in fields, gardens, and at feeding stations.

Feeding

Goldfinches are seedeaters in all seasons, consuming a huge variety of weed, grass, and plant seeds as well as tree buds. In goldfinch nests par-asitized by brown-headed cowbirds, young cowbirds are unable to survive the all-seed diet fed to nestling goldfinches. Goldfinches are agile birds, able to exploit seed sources that other finches cannot, by hanging upside down from seedheads, plant stalks, and bird feeders.

Nesting

Goldfinches' nesting season begins late, a timing adaptation so that nesting occurs when there is the greatest natural abundance of seeds, as well as the soft thistle down that goldfinches use to line their nests. Late June is the earliest nesting time, but peak nesting season is late July, though some nesting occurs as late as September. The nest site is in a shaded spot in a sapling or shrub and is selected by the pair. The female builds the open-cup nest from twigs (attached with spider web), rootlets, and plant stems, and she lines it with soft thistle down or a similarly soft material. Four to six eggs are incubated by the female for about two weeks, with the male bringing food to her on the nest. Both parents tend the nestlings for 12 to 17 days before they fledge.

Backyard & Beyond

The twittering calls of goldfinches will alert you to the presence of these energetic songbirds. At bird feeders, goldfinches especially like thistle seeds (sometimes called Niger seeds), sunflower seeds and bits, and peanut bits. Goldfinches love to drink and bathe in shallow birdbaths and are especially attracted to moving water.

House Sparrow

Passer domesticus

Introduced to North America in the early 1850s from England to help control wireworms, the house sparrow population spread across the continent in just 50 years. The house sparrow enjoys a close association with humans, almost always nesting and living in proximity to our settlements. It is one of the world's most successful and widespread species.

All About

The chunky little house sparrow is known for its constant *cha-deep, cha-deep* calls and for the male's black bib in breeding plumage. Breeding males have a black bill and a contrasting black, gray, and brown head and face pattern. Winter males are a muted version of the breeding plumage. Females are drab gray-brown overall and lack the bib. House sparrows are constantly chirping and are aggressive competitors at feeders and nest sites.

Habitat & Range

House sparrows are year-round residents. It's easier to describe where you *won't* find house sparrows because they are utterly ubiquitous. Pristine natural habitats—forest, grassland, or desert—that are lacking human development will also lack house sparrows. Historically, the house sparrow associated with horses (and the seeds and insects in their droppings) and other livestock. Today, house sparrows are found in the most urban of habitats, living on food scraps and nesting in building crevices—though they are still a common inhabitant of horse barns, farmyards, and feedlots.

Feeding

Seeds and grains will be on the house sparrow's normal menu throughout the year. In spring and summer, they take advantage of bountiful insect populations. At any time, house sparrows are quick to take food at bird feeders or scraps of food offered directly or indirectly by humans in parks, picnic areas, fast food restaurants, and strip malls. Cracked corn, sunflower seeds, peanut bits, and bread products are favorite foods.

Nesting

Males choose a cavity and sing by it to attract the female. Both build the messy nest of grass, weed stems, feathers, paper, and string. House sparrows will appropriate nest boxes from bluebirds, swallows, and purple martins (forcing many nest box landlords to use controls and special housing to discourage house sparrows), and they may even kill nest box competitors. The female lays between three and six eggs, which are incubated by both parents for 10 or more days. The parents share feeding duties until the nestlings are ready to fledge at about two weeks.

Backyard & Beyond

House sparrows are feeding station regulars, especially in towns and cities. To discourage house sparrows from dominating nest boxes, use boxes with interiors less than 5 inches deep, remove their nesting material regularly, and place nest boxes far from buildings and thick shrubbery.

Solutions for Common Feeding Problems

Lack of Birds

- During spring and summer, the diet of many of our seed-eating feeder visitors shifts to a greater reliance on insects, fruits, and other natural, abundant food sources. Even during the traditional fall and winter bird-feeding seasons, birds may not immediately find a feeding station. Once the first chickadee, goldfinch, or titmouse "tunes in" to your feeders, the word will spread quickly and other birds will show up. Temporary loss of birds at a feeder can be caused by the presence of a hawk, a cat, or by stale birdseed.

Discouraging Squirrels

- It is a battle that has been going on for nearly a century: humans trying to keep squirrels from getting to bird feeders. There are many squirrel-proof feeders available, but squirrels figure out many of these after a time. Placing your feeders on baffled poles far from any tree, deck railing, or other potential launching pad that a squirrel could use seems to be the most successful strategy. Alternatively, offer the furry menaces some cracked corn (or ears of field corn) far away from your feeders. Keep squirrels happy elsewhere, and you may keep them off your feeders.

Blackbirds, Pigeons, Jays, and Sparrows

- Certain birds can hog all the space and food at your feeders to the exclusion of the smaller, less aggressive species. You can limit the impact of these "feeder hogs" by removing their preferred food from the menu. For blackbirds, pigeons, and doves, limit the cracked corn and mixed seed; for jays and crows, limit the suet, peanuts, cracked corn, and table scraps; for sparrows, limit the cracked corn and do not feed bread. Larger birds (such as grackles, rock pigeons, and blue jays) can also be discouraged through the use of small tube feeders with short perches—small birds can use 'em, but big birds can't.

Hawk at Feeders

- Cooper's hawks and sharp-shinned hawks are songbird specialists that can be attracted to the bird activity at your feeders. Their tactic is a quick surprise attack, scattering the feeder visitors and perhaps catching a slow, sick, or unwary individual. As unpleasant as it may seem, it is perfectly natural and is an important aspect of nature's balance.

Cat at Feeders

- Place your feeders a short distance away from thick cover where hunting cats might lurk. Mount your feeders high enough (above 4 feet) that a leaping cat cannot reach feeding birds. A circle of short (1-foot-high) wire fencing can make it more difficult for charging cats to catch birds.

Night Marauders

- If your feeders empty out overnight, you probably have a mammal making nocturnal visits to your feeder. This furry critter could be a raccoon, an opossum, a flying squirrel, deer, or even a bear! Feed only as much seed as can be eaten by your birds during a single day, and you'll discourage these late-night diners.

Sick Bird at Feeders

- Sick birds often show up at feeders, desperate for an easy meal, and they usually succumb to their illness within a short while. Although most bird illnesses are not transferable to humans, it pays to be cautious. Contact your local wildlife officials about any sick birds you see at your feeders—they often monitor wildlife health trends. If you find a dead bird, avoid making direct contact with it (wear gloves or use a plastic bag to pick it up), and bury it or discard it in the trash. Clean your feeders thoroughly and consider halting your feeding for a few days to allow the healthy birds to disperse temporarily.

Food and Feeder Chart

Species	Food
Quail, pheasants	Cracked corn, millet, wheat, milo
Pigeons, doves	Millet, cracked corn, wheat, milo, Niger (thistle seed), buckwheat, sunflower, baked goods
Hummingbirds	Plant nectar, small insects, sugar solution
Woodpeckers	Suet, meat scraps, sunflower hearts/seed, cracked corn, peanuts, fruits, sugar solution, mealworms
Jays	Peanuts, sunflower, suet, meat scraps, cracked corn, baked goods
Crows	Meat scraps, suet, cracked corn, peanuts, baked goods, leftovers, dog food
Titmice, chickadees	Peanut kernels, sunflower, suet, peanut butter, mealworms
Nuthatches	Suet, suet mixes, sunflower hearts and seed, peanut kernels, peanut butter, mealworms
Wrens, creepers	Suet, suet mixes, peanut butter, peanut kernels, bread, fruit, millet (wrens), mealworms
Mockingbirds, thrashers, catbirds	Halved apples, chopped fruit, mealworms, suet, nutmeats, millet (thrashers), soaked raisins, currants, sunflower hearts
Robins, bluebirds, other thrushes	Suet, suet mixes, mealworms, berries, baked goods, chopped fruit, soaked raisins, currants, nutmeats, sunflower hearts
Kinglets	Suet, suet mixes, baked goods, mealworms
Waxwings	Berries, chopped fruit, canned peas, currants, dry raisins
Warblers	Suet, suet mixes, fruit, baked goods, sugar solution, chopped nutmeats
Tanagers	Suet, fruit, sugar solution, mealworms, baked goods
Cardinals, grosbeaks	Sunflower, safflower, cracked corn, millet, fruit
Towhees, juncos	Millet, sunflower, cracked corn, peanuts, baked goods, nutmeats, mealworms
Sparrows, buntings	Millet, sunflower hearts, black-oil sunflower, cracked corn, baked goods
Blackbirds, starlings	Cracked corn, milo, wheat, table scraps, baked goods, suet
Orioles	Halved oranges, apples, berries, sugar solution, grape jelly, suet mixes, soaked raisins, dry mealworms, currants
Finches, siskins	Thistle (Niger), sunflower hearts, black-oil sunflower seed, millet, canary seed, fruit, peanut kernels, suet mixes

Nest Box Chart

Species	Interior Floor Size of Box (inches)	Interior Height of Box (inches)	Entrance Hole Diameter (inches)	Box Mounting Height (feet)	Habitat for Box Placement
Chickadees	4x4	9–12	$1^1/8 - 1^1/2$	5–15	Open woods and edges
Prothonotary Warbler	4x4	12	$1^1/4$	5–12	Wooded areas, swamps and streams
Titmice	4x4	12	$1^1/2$	5–12	Wooded areas and edge habitat
White-breasted Nuthatch	4x4	12	$1^1/2$	5–12	Wooded areas and edge habitat
Carolina Wren	4x4	9–12	$1-1^1/2$	5–10	Old fields and thickets
Eastern Bluebird	4x4	12	$1^1/2$	5–6	Open land with scattered trees
Tree Swallow	5x5	10–12	$1^1/2$	5–10	Open land near pond or lake
Purple Martin	6x6	6	$2^1/8$	15–25	Open country near water
Great-crested Flycatcher	6x6	12	$1^3/4 - 2$	6–20	Open woods and edges
House Finch	5x5	10	$1^1/2$	5–10	Backyards and porches
Downy Woodpecker	4x4	12	$1^1/2$	5–20	Forest openings and edges
Hairy Woodpecker	6x6	14	$1^1/2$	8–20	Forest openings and edges
Red-bellied Woodpecker	6x6	14	2	8–20	Forest openings and edges

Nest Box Chart

Species	Interior Floor Size of Box (inches)	Interior Height of Box (inches)	Entrance Hole Diameter (inches)	Box Mounting Height (feet)	Habitat for Box Placement
Red-headed Woodpecker	6x6	14	2	8–20	Forest openings and edges
Northern Flicker	7x7	16–24	2$\frac{1}{2}$	10–20	Farmland, open country
Pileated Woodpecker	12x12	24	4	15–25	Mature forest
Bufflehead	7x7	17	3	5–15	Wooded lakeshores, swamps
Wood Duck	12x12	24	3x4 oval	5–20	Wooded swamps, bottomland
Hooded Merganser	12x12	24	3x4 oval	5–30	Wooded swamps, bottomland
Goldeneyes	12x12	24	3$\frac{1}{4}$x4$\frac{1}{4}$ oval	15–20	Wooded lakeshores, swamps
Common Merganser	12x12	24	5x6 oval	8–20	Wooded lakeshores, swamps
Saw-whet Owl	7x7	12	2$\frac{1}{2}$	8–20	Forest clearings and edges
Eastern Screech-owl	8x8	18	3	8–30	Farmland, orchards, woods
Barred Owl	14x14	28	8	15–30	Mature bottom-land forest
Barn Owl	12x36	16	6x7 oval	15–30	Open farmland, marshes
American Kestrel	9x9	16–18	3	12–30	Farmland

A Glossary of Common Bird Terms

- **Avifauna:** The community of birds found in a given region or habitat type.

- **Cavity nester:** A bird that nests inside an enclosed area such as a hollow tree, an old woodpecker hole, or a bird house.

- **Crown:** The top of a bird's head.

- **Diurnal:** Active during daylight hours.

- **Edge habitat:** A place where two or more habitats come together, such as where woodland meets an old meadow. Edge habitat typically offers a rich diversity of birds.

- **Endemic:** A breeding species that is unique to a given geographical region.

- **Extinct:** A bird that no longer exists in the wild. The Carolina parakeet is an example of an extinct species.

- **Extirpated:** A bird that once was present in a given area but no longer is. It does exist in other areas, however. For example, the red-cockaded woodpecker has been extirpated from much of its original range throughout the South, but remains in small pockets of its former range.

- **Eyeline:** Refers to a line of contrasting colored feathers over or through a bird's eye, often used as a field mark for identification.

- **Field mark:** An obvious visual clue to a bird's identification. Field guides are based on describing field marks of birds.

- **Fledgling:** A bird that has left the nest, but may still be receiving care and feeding from a parent.

- **Hotspot:** A location or habitat that is particularly good for bird watching on a regular basis.

- **Juvenile/Juvenal:** *Juvenile* (noun) refers to a bird that has not yet reached breeding age. *Juvenal* is an adjective, referring to the plumage that a juvenile bird wears.

- **Life bird:** A bird seen by a bird watcher for the first time is a life bird. Life birds are usually recorded on a birder's life list, a record of all the birds he or she has seen at least once.

- **Lores:** The area between a bird's bill and its eyes.

- **Migrant:** A bird that travels from one region to another in response to changes of season, breeding cycles, food availability, or extreme weather. Many of our warbler species that spend the spring and summer in North America *migrate* to Central or South America for the winter.

- **Mimic:** A term used to describe birds that imitate other sounds and songs. Three common bird species are mimics: the northern mockingbird, gray catbird, and brown thrasher.

- **Nape:** The back of a bird's neck, often referred to in reference to a field mark for identification.

- **Neotropical migrant:** Refers to migratory birds of the New World, primarily those that travel seasonally between North, Central, and South America.

- **Nestling:** A bird that is still being cared for in the nest.

A Glossary of Common Bird Terms

- **Peeps:** A generic term for groups of confusingly similar small sandpipers.

- **Pishing (or spishing):** A sound made by bird watchers to attract curious birds into the open. Most often made by repeating the sounds *spshhh* or *pshhh* through clenched teeth.

- **Plumage:** Collective reference to a bird's feathers, which can change both color and shape through the process of seasonal molt. During a molt, a bird loses some or most of its old worn-out feathers and grows new healthy feathers to replace them. Breeding plumage is worn by birds during the breeding season and this is often when a bird is at its most colorful. Non-breeding or winter plumage is worn during fall and winter, generally, and is often less colorful than breeding plumage.

- **Primary feathers (primaries):** The long flight feathers originating from the "hand," or end, of a bird's wing.

- **Raptor:** A term used to refer to a bird of prey, including hawks, owls, osprey, and vultures.

- **Resident:** A non-migratory species—one that is present in the same region all year.

- **Spotting scope:** A single tube optical device mounted on a tripod and used to look at distant birds. Most birding scopes are between 15x and 60x in magnification power.

- **Suet:** The large chunks of hard, white fat that form around the kidneys of beef cattle. Suet is used by bird watchers as a high-energy winter food for birds.

- **Tail spot:** Spots, usually white, on a bird's tail, often used as a field mark for identification.

- **Underparts:** A term referring to the lower half of a bird (breast, belly, undertail), often used in relation to a field mark.

- **Upperparts:** A term referring to the upper half of a bird (crown, back, top of tail), often used in relation to a field mark.

- **Vagrant:** A bird that wanders far from its normal range.

- **Wing bars:** Obvious areas of contrasting color, usually whitish, across the outer surface of a bird's wings.

Frequently Asked Questions

General

Q. There is a bird in my backyard that not only sings throughout the day, but also *all night long!* This particular bird has many, many songs. Do you have any idea what kind of bird this is?

A. Your bird is most likely a northern mockingbird. Don't worry, male mockingbirds only perform this nocturnal singing in the spring and summer, during the time of the full moon. Try running an electric fan (to create a buffer of sound) or using your earplugs on those nights when the male mockingbird is singing. Having a mocker around is a good thing—some would even consider you lucky!

Q. A female robin recently built a nest in a tree on my patio. On May 10, she started laying her eggs—four in total. How long before they hatch, and how long after that do they still need the nest?

A. Robins incubate their eggs for 12 to 14 days. Once hatched, the nestlings remain in the nest for another 14 to 16 days before fledging. Two weeks is normally the incubation period for most songbirds. Another two weeks is an average time before the young leave the nest.

Q. Many times I have seen hawks being mobbed by American crows. Is this a common phenomenon, and why does it occur?

A. Mobbing behavior by crows is common. The crows are reacting to the potential threat that the hawk poses as a predator to the adult crows and their offspring. The mobbing often serves to harass the hawk into leaving the area. Occasionally, a mobbed hawk will turn the tables and attack and kill a crow.

Q. A woodpecker is pecking holes in my house siding. Is there anything I can do to get it to stop?

A. A woodpecker drilling on your wooden house is only doing what comes naturally—drilling into wood in search of shelter or food. Most house-wrecking woodpeckers do their damage in fall, which is when they begin making their winter roost holes. Try mounting a nest box with an appropriately sized hole over the drilled area. Fill the house with wood chips, and you may divert the bird's attention and gain a tenant.

Woodpeckers also use wood and sometimes metal parts of houses as drumming sites. They drill their bills against the surface in a rapid staccato beat. This drumming noise is a territorial announcement and a method for attracting a mate. Drumming happens most regularly in spring. There are several things you can try; one of them may work.

1. Place some sheet metal or heavy aluminum foil over the area the bird is using.

2. Hang some aluminum pie plates around the affected area. Make sure they move in the wind (to scare the bird away).

3. Place a rubber snake near the drilling area (to scare the bird away).

4. Repeatedly frighten the bird by yelling or clapping when it lands on your house.

5. If nothing else works, call your local wildlife official to see if someone can come to your house to remove the offending bird.

Q. Is seeing a robin a true sign of spring's arrival? Where do they go in winter?

A. American robins are surprisingly hardy as long as they have access to their winter food sources: fruits. They switch over in winter from their mostly insect-based summer diet. As such, robins are *facultative migrants*. This means that they will migrate only as far south as they need to or are forced to by bad weather or food shortages. During ice storms, when fruits are covered in a thick coating of ice, many robins flock together and move south. In the same way, if a robin spends the winter in your region, it's probably because there's enough food to see it through.

The idea that robins are the first true sign of spring is somewhat mythical. In much of northern North America, a few robins overwinter, but they stick to woods and thickets where they can find fruit. Most backyard bird watchers do notice the robins' return when these birds appear on lawns with the onset of warm weather, seeking their warm-weather food: earthworms, grubs, caterpillars, and other insects.

Q. Do all birds mate for life?

A. No. Some species have unusually strong pair bonds between mated birds. These species include some eagles, cranes, swans, geese, and ravens. Being mated "for life" means, really, for as long as both birds are alive. When one of the pair dies, the other will take a new mate. Most North American bird species pair up primarily to reproduce, and then go their separate ways soon after they have nested. In some species, the pair bond is brief. In the case of ruby-throated hummingbirds, the pair bond lasts only as long as courtship and copulation. The male has nothing to do with the incubation or raising of the young birds.

Q. Do all birds migrate?

A. Not all bird species migrate, but most do. Migration in North America is defined as the seasonal movement of birds, northward in spring from the wintering grounds, and southward in fall from the breeding grounds. Among the birds that are *resident*, or that do not migrate, are many grouse, ptarmigan, and quail species; many owl species; pileated, red-bellied, downy, and hairy woodpeckers along with white-breasted nuthatch, Carolina wren, northern cardinal, wrentit, ring-necked pheasant, Townsend's solitaire, common raven, gray jay, and northern mockingbird.

Bird Care

Q. Is it true that if you find a baby bird out of the nest, you should not touch it because the parent birds will detect your scent and abandon the nest?

A. No, most birds do not have a well-developed sense of smell. However, most mammalian predators (skunks, foxes, raccoons, weasels, and so forth) do have a good sense of smell and may follow your scent trail to a bird's nest. If you are going to handle a baby bird be sure to place it out of harm's way, back in the nest or in an open-topped cardboard box propped in a tree. Many bird species are equipped to survive outside the nest at a very young age. These species include many shorebirds, gamebirds, and birds such as robins and wrens.

Q. If I find a baby bird that has fallen from a nest, what should I do?

A. Try to place the nestling back in its nest if at all possible. This will be the baby bird's best chance at a normal life. If you can't find the nest or a place to put the nestling out of harm's way, you will need to get the bird to a licensed rehabilitator as soon as possible.

Baby birds are unable to *thermoregulate* (regulate their body temperature), and so must be kept in a protected area with a heat source. A soft nest made of tissues inside a small cardboard box, placed on a heating pad set on LOW temperature, is a good example of a temporary home. A moist sponge placed in the box will add a touch of desired humidity. This will warm the bird.

Try to contact a wildlife rehabilitator as soon as possible. Your state fish and wildlife officers are responsible for licensing and regulating the activities of rehabilitators and have listings for those in your region. Make sure anyone else giving you advice is familiar and current with the specialized needs of wildlife.

Q. I found an injured bird. What should I do with it?

A. A person must have special permits from the federal, state, or provincial government to handle injured or dead non-game bird species. While your first instinct may be to call your local veterinarian, many vets are unwilling to care for "wildlife cases." In many situations, the best thing to do is to let nature take its course. Birds and other creatures are part of nature's natural cycle of life and death. An injured or dead bird may be a meal for another animal. If you feel you *must* do something to help an injured bird, call your local wildlife office, department of the environment, fish and game, or extension office. Your local vet may take rehabilitation cases—or may know of a licensed rehabilitator in your area.

Window Strikes

Q. A bird is flying from window to window, butting its head against the glass while looking into the house. Can you explain this behavior?

A. Your bird is fighting its reflection in the windows, thinking that the reflection is a rival bird. The behavior will last through the breeding season. One solution is to place screens over the outside of the window. Plastic wrap stuck to the outside will also work—anything that will break up the reflection will do. You may also offer your bluebirds places to perch, such as snags and posts, far from windows. Bluebirds love a perch in the middle of a lawn or field. This has worked to distract the birds from windows.

Q. How can I keep birds from flying into my windows?

A. Silhouettes of flying hawks or falcons do work, but they perform best when applied on the outside of the glass. Hanging ornaments such as wind chimes, wind socks, and potted plants also helps. Misting the outside of the window with a very weak detergent or soda solution will eliminate the reflection, but will also impair visibility for you. Awnings, eave extensions, and window screens will eliminate reflection and stop the collision problem. Plastic cling wrap applied to the outside of the window can also be effective. One of the most effective solutions we have found is FeatherGuard, a series of bright-colored feathers strung on fishing line and hung over the outside surface of the glass.

Bird Feeding

Q. What is the best seed to offer birds?

A. Black-oil sunflower seed is the most universally eaten seed at bird feeders. But there are many other seeds and foods to offer birds. What is most popular with your birds depends on where you live and what birds are present.

Q. What is the best feeder for bird feeding?

A. There is no single best feeder for bird feeding. A well-rounded feeding operation will include a platform feeder, a tube feeder, a hopper feeder, a suet feeder, and a peanut feeder. And don't forget the birdbath!

Q. I recently purchased a bird feeder, but have yet to see any birds. What am I doing wrong?

A. You're not doing anything wrong. It takes time for birds to locate a new feeding source. A spell of bad weather always drives birds to concentrate at feeders. Try putting your feeder in a new location far from your house and the portion of your yard where you are active. Put the feeder in or near a tree that the birds regularly use.

Q. Do birds that eat at feeders lose their ability to find food naturally? If I stop feeding them, will they starve?

A. No. Birds are not totally reliant on the food offered at your feeding station. Birds are programmed by instinct to forage for food, and they have evolved over millions of years to be very mobile in their food-finding habits. Because they can fly, birds are efficient at going to where the food is. Though feeding stations have been linked to slightly improved survival rates for birds in harsh weather conditions, overall bird feeding does not drastically affect the birds' survival. Also, when warmer weather comes, many of the seed-eating birds that frequented your feeders during winter switch to an insect-based diet in spring.

Q. How do I keep squirrels away from my bird feeders?

A. Baffling your feeders (preventing squirrels from gaining access to the feeders) is the best way. Feeders can be strung from a thin wire, far from any object from which the squirrels can leap. String the wire with empty 35mm film canisters (with the lids on) or short lengths of 1-inch PVC pipe, which will spin and dump the squirrels off. There are many squirrel-proof feeders on the market. These may give the squirrels a small electric shock, may prevent them from reaching the seed, or may rotate or bounce to dump the squirrels off. But be forewarned: Squirrels have been known to outsmart the most ingenious of the squirrel-proof inventions.

And if you can't beat 'em, join 'em! Feed squirrels ears of dried corn, but place the corn away from your bird feeders. Given the choice, squirrels will always go for the easiest food, and they *love* corn.

Q. What can I do to protect the birds in my yard from cats?

A. Hang feeders at least 5 feet above the ground. For ground-feeding birds, arrange ornamental border fencing in two or three concentric circles about 16 inches to 2 feet apart, to disrupt a cat's ability to leap at feeders or to spring on birds. Harass offending cats with a spray of water to train them to avoid your yard. If all else fails, use a live trap to catch the cats and take them to the local animal shelter. If the cats belong to your neighbors, ask them to restrain their pets from accessing your yard.

Hummingbirds

Q. What is the best ratio of water to sugar to use for feeding hummingbirds?

A. Four parts water to one part sugar (a 4:1 ratio) has been shown to be the closest to the sucrose content of natural flower nectar. Concentrations stronger than this (such as a 3:1 ratio or stronger) are readily consumed by hummers, but no scientific evidence exists regarding the potential helpful or harmful effects on hummingbirds.

Q. Can I use molasses or honey instead of sugar to make my hummingbird nectar?

A. No. White table sugar is the only human-made sweetener that, when mixed with the right amount of water, closely resembles natural flower nectar. Resist the urge to use other sweeteners, which spoil quickly and may not be good for hummingbirds to consume.

Q. Is the red dye found in premixed solutions bad for hummingbirds?

A. Though no conclusive scientific evidence exists showing harmful effects of red food dye on hummingbirds, this chemical additive is certainly not a necessary ingredient in hummingbird solution.

Many commercially available brands of hummingbird solution contain red food coloring that is meant to be attractive both to hummingbirds and to shopping bird watchers. Brightly colored flowers are nature's way of attracting the eye of a foraging hummingbird, so the red solution in feeders is aimed at attracting hummingbirds. Bright red feeder parts (which most hummer feeders have) or a bright red ribbon hung near the feeder can be just as attractive as red-dyed solution. Red dye or food coloring may or may not be harmful to hummingbirds, but it is completely unnecessary.

Q. How do I foil a "bully" hummer?

A. Many hummingbird species defend feeding territories, and assemblages at feeders usually develop hierarchies. The behavior exemplifies natural selection at work, and you should do nothing except enjoy it.

If you're worried about hungry hummers, put up several more feeders near your original one. The bully will be overwhelmed by the sheer numbers of other birds and will quit being so territorial.

Q. Do hummingbirds migrate on the backs of Canada geese?

A. No. This is either a Native American myth or just an old wives' tale. Hummingbirds are excellent, strong-flying migrants. A healthy ruby-throated hummingbird can easily handle the 500-mile flight across the Gulf of Mexico.

Q. Is it true that hummingbirds at my feeder will not migrate if I leave my feeder up in the fall?

A. No. This is another in a long line of bird myths. Birds are genetically programmed to migrate when their internal "clocks" tell them to do so. They will depart when the time is right—whether your feeders are up or not. However, leaving your feeders up in fall, and getting them up early in spring may help early or late migrants that are passing through your area.

How to Build a Simple Birdhouse

These plans are designed to help you build a simple birdhouse—one that is easy to put together and will attract a number of species. The 1½-inch entrance hole will allow birds as large as bluebirds to enter the house, but even tiny house wrens and chickadees will find this house appealing.

Before you begin the building process, read through this entire plan. This will make the building go more smoothly and should prevent costly, frustrating errors. Study the instructions and drawings together. The letters in the instructions refer to the drawing that illustrates a particular section of directions.

Now, let's look at materials. Cedar will last, but it can be expensive. Pound for pound, cedar is the most durable, weather resistant, and provides the best insulation—so if your budget permits it, cedar is the best wood to use for birdhouses. After years of weather, nails in cedar can become loose, so I suggest using screws in place of nails for cedar construction. Pine is easy to nail and does not split easily, but it will decay unless preservatives are used (on the outside of the box only).

An excellent alternative material is ⅝-inch thick exterior plywood. It is tough, weathers well, and will not split along the edge if you use nails of the proper size, usually four-penny galvanized box nails. Called T 1-11, this wood has vertical grooves to resemble boards and is often used for exterior siding on homes. Most lumber yards and home centers sell T 1-11 in large 4-x-8-foot sheets. When assembling a birdhouse using exterior plywood, always remember to keep the weather surface of the wood on the outside of the birdhouse. It is an obvious point, but one that is easily forgotten in the midst of the building process.

Unless otherwise instructed, use four-penny galvanized box nails for nailing house parts together. Remember to use screws when using cedar or pine or when you feel extra strong binding is necessary.

It's impossible to predict which bird species is most apt to settle in your new birdhouse. Half a dozen cavity-nesting birds prefer a box with a single slant roof and a 1½-inch-diameter entrance. Depending on your location, it could be tree swallows, hairy or downy woodpeckers, or perhaps titmice, chickadees, Carolina or house wrens, or even bluebirds.

Good luck with your building—and with being a landlord to the birds!

Materials:
western red cedar, exterior plywood, or T 1-11
   siding scraps (⅝ inch thick, 31 × 14 inches),
   which will be cut into the following pieces:
bottom: 5 × 5 inches
sides (cut 2): each 10 × 9 × 5 inches
back: 12 × 6¼ inches
front: 9½ × 6¼ inches
roof: 8¼ × 8¼ inches
four-penny galvanized box nails
right-angle screw hook, about 1½ inches long
caulking compound
sixteen-penny galvanized framing nails
2 galvanized siding nails (or wood screws),
   1¾ inches long

Tools:

square	2 C clamps (optional)
ruler	rasp
pencil	hammer
saw	wood blocks of
plane	various sizes
drill or brace,	drill, with assorted
with 1½-inch	small bits
expansion bit	
and ½-inch	
diameter bit	

Instructions:

1. On the weather surface of the plywood, measure and mark with a pencil the exact outlines of each piece. Be sure the grain of the wood runs vertically on the two side pieces, the back, and the front. The T 1-11 siding has a vertical groove running down it. This won't hurt anything—but when laying out the parts, keep the groove away from the edge of each piece to avoid problems with nailing later on.

2. Lay out the two side pieces with a common line along the 9-inch dimension so that the tops angle toward the center line, making a shallow V. In this way, when you assemble the house, the weather surface will end up on the outside.

3. After checking the measurements once more, carefully saw or cut out all the parts. Trim the rough edges with a plane to knock off splinters. You won't need to sand anything—this is going to be rustic!

4. Lay the parts on the workbench and mark them, just to keep track. There are six parts— two sides, a roof, a bottom, a front, and a back.

5. To accommodate the roof slant, you will need to bevel the top edges of the front and back panels with a plane. Set the two pieces in front of you, just as they will be when assembled. On the weather surface of the front panel and on the inside surface of the back, draw a horizontal line $1/8$ inch down from the top. Then bevel off $1/8$ inch from each piece individually.

6. On the front panel, center a vertical line running 3 inches down from the top. Put a cross

A Simple Birdhouse

Note: Dimensions are in inches

mark on the line, $13/4$ inches from the top. Open the expansion bit to precisely $11/2$ inches, then test it on a scrap board and measure the hole. Now, to ensure a clean cut, clamp the panel tightly to a board. Center the bit on the cross mark and drill the hole. (If you have no C clamps, lay the panel on a board and drill halfway. Turn it over and drill through the other side.) Round off the sharp edges with a rasp.

7. On the bottom piece, measure $3/8$ inch in on each side of each corner and mark. Place a ruler diagonally across each corner and connect the two marks. Saw off the four corners at these points. The resultant openings in the finished house will allow adequate drainage and air circulation for the birds.

8. On the back panel, with the weather side up, center a vertical line—2 inches long—down from the top. At the bottom of the line, drill a ½-inch hole.

9. Mark a line across the weather surface of both side panels, 1 inch up from the bottom. On the right panel, extend the bottom line across the edges. Mark a line across the face of the front panel, 1 inch up from the bottom. It, too, should extend across the edges.

10. Now, mark a line across the weather surface on the back panel, 2½ inches up from the bottom, and extend it across the edges.

B

1. You are now ready to start putting things together. Lay the right-hand side panel (the one on the right when the entrance of the completed birdhouse faces you), weather surface up, on the bench. Start two nails, each 1½ inches in from the edge and ¼ inch below the bottom line. Drive them in until they barely peek through the other side. Be sure they are straight.

2. Place the bottom panel (weather side toward you) on edge and at a right angle to the bench, against a flat wall or solid surface. (When the corners are cut off, it is easier to get the side and bottom flush when both are pressed against a flat wall.) Lay the right side panel (weather side out) across the upper edge of the bottom piece, matching the line on the side panel with the interior surface of the bottom. (Place a block under the other end of the right panel.) Drive the nails in part way—just enough to hold.

C

1. Turn the assembled pieces over so the right side faces you. Place two nails in the weather surface of the back panel, ¼ inch below the line you marked earlier and 1½ inches from the ends of the bottom panel. Drive them in until they begin to show on the other side.

2. Put the back piece on the two pieces that you assembled. Make sure that the lines marked on the bottom match, and that the edges are flush with the outside of the side panel.

B.

C.

How to Build a Simple Birdhouse

D.

3. Drive the nail into the bottom, nearest the side panel, enough to hold. Start another nail along the edge of the back panel, 2 inches down from the top and about 1/4 inch from the edge. Check to see that the back panel edge and the side are flush. Drive the nail in part way.

4. Now check the bottom. Its outer corner may be sprung slightly. Press it into alignment with the back panel marks, hold, and drive the other bottom nail in part way. Check it over to see if the bottom is lined up. If so, place one more nail along the edge, 4 inches up from the bottom of the back panel, and drive in all the nails.

D

1. Turn the unit on its back. Lay out the front panel, weather side up—racing stripe dazzling your eyes—and start two nails 1/4 inch below the bottom line and 1 1/2 inches in from each edge. Be sure the points have just come through the other side.

2. Put the front in place, matching the lines marked at the bottom with the interior surface of the bottom panel. There should be about a 1/2-inch gap at the top of the right side when the roof is on.

3. Drive the nail into the bottom, nearest the enclosed side, until the nail holds. Then start a nail 2 inches down from the top of the front panel and 1/4 inch in from the edge. Make sure that the front panel edge and the side are flush. Drive the nail in part way. Spring the bottom corner into alignment, and drive the nail near the open edge part way into the bottom. Start another, 2 inches up from the bottom, and drive it in part way. If everything looks good, pound in all the nails.

E.

E

1. Fit the left-hand side panel into position. If it is tight, plane down the edge for a looser fit. You want this "door" to open easily even when the wood swells in wet weather, so you can inspect the nest and clean out the house at the season's end.

2. Check for about a ¹/₂-inch gap at the top. Drive two nails—one into the bottom and one into the front, halfway up—part way in to hold temporarily. (They will be removed later.)

3. On the left edge of the front panel, make a mark 1 inch from the top. Using a square, draw a horizontal line across the left side panel on the mark. At one end of this line, drive a nail through the front panel into the edge of the left panel. At the other end of the line, drive a nail through the back panel into the edge of the left panel. These nail hinges will allow the "door" to be opened.

4. Put a mark on the front panel 2 inches up from the bottom and centered over the edge of the door. Drill a small hole, about 2 inches deep, at the mark. Use a right-angle screw hook twisted into place as a lock nail. It is not likely to fall out of the hole, as a nail might, when the box is tipped forward. Remove the temporary nails and test the door.

F

1. On the roof, start two nails, each ¹/₄ inch in from the back or top edge of the roof, and about 2 inches in from the left and right sides. Remember that the roof slants, and you want the nail angled so it goes straight into the edge of the back panel. Stand the box upright with a block under the front. Run a strip of caulking compound along the top edge of the back panel. Place the top on, with the wood grain running down the slant, not across it.

2. Adjust the roof for equal overhang on each side. It should be flush with the back. Drive the nail in part way.

3. Sight along the front and drive two more nails—gingerly—into the top edge of the front panel until they hold. If it looks right, hammer them in.

G

1. Now for hanging the birdhouse. If there are predators in your area, resist the temptation to hang your house on a tree or fencepost. If your area is predator-free (and not many areas are in North America), trees or fenceposts may be acceptable. To be safe, I suggest baffling all of your bird houses.

F.

Wall

Roof

Hanger hole

Nail hinge

Back

Left side (door)

Lock

Block

Workbench

G.

Hooked on nail at back

2 nails

Bird-Friendly Plants for Your Yard

TREES

Common Name	Latin Name	Good For/Other Notes
Apples	*Malus* spp.	Fruit, insects, cavities
Ashes	*Fraxinus* spp.	Seeds, insects, cover
Aspens	*Populus* spp.	Seeds, insects, cover, cavities
Birches	*Betula* spp.	Seeds, insects, cover
Cedars	*Juniperus* spp.	Fruit, year-round cover
Cherries	*Prunus* spp.	Fruit
Chokecherry, common	*Prunus virginiana*	Fruit
Cottonwoods	*Populus* spp.	Cavities, shelter
Crabapples	*Malus* spp.	Fruit, insects
Dogwoods	*Cornus* spp.	Fruit
Firs	*Abies* spp.	Year-round cover
Hackberries	*Celtis* spp.	Fruit, cover
Hawthorns	*Crataegus* spp.	Fruit, cover, nesting
Hemlocks	*Tsuga* spp.	Seeds, insects, shelter
Hollies	*Ilex* spp.	Fruit, year-round cover
Junipers	*Juniperus* spp.	Year-round cover
Larches	*Larix* spp.	Seeds
Madrones	*Arbutus* spp.	Fruit
Maples	*Acer* spp.	Seeds, cover
Mesquites	*Prosopis* spp.	Shelter
Mountain ashes	*Sorbus* spp.	Fruit
Mulberry, red	*Morus rubra*	Fruit
Oaks	*Quercus* spp.	Acorns, cover, insects
Pines	*Pinus* spp.	Year-round cover, insects
Poplars	*Populus* spp.	Cavities, shelter
Sassafras	*Sassafras albidum*	Fruit, cover, cavities
Shadbush, or serviceberry	*Amelanchier laevis*	Fruit, flowers
Spruces	*Picea* spp.	Year-round cover
Sycamores	*Platanus* spp.	Cavities, shelter, insects
Willows	*Salix* spp.	Cavities, shelter, insects

Bird-Friendly Plants for Your Yard

SHRUBS

Common Name	Latin Name	Good For/Other Notes
Arrowwood viburnum/ Viburnums	*Viburnum dentatum/ Viburnum* spp.	Fall fruit. Tolerates shade
Bayberry, northern	*Myrica pensylvanica*	Fruit. Male & female plants needed for fruit
Blackberry, American	*Rubus allegheniensis*	Fruit, dense cover, nesting
Blueberry, highbush	*Vaccinium corymbosum*	Fruit, flowers, cover. Needs acid soil
Chokeberry, red	*Aronia arbutifolia*	Fruit. Moist soil preferred
Cranberry, highbush	*Viburnum trilobum*	Fruit. Shade tolerant
Dogwoods	*Cornus* spp.	Fall fruit, dense cover
Elderberry, American	*Sambucus canadensis*	Fruit, dense cover
Hercules' club	*Aralia spinosa*	Fruit
Hobblebush	*Viburnum alnifolium*	Fruit. Shade tolerant
Hollies, deciduous	*Ilex decidua, Ilex* spp.	Winter fruit. Male & female plants needed for fruit
Huckleberry, black	*Gaylussacia baccata*	Fruit. Sandy soil preferred
Inkberry	*Ilex glabra*	Fruit. Thicket-forming. Needs acid soil
Mahonia	*Mahonia aquifolium*	Fruit, year-round cover
Manzanitas	*Arctostaphylos* spp.	Early fruit, thick cover
Nannyberry	*Viburnum lentago*	Fruit. Shade-tolerant
Pokeweed	*Phytolacca americana*	Fall fruit.
Roses	*Rosa* spp.	Winter fruit. Summer flowers
Shadbushes	*Amelanchier* spp.	Early fruit
Spicebush	*Lindera benzoin*	Fruit. Needs moist soil
Sumacs	*Rhus* spp.	Fruit available all winter
Winterberry, common	*Ilex verticillata*	Fruit. Male & female plants needed for fruit
Yews	*Taxus* spp.	Year-round cover. Some fruit

VINES

Common Name	Latin Name	Good For/Other Notes
Ampelopsis, heartleaf	*Ampelopsis cordata*	Fruit. Resembles a grape vine
Bittersweet, American	*Celastrus scandens*	Fruit. Avoid Asian species.
Grapes, wild	*Vitis* spp.	Fruit attracts 100 species, cover

Bird-Friendly Plants for Your Yard

VINES

Common Name	Latin Name	Good For/Other Notes
Greenbriars	*Smilax* spp.	Fruit, thick cover
Trumpet honeysuckle	*Lonicera sempervirens*	Nectar, fruit, cover. Avoid Asian species
Trumpet vine	*Campsis radicans*	Nectar, summer cover
Virginia creeper	*Parthenocissus quinquefolia*	Fruit attracts 40 species

FLOWERS

Common Name	Latin Name	Good For/Other Notes
Asters	*Aster* spp.	Flowers attract butterlies, seed
Bachelor's button	*Centaurea cyanus*	Seed
Black-eyed Susan	*Rudbeckia serotina*	Seed
Blazing star	*Liatris* spp.	Seed, flowers attract butterflies
California poppy	*Eschscholzia californica*	Seed
Coneflower, purple	*Echinacea purpurea*	Seed, flowers attract butterflies
Coreopsis	*Coreopsis* spp.	Seed, flowers attract butterflies
Cornflower	*Centaurea cyanus*	Seed
Cosmos	*Cosmos* spp.	Seed
Daisy, gloriosa	*Rudbeckia* cv.	Seed
Goldenrods	*Solidago* spp.	Flowers for butterflies, winter cover
Joe-Pye weeds	*Eupaorium* spp.	Flowers for butterflies, winter cover
Marigolds	*Tagetes* spp.	Seed
Penstemons	*Penstemon* spp.	Nectar, seed
Poppies	*Papaver* spp.	Flowers attract butterflies, seed
Primroses	*Oenothera* spp.	Seed
Sedums	*Sedum* spp.	Flowers attract butterflies, seed
Sunflowers	*Helianthus* spp.	Seed
Thistles, globe	*Echinops* spp.	Flowers, seed, nesting material
Zinnias	*Zinnnia elegans*	Seed, flowers attract butterflies

Bibliography

American Bird Conservancy. 2003. *Guide to the 500 Most Important Bird Areas in the United States*. New York: Random House.

American Ornithologists' Union. 1998. *Check-List of North American Birds*. 7th edition. Washington, DC: American Ornithologists' Union.

Choate, E. A. 1985. *The Dictionary of American Bird Names, Revised Edition*. Boston: Harvard Common Press.

Ehrlich, P. R.; Dobkin, D. S.; and Wheye, D. 1988. *The Birder's Handbook*. New York: Fireside Books.

Kaufman, K. 1996. *Lives of North American Birds*. Boston: Houghton Mifflin Co.

Kaufman, K. 2000. *Birds of North America, A Kaufman Focus Guide*. Boston: Houghton Mifflin Co.

National Geographic Society. 1999. *Field Guide to the Birds of North America*. 3rd edition. Washington, D.C.: National Geographic Society.

Peterson, R. T. 1996. *A Field Guide to the Birds* (Eastern). Boston: Houghton Mifflin Co.

Poole, A., and Gill, F., eds. 1992–2002. *The Birds of North America*. Philadelphia, PA: American Ornithologists' Union/Birds of North American, Inc.,

Sibley, D. A. 2000. *The Sibley Guide to the Birds*. New York: Alfred A. Knopf, Inc.

Stokes, D., and Stokes, L. 1996. *Stokes Field Guide to Birds: Eastern Region*. Boston: Little, Brown and Co.

Terres, J. K. 1995. *The Audubon Encyclopedia of North American Birds*. New York: Wings Books.

Thompson III, B. 1995. *An Identification Guide to Common Backyard Birds*. Marietta, OH: Bird Watcher's Digest Press.

Thompson III, B. 1997. *Bird Watching For Dummies*. New York: John Wiley & Sons.

Thompson III, B. 2003. *The Backyard Bird Watcher's Answer Guide*. Marietta, OH: Bird Watcher's Digest Press.

Zickefoose, J. 1995. *Enjoying Bird Feeding More*. Marietta, OH: Bird Watcher's Digest Press.

Zickefoose, J. 2001. *Natural Gardening for Birds*. Emmaus, PA: Rodale Organic Living Books.

National Organizations for Bird Watchers

National Organizations

American Bird Conservancy
P.O. Box 249
The Plains, VA 20198
(540) 253-5780
www.abcbirds.org

American Birding Association
P.O. Box 6599
Colorado Springs, CO 80934-6599
800-850-2473
www.americanbirding.org

Cornell Laboratory of Ornithology
Attn: Communications
159 Sapsucker Woods Road
Ithaca, NY 14850
800-843-2473
www.birds.cornell.edu

National Audubon Society
700 Broadway
New York, NY 10003
(212) 979-3000
www.audubon.org

National Wildlife Federation
11100 Wildlife Center Drive
Reston, VA 20190-5362
800-822-9919
www.nwf.org

The Nature Conservancy
4245 North Fairfax Drive, Suite 100
Arlington, VA 22203-1606
800-628-6860
www.tnc.org

Field Guides to Birds

Griggs, J. L. 1997. *All the Birds of North America*. New York: Harper Collins.

Kaufman, K. 2001. *Birds of North America (Kaufman Focus Guides)*. Boston: Houghton Mifflin Co.

National Geographic Society. 1999. *National Geographic Field Guide to the Birds of North America, 3rd edition*. Washington, D.C.: National Geographic Society.

Peterson, R. T. 2002. *A Field Guide to the Birds of Eastern and Central North America (Peterson Series). 5th ed.* Boston: Houghton Mifflin Co.

Robbins, C. S., et al. 1983. *Birds of North America: A Guide to Field Identification (Golden Field Guide Series)*. Revised edition. New York: Golden Press.

Sibley, D. A. 2000. *The Sibley Guide to the Birds. New York:* Alfred A. Knopf, Inc.

Stokes, D., and Stokes, L. 1996. *Field Guide to the Birds of North America*. Boston: Little, Brown and Co.

Audio Guides to Birds

Elliott, L. 2004. *Know Your Bird Sounds, volumes 1 and 2.* Mechanicsburg, PA: Stackpole Books.

Elliott, L.; Stokes, D.; and Stokes, L. 1997. *Stokes Field Guide to Bird Songs: Eastern Region (Stokes Field Guide to Bird Songs).* New York: Time Warner Audio Books.

Peterson, R. T. 2002. *A Field Guide to Bird Songs of Eastern and Central North America. Revised edition.* Boston: Houghton Mifflin Co.

Walton, R. K., and Lawson, R. W. 1989. *Birding By Ear, Eastern and Central North America (Peterson Field Guide Series).* Boston: Houghton Mifflin Co.

Walton, R. K., and Lawson, R. W. 1994. *More Birding By Ear (Peterson Field Guide Series).* Boston, MA: Houghton Mifflin Co.

Periodicals for Bird Watchers

The Backyard Bird Newsletter
P. O. Box 110
Marietta, OH 45750
800-879-2473
www.birdwatchersdigest.com

Bird Watcher's Digest
P. O. Box 110
Marietta, OH 45750
800-879-2473
www.birdwatchersdigest.com

Living Bird
Cornell Laboratory of Ornithology
159 Sapsucker Woods Road
Ithaca, NY 14850
800-843-2473
www.birds.cornell.edu

Photography Credits

Arthur Morris/Birds as Art: Pages 35, 46, 47, 48, 49, 50, 51, 52, 53, 54, 55, 56, 59, 61, 63, 64, 65, 66, 67, 68, 69, 70, 73, 74, 75, 76, 77, 79, 82, 85, 87, 88, 89, 91, 93, 95, 96, 98, 99, 101, 102, 103, 104, 106, 107, 109, 111, 112, 113, 114, 115, 116, 117, 119, 122, 125, 127, 129, 131, 132, 133, 134, 135, 136, 137, 138, 139, 140, 141, 144, 145

Bird Watcher's Digest: Pages 34, 37, 38 (both photos), 39 (both photos), 40, 41

Tom Vezo: Pages 60, 72, 80, 81, 92, 108, 118, 130

Maslowski Photography: Pages 78, 84, 86, 142, 143

Robert McCaw: Pages 71, 90, 100, 105, 123

Cliff Beittel: Pages 57, 62, 124

Brian Henry: Pages 94, 110, 121

Barth Schorre: Pages 120, 126

Julie Zickefoose: Pages 43, 176

Ron Austing: Page 83

Bill Bevington: Page 128

Randall Ennis: Page 33

Charles Melton: Page 42

Gary Meszaros: Pages 58

Marie Read: Page 97

Index

Sighting Notes

Date	Species/Description	Location

Sighting Notes

Date	Species/Description	Location

Sighting Notes

Date	Species/Description	Location

Meet Bill Thompson, III

Bill Thompson, III is the Editor of Bird Watcher's Digest, *the popular bimonthly magazine devoted to birds and bird watching. From an early age, Bill knew his life would be intertwined with birds and bird watching. One of his first words was "junco" and one of his early memories is of seeing a male cardinal in a tree. In 1978, his parents, Bill and Elsa Thompson, founded* Bird Watcher's Digest *in their living room, fulfilling their dream. It has been published continuously since its inception.*

In addition to this book for Cool Springs Press, Bill Thompson is the author of the Southern series of state bird watching books for Cool Springs Press. He is the author of the best-selling book, *Bird Watching for Dummies*. He is also the author of many booklets published by *Bird Watcher's Digest*. His articles on bird watching have appeared in numerous books and magazines, including *National Gardening*. Bill is a frequent guest lecturer and speaker for many events. In addition, he is a longtime member of The American Birding Association and is a Director of the Ohio Ornithological Society.

Bill, his wife Julie Zickefoose (an acclaimed artist and nature writer), and their two children enjoy life on an 80-acre farm in Whipple, Ohio. One of their life dreams became a reality when they added a 50-foot-tall bird-watching observation tower to their home. To date, they have recorded sightings of more than 181 bird species. When he's not serving as an editor, traveling, lecturing, or writing books, Bill enjoys playing guitar in his band, *The Swinging Orangutangs*, with his wife, Julie, and brother, Andy.